The
Pirates of Manhattan

Systematically Plundering the American Consumer & How to Protect Against It.

By Barry James Dyke

Copyright

Manufactured in the United States
Cover by Alison Vallocchia
Library of Congress Cataloging-in Publication Data
Dyke, Barry James
The Pirates of Manhattan: Systematically Plundering the American Consumer & How to Protect Against It.

For additional copies and further communication, contact us at:
www.thepiratesofmanhattan.com

Dedication

This book is dedicated to my children Rachael, Warren and William, and to those who have gone before me, my father Warren, my mother Eleanore and my brother Bruce.

And it is also dedicated to financial advisors everywhere who are missionaries for the truth about money.

PREFACE

In 1997, the research for this book began. Finishing this book is just as much about overcoming obstacles as it is about educating the agent and consumer about the mechanics of the monetary system and the benefits of life insurance.

In the fall of 1999, the author's mother died. Twelve months later, the author and his then wife and children formally separated, which led to heartbreaking consequences and a nasty divorce. Approximately twelve months after the separation, the author underwent an operation for skin cancer on a day, which will go down in infamy in American history—September 11, 2001.

During this time, the author, a financial and consulting professional, felt like the world was coming to an end. On the one hand, he was losing significant revenue as successful clients sold their businesses to larger entities, and on the other hand, competitors were successfully stealing many existing clients who got wind of the author's acrimonious divorce. He had to let go of staff that had once helped him. The world of business was like running on a treadmill from hell.

Incoming legal invasions were devastating, like rocket attacks from the Vietnam conflict. Early morning appearances from sheriffs serving legal notices became as routine as brushing his teeth. Visits to therapists increased. Nothing seemed to help, not even prayer.

Moreover, it got worse. The author, who had built up a Tiffany credit report and a successful financial planning and benefits consulting practice over twenty years of hard work, determination, and sweat equity, watched competitors and creditors begin to tear him apart. Major banks, who are portrayed as some of America's most admired financial institutions, got very nasty and verbally abusive. The author wondered if Tony Soprano had trained them.

Every week law firms representing banks sent certified legal notices to the author at a time when the author had no funds to defend himself. The humiliation was devastating and incomprehensible. The author's marital home was in the process of foreclosure. The notice of public auction was heartbreaking. It was quite difficult to sleep. The American dream had not only fallen apart; it had been shattered into a million little pieces.

After the foreclosure, the author's final divorce agreement was handed out. It was not kind to the author. However, no one wins in a divorce; the collateral damage hits everyone in its path.

One of the mortgagees who had a lien on the marital residence was not happy with the author. Creditors continued to hound him day and night at his business and home. Bottom-fishing predatory creditor counseling agencies hounded the author as well, leaving as many as a half dozen calls per day, sometimes invading the author's privacy with automatic auto-dialers. Bankruptcy was the only logical choice and the process of filing was not cheap.

However, even in the bankruptcy court the author was hammered. After the author filed at the courthouse, the creditors filed liens against the author's ex-spouse. The ex-spouse filed suit against the author in federal bankruptcy court. The author lost once again. The idea of a fresh start in bankruptcy was an absolute hallucination.

In addition, during the calamity of losing another battle in a courtroom, which favored the rights of a bank over the rights of an individual, the Internal Revenue Service was turning up the heat for unpaid taxes with a new salvo of registered letters, penalties, and interest. All the while, the author continued to work on this book. For months at a time, he would drop the research, only to pick it up again. Something within the author compelled him to get out his story.

On a business trip to New York, the author, while driving absent-mindedly and in a rush, slid into a guardrail in Westchester. He totaled his old car, with a laptop computer in the trunk. The car and the laptop were insured, but all the files and original chapters of this book were lost in the accident. In 2004, from memory and notes, the author started the writing all over again.

In a way, the author's life was a modern day Book of Job. In spite of it all, the author still had a great deal of gratitude for knowing that he had his physical health, wonderful children, amazing friends and an incredible depth of experience and passion for the work he has done which has benefited others. He lives in a beautiful place. Outside his window, he can see the Atlantic Ocean. He has been given the gifts of a sharp intellect and the persistence of a prizefighter. To try to hide the author's wreckage of the past would be a major mistake, so, Dear Reader, you now know the absolute truth—warts and all.

Where this work will take the author no one really knows, but from the bottom of the author's heart, he is pleased that he can write a book like *The Pirates of Manhattan*. It is a David versus Goliath story and originates in the heart of an underdog—a persona found somewhere in all of us.

For those of you who face challenges in your life, the author wants you to know that others have gone through financial and moral devastation and have come out stronger on the other side. Ultimately, rejection and destruction have the potential to become the ultimate blessing. As Charles Dickens once commented, *"the best steel goes through the fire."* Above all else, have faith and just take things one day at a time. There are literally hundreds of examples of the power of persistence, but some of the more notable examples are people who have overcome tremendous financial and devastating setbacks.

Immanuel Nobel, father of Alfred Nobel went bankrupt twice in his life. Alfred went on to become the world's largest manufacturer of explosives and later one of the world's greatest philanthropists with the creation of the Nobel Peace Prize.

Phineas Taylor (P.T.) Barnum filed for bankruptcy due to losses he incurred for embarking in unwise business ventures. P.T. was so devastated that at one point he contemplated suicide. After bankruptcy, Barnum organized his famous circus, "The Greatest Show on Earth." Later, he would merge his circus with that of another famous competitor, James Bailey, to form the Barnum and Bailey Circus. Barnum would go on to make millions after his bankruptcy.

Henry John Heinz manufactured condiments and sold horseradish, pickles, sauerkraut, and vinegar using a variety of family recipes. His company would file for bankruptcy when an unexpected bumper crop gave the company a demand to which it could not live up. The company became so over-extended it could not meet payroll. After bankruptcy, Heinz immediately started a new company, the H.J. Heinz Company that manufactured a new product known as tomato ketchup. The rest is history.

L. Frank Baum is one of the author's favorite examples of a comeback story. Baum was the author of *The Wonderful Wizard of Oz*. After running a retail store in South Dakota into bankruptcy, Baum went on to become an author and write one of the most popular books in American children's literature. At face value, it appears to be an innocent fairy tale about love and family. Yet in many circles, *The Wonderful Wizard of Oz* is considered an allegory and a sophisticated commentary and parable of economic and political issues, which faced America during the Populist era. In part, the story was an illustration illuminating a number of issues during the Gilded Age such as the growth of Populism and the silver movement, the Gilded Age presidency, the problems of labor, and the insurrection in the Philippines. Baum wanted to make *Oz* youthful entertainment first but the underlying allegories are impressive and apparent.

Oz is the abbreviation for an ounce of gold. The Yellow Brick Road is symbolic for the "banker's gold standard" with all of its dangers. The Cowardly Lion represents William Jennings Bryant—a Populist presidential candidate who at one point challenged the nation's banking system and Wall Street. The Scarecrow was the wise but naïve western farmer. The Tin Woodsman stood for the dehumanized industrial worker of the time. The Deadly Poppy Field, where the Cowardly Lion slept but could not move forward, was considered to symbolize how the country was stuck because of the Spanish-American War and the imperialism in the Philippines. The Emerald Palace represented the White House, while the Emerald City represented a fantasy version of Washington. The Wizard, who was a bumbling old man, could have passed as one of the Gilded Age presidents.

The Wicked Witch of the East stood for eastern manufacturing, banking, and Wall Street interests, which controlled the financial agenda of America, and the Munchkins represented the people they controlled. The slippers Judy Garland wore in the movie are ruby colored, but in Baum's book, they were silver as silver coinage was a way to make the money supply more plentiful for average Americans over the interest of bankers.

Another great story is that of Mark Twain. Twain lost all of his money investing in a worthless machine called the Paige Compositor. In bankruptcy, Twain discharged all of his debts but he was determined to repay what he owed. Twain gave lectures to large audiences and spent four years traveling Europe doing so. He used the money he earned to repay his debts and wrote successful books such as *The Adventures of Tom Sawyer* and *Pudd'nhead Wilson.*

Henry Ford's first company also ended in bankruptcy. The second company he started ended in a disagreement with a business partner. His third company, the Ford Motor Company, almost went under as well, but then he sold his first car and the rest is history.

Milton Snavely Hershey started four candy companies that failed and Hershey filed for bankruptcy, too. Hershey, who only had a fourth grade education, started a fifth company, the Hershey Chocolate Company, with the determination that the public would buy a good product at a fair price. His last attempt was obviously quite successful.

Walt Disney, who will be discussed later in this book in regards to how he used his life insurance cash values to form Walt Disney theme parks in 1952, went bankrupt for the first time in 1923 after he had created the Laugh-O-Gram Corporation in 1921. Walt would go on to realize phenomenal success.

Charles Goodyear went bankrupt several times and he even spent time in debtor's prisons in Philadelphia, New Haven, and Boston. With his wife's incredible loyalty, relentless perseverance, and tenacity between jail times, Goodyear would go on to develop the process to vulcanize rubber.

Larry King, the famous talk show host, went bankrupt in 1978. King is now known as one of America's greatest talk show hosts and one of the country's best-selling authors.

The rock-and-roll world has its share of success stories, too. For example, Tom Petty went bankrupt over a record company dispute in 1979. Soon afterward, Petty came up with a new record contract and produced a hit album "Damn the Torpedoes." Petty bolted to rock star fame, earning a $20 million record contract with Warner Brothers. He played with the group "The Traveling Wilburys" which included Roy Orbison, George Harrison, and Jeff Lynne and featured Bob Dylan. Today, Petty even has his own radio show on *XM Satellite Radio.*

Wayne Newton, the performer, went bankrupt after finding himself over $20 million in debt. Later, under a new contract with Stardust Hotels, Newton allegedly made $25 million per year under a ten-year contract, which started in the late 1990s.

That brings us to one of the most remarkable comeback stories of all time, "The Donald." Donald Trump is one of the wealthiest people in America, but in the early 1990s, things were not looking so good. Trump's personal liabilities approached $900 million. His three casinos and posh Plaza Hotel were forced into bankruptcy. Trump lost his yacht and his airline, the Trump Shuttle. His ex-wife Ivana snagged his mansion and another $14 million in a divorce settlement.

In late 2004, Trump Hotels & Casinos Resorts announced a restructuring of debt. Trump Hotels was forced to seek voluntary bankruptcy protection to keep itself afloat. In 2005, the company re-emerged from bankruptcy as Trump Entertainment Resorts, Inc.

As we now know, Donald Trump also went on to become the executive producer of the NBC reality show *The Apprentice*. The first year that Trump did the show, he was paid about $50,000 per episode. Today, he reportedly earns $600,000 per episode. This makes Trump one of the highest paid entertainers in the media industry.

So keep your sunny side up. Live one day at a time. Tomorrow is another day. *Now to the acknowledgements...*

ACKNOWLEDGEMENTS

No book would be possible without the support of others.

First of all, to my children, Rachael, Warren, and William. Thank you for listening to me for all my ranting about the Federal Reserve System and all things economic. I am passionate about this stuff because I want you to know what is going on in the American Empire. Be prepared for the days ahead. Pray for the best; plan for the worst.

To Mark Morrisse, I have never said it enough but your encouragement has been invaluable. You know, probably better than anybody, all the research and work I have put into this. You have been in tune all along to what is going on in Casino America—thank you.

To Barbara Campagna and David Michel. I cannot say enough about you two. You provided an oasis to me in a very turbulent time. Sophia Zlatin, you are a wizard on the Internet...Crystal Williams, an awesome job in the editing department—only you could untangle my verboseness. Alison Vallocchia, hats off to an awesome book cover; you gave the book the visual punch it needed...

To Phil McDonough, your friendship has been invaluable. You made me realize that it is not about me; it is about what we can do for others. Stewart Berman, that is a ditto.

To Gretchen Harb, Darlene Trombly, Terry Marcille, Karen McCormick, and Suzanne Trumbore. The old Andover crew cannot believe all you guys are in my life but I am most thankful. Your support and kind words have proven invaluable. Lewis Trumbore, thank you for taking the time to read that charitable thing in 2002. That did not fly, but your encouragement that I was on to something proved invaluable; I ran with it. Jay Leno, if you had not turned me down, I probably would not have done this. The ultimate rejection ended up being the ultimate blessing. Thank you, Jay. If everyone displayed the courtesy you continue to show, the world would be a better place. Now you know in what Angelo and Warren were involved. Thank you for your friendship and your power of example in the persistence department.

To Mary Lou and Patrick Small, your encouragement and friendship have proven invaluable as well. Fred Bradley, ahoy! All the McCarthys—Jane and Allen, Lisa, Jay, Taryn, Steven, Susan, and Timmy—and their spouses, Bob, Lee Ann, Bob, Nina, and Bob.

To my accountant, Steve Troian, I thank you; I could not ask for a better advisor and friend. Twenty-four years go by very quickly—thanks for all the support. Tony DiMaio, without an information technology guy like you, I would be nowhere. Thanks for keeping me up and running.

To Larry Ragone. Thank you for the encouragement. It has been invaluable. Len Martin and Lew Merrow...thank you. Lenny, you have always been one of the cutting-edge guys in the life insurance business; your energy and enthusiasm are contagious. Lew, thanks for all the stuff about all the problems with probate; it opened my eyes. Roger Bell and Keith Baumgarn, thanks for the encouragement. Fellow agents—Al Dauphin, Jerry Hines, Erland Reuter, Dave Evans, John Wain, Jim Byers, Ray Poteet, David Cobb, Dan Rust, Joe Bedwell, Alan Eckstrand, Joe Pantozzi, Tim Cooper, Dan Manoff, Steve Sappington, Dan Savard, Jon Betts, Chuck Tiedje and all the rest—thank you for the encouragement, insights and support.

To Bruce and Ruth Schlappi, you folks are special. It is always wonderful to talk with you. R. Nelson Nash and David Stearns, what can I say? I cannot thank you enough for getting me interested in Austrian economics, the Mises Institute and the nation's monetary system. Thank you for supporting my thesis that people cannot truly understand the beauty of life insurance unless they understand the monetary system. Don Blanton, thank you for your support and passion. It is all about what we can do for others. Rich Moss from Clark Capital, thanks for the statistics and facts about the real costs of mutual funds. Mae Bradshaw, Esquire, thank you for the encouragement. Nancy Risely and Kris Stecker, thank you; your unfailing encouragement, as well as the meditation I learned from you proved invaluable. Cathy Stickney, thanks; the personal training helped create the strength to write this.

To Bill Strauss of FutureMetrics, thank you. Your analysis on the actual rates of returns on corporate pension plans within America proved invaluable near the end. Steve Leimberg, Esquire. Steve, thank you for the encouragement and for setting me straight on the Dow Chemical case. Gideon Rothschild of Moses & Singer, thank you for your encouragement, the original work you have done on asset protection, and for pointing out some of the additional pitfalls.

To Gretchen Morgenson, of the *New York Times*, great work on exposing the mutual fund industry and Wall Street. You gave me some awesome insights and inspiration to look even deeper. Keep up the great work. Thank you for the encouragement.

To David Swensen, author of *Unconventional Success*, great insight into the mutual fund business. Thanks for the encouragement. Lew Rockwell of the Ludwig von Mises Institute, thank you for your encouragement. Jesus Huerta De Soto, author of *Money, Bank Credit and Economic Cycles*, thank you for your insight in regards to the Austrian School treatment of life insurance and information about John Maynard Keynes. Bill Bonner and Addison Wiggin, authors of *Empire of Debt, the Rise of an Epic Financial Crisis,* thank you very much. Thank you for giving me permission to use some of your work and thank you for the encouragement. William Black, author of *The Best Way to Rob a Bank is to Own One.* Bill, thanks for your intricate exposé on the banks and the Savings and Loan crisis. It should be a must-read for every American. Thanks for the encouragement. Philip Augar, author of *The Greed Merchants: How the Investment Banks Played the Free Market Game.* The book is well done and one about the power of banks that needed to be written. Thank you for your encouragement and permission to use some of your work. Dan Reingold, author of *Confessions of a Wall Street Analyst.* Dan, thanks for the encouragement and permission to use some of your conclusions about the stock market. It is a story that needs to be heard now more than ever.

Thank you, John Perkins, author of *Confessions of an Economic Hit Man.* Thank you for your permission to use material and thank you for the encouragement. Good to know you are from New Hampshire, too.

To Bob Castiglione, you are a brilliant man. The development of an economic model for financial planning is a chassis everyone needs. Your application of universal mathematics proves that most financial products, other than life insurance, are all subject to the ravages of inflation, taxation, lost opportunity costs, and loss of control and utility for the consumer.

THE PIRATES OF MANHATTAN

Contents

Introduction

In the fall of 2005, the author's work as a life insurance professional was reaffirmed in a number of ways—through a series of enlightening events. First, a female client used her life insurance accelerated benefits to pay for experimental cancer treatments at the end stages of her life. Although she eventually died, the cash made available prior to her death gave her the opportunity to spend some meaningful time with the ones she loved.

In another situation, an executive of a public company, whom the author had known well for at least fifteen years, died in a coma. The group life insurance he had negotiated and brokered for the corporation was a major tax-free benefit for his heirs. In addition, while assisting another client settle an estate, it was clear that life insurance proceeds were the ideal economic shock absorber to pay the numerous expenses the estate would ultimately incur.

Lastly, in late 2006 and early 2007, the author had two additional life insurance claims on two successful business owners. Once again, life insurance proved to be an economic shock absorber and the least taxed asset in the estates. Most agents and planners who have sold life insurance have only had about five or six claims before they reach the age of sixty-five. For the author, it has been different. Since he has designed and implemented dozens of corporate benefit and retirement plans with pre-retirement death benefits, he has had at least four dozen death claims, probably more.

Each time one processes a life insurance claim it leaves a mark. Sometimes it can be reaffirming in knowing that you helped those left behind. Other times you can feel despondent when a beneficiary demands, "Why didn't you sell him more?"

The unexpected, the author has come to learn, happens all the time. We live in a volatile world. No one can predict the future. Situations can change overnight. No one ever dies at the right time. No one ever dies with too much cash. The author is not in charge. Someone else certainly is calling the shots.

The author knows firsthand that life insurance has the power to do good things. Life insurance proceeds helped his mother maintain her dignity and her lifestyle when his father died of cancer at a young age. Moreover, when his only brother, who was also his best friend, took his own life, he not only left shattered dreams and incomprehensible sadness, but also a mountain of bills and costs to which the author had to attend. Without the proceeds of his brother's personal and group life insurance, the author questions how he would have addressed the financial burden that his brother left behind.

Professional Background

The author has been a life insurance professional for about two and a half decades. He has been more entrepreneurial than most, having started a pension administration business, a third-party cafeteria benefits administration firm, an employee benefits practice, which served private and publicly traded corporations, and a registered investment advisory firm. He has sold a great number of financial products to an upscale clientele—life insurance, disability insurance, health insurance plans, pensions, 401(k)s, equities, limited partnerships, mutual funds, rare coins, consulting services, investment advisory work, annuities, separate accounts, communication services, reinsurance and more.

The clientele has been diverse. Although mostly small businesses have made up the clientele, products and consulting services have been sold to physicians, legal firms, public corporations, non-profits, government entities, professional athletes, venture capital firms, high-tech start-ups, and just everyday people. Some clients have had a negative net worth. Others have had assets valued at over $100 million.

A Passion for Economics

The author's father always said that economic issues controlled the world. Most wars, when you really analyze what caused them, the author's father would say, had their roots in economic fundamentals.

His father was a Marine in World War II. He served in Guadalcanal, a place were fifteen thousand American men died in battle. Before he died he told the author about some of the horrific atrocities of war—the maiming, the slaughter and the senseless loss of life. He spoke in brutal frankness about what it took to survive in the jungle. However, in the end, he said that all root causes of wars were tied to *economic issues.*

The author's father never totally escaped Guadalcanal. He was as kind as a man could be, but as a child, the author can vividly remember horrifying nightmares awakening his father in the middle of the black night. In his dreams, he was back in the steamy hot night jungles of Guadalcanal. The shouts he let out and the sheer panic he felt when having one of these gruesome dreams echoed the terrors of wars.

Needless to say, the comments that the author's father made about economic issues controlling the world made an everlasting impression. Economics, in the final analysis, is the study of how what limited resources we have are allocated. Our decisions concerning our economic purchases should be to maximize the benefits we receive with our purchases, and the benefits received should exceed the amount we paid for something. In regards to financial products, permanent life insurance maximizes economic benefits better than any other product in the marketplace. Unfortunately, this is something mainstream America has forgotten.

Most Financial Products Do not Work over the Long Haul

For about the past ten years or so, the author has passionately studied economics and the financial services industry within America. What he learned along the way was life changing. Many financial products and concepts sold to the American consumer simply do not work over an extended period. Popular strategies in today's financial planning such as dollar cost averaging into mutual funds,[1] maximizing your 401(k) program,[2] and buying term life insurance and investing the difference, which directly affects all of our financial lives, simply do not work over the long haul.

Yet these strategies and the products associated with them are promoted incessantly. They are not promoted because they work over the long haul for consumers, but because they are extremely profitable to the financial institutions that manufacture and market these products.

In the absence of guarantees, most financial products fall apart and fade away. No one knows what the stock market will do, not even the professionals who manage money. The concept that mutual funds offer a surefire road to wealth is an absolute hallucination. However, as we will later see, the mutual fund business has been a Klondike gold rush for mutual fund owners, managers, and other financial intermediaries who do business within that industry.

Maximizing a retirement plan such as a 401(k) looks great on paper and it would work in an imaginary Alice in Wonderland world where there are no taxes or market risk. However, when you factor in the inevitable *real world* of market risk, management fees, inflation, trading costs, taxes and lost opportunity costs of the money within that retirement plan, the 401(k) falls apart. The 401(k) plan was originally meant to be a side dish of retirement savings, but today it is served up as the main course.

Another popular concept, buy "term life insurance and invest the difference" never works for consumers, but this unsupported strategy is promoted by financial gurus who are more interested in promoting their agenda, and life insurance companies do not object because they make a great

---

[1] Carolyn T. Greer, "The Dollar Cost Fallacy" *Forbes,* April 10, 1995. For years, the author has realized that dollar cost averaging is a marketing tool for mutual fund companies. This article shows there is no scientific, mathematical, or historical validity to support the dollar cost averaging theory. An additional study by Wright University reports similar findings.
[2] William Wolman and Anne Colamosca, *The Great 401(k) Hoax* (Cambridge, MA: Perseus Publishing, 2002).

deal of money on term life insurance. Moreover, the "buy term and invest the difference" strategy certainly worked out well for Arthur L. Williams. Williams was known as "The Coach" and convinced swarms of agents to follow him blindly so that they could cannibalize and replace a lot of good, in-force, permanent life insurance with expensive term life policies that his company offered. Although both consumers and agents were shafted, Williams hit the lottery. He sold his company, the A.L. Williams Insurance Company, to Travelers Insurance, which merged with Citigroup. Today, Williams is one of the richest men in America ($1.7 billion) for promoting a concept, which does not work over the long haul.

Williams' company lives on, continuing to push the "buy term and invest the difference" strategy under the name Primerica, which is a major subsidiary of the Citigroup financial company, the largest bank in the world.

Yet Citigroup does not buy into the "buy term and invest the difference" strategy in regards to life insurance for its own account. It has bought into the benefits of permanent cash value life insurance in a big way. As a matter of public record, as of June 30, 2006, Citibank and its Banamex USA subsidiary owned more than $2.247 billion in cash surrender value life insurance on its balance sheet. By December 31, 2006, Citibank's aggregate cash surrender values soared to $3.315 billion, meaning that Citibank had deposited more than $1 billion in additional permanent life insurance protection in a little over six months time.

The Life Changing Event...The Beginning of Enlightenment

"That which hurts instructs."
Benjamin Franklin

The experience of enlightenment or *satori* came about when the author discovered, beyond a shadow of a doubt, that the Federal Reserve System in the United States, which is the alleged fountainhead of wisdom and supreme authority on all financial and economic issues in the nation, is not federal. It has *no reserves*. It has never operated over an extended period as a successful economic system. In fact, The Fed has contributed immensely to economic upheavals, instability, and speculation by its special powers to expand and contract the nation's money supply. The Fed has actually operated as a bailout mechanism for Wall Street speculators. Nobel Prize-winning economist Milton Friedman, as well as many other renowned economists, acknowledge that the vast expansion of money and credit by the Federal Reserve caused overspeculation and the Crash of 1929, and the Fed's subsequent contraction of the money supply during the 1930s caused the Great Depression.

The reality, Dear Reader, is that the Federal Reserve System is a *private corporation* owned by *commercial banks*. Non-elected government officials who have very privileged tenures in office, which can last up to fourteen years, run the Fed. The Fed reports to no one. It has never been audited. The Federal Reserve System has about as much in common with the federal government as Federal Express does. The Federal Reserve System is an economic cartel of commercial banks as much as OPEC is a cartel for oil-producing countries.

Once the author thoroughly understood that the Federal Reserve System was the ultimate con job over the American people, he began to question the integrity of *all* financial institutions and *all* financial products.

Lessons Learned

Once the author understood that the Federal Reserve System was not a federal government institution, he began to understand the inherent problems of having a private central bank in control of the nation's money supply. These problems will be later addressed in a second book, probably something like *The Pirates of Manhattan II*. Nevertheless, for a brief summary, here are the problems with having a private central bank and the effect it has on the American economy and its people. Lessons learned included:

Lesson One. The regional Federal Reserve Banks throughout the country own the Federal Reserve System. Commercial banks own those regional Fed banks. The Fed has worked clearly and consistently in favor of the nation's banking systems first and not necessarily for the benefit of the American taxpayer. Wealthy private Wall Street bankers such as J.P. Morgan and John D. Rockefeller conceived the private central bank on Jekyll Island off the coast of Georgia in November of 1910[3] and lobbied for it. On December 23, 1913, when Congress created the Federal Reserve System—the Founding Fathers' worst nightmare came true—a private corporation took control of the nation's money supply. America has suffered the consequences ever since. Before his death, Woodrow Wilson, the president who originally signed the Federal Reserve Act, regretted that he had participated in the Fed's creation.

By giving a private central bank the lever to control interest rates and the privilege to create currency and credit out of thin air, Wall Street, the banking industry, the federal government and contractors who do business

---

[3] Griffin, G. Edward, *The Creature from Jekyll Island, A Second Look at the Federal Reserve* (Westlake Village, CA: American Media, 1998). Irrefutable information in regards to the creation of the Fed and historical background about the Fed.

with the federal government benefit immensely. After all, money is their stock in trade as they do not produce or manufacture anything. These parties benefit the most because they are the first to get their hands on the currency before it loses its value. With the Fed's continual ability to sell IOUs, which only the taxpayers' ability to pay backs up, the Federal Reserve System creates the worst tax of them all—*inflation*. With the Fed's continual ability to sell IOUs or treasury bills to investors and foreigners, politicians have successfully buried this generation and future generations with massive debts and inflation.

The Fed may deny inflation exists every single day, but regular everyday people know that inflation is real. Each year we are working harder and harder and seeing our paychecks purchase less and less. Prices for food, housing, energy, education, and healthcare for everyday people have gone through the roof. The Fed actually excludes the costs of food and energy from its core inflation rate. By creating vast amounts of money or IOUs out of thin air, the Federal Reserve System dilutes the value of our purchasing power. Since 1971, when the country went off the gold standard, the printing presses of money creation have been on a rampage. The dollar has lost at least 80 percent of its value since 1971 and the value of the dollar continues to decline because of the amount that we borrow overseas everyday. By the way, the dollar is not really a dollar; it is a *Federal Reserve Note.* Open your wallet; take a peak.

Lesson Two. After the Federal Reserve System creates money out of thin air by printing paper IOUs or electronic checkbook entries (known as *fiat currency* in economics), this currency is in turn deposited into the nation's banks and multiplied again. For every dollar a bank now has on deposit of its own or other people's money, the bank through the *multiplier effect* or *fractional reserve banking,* lends out $10 to the public. This is all perfectly legal and no other agent within society enjoys this money creation privilege as banks do.

However, fractional reserve banking, because it is highly leveraged with a minimum of a ten-to-one ratio, is also highly unstable and sometimes even results in a *run on the bank.* During the Great Depression of the 1930s, over ten thousand banks failed. More recently, during the Savings and Loan crisis of the 1980s and 1990s, fractional reserve banks, many of which had only three percent reserves—and some had no reserves whatsoever—once again proved highly unstable. This time, over twenty-nine hundred banks failed. Major banks such as Continental Illinois needed a massive taxpayer bailout of $4 billion in 1984. The Bank of New England needed an injection of $4 billion before it closed its doors. In the early 1990s, Citibank would almost certainly have gone under had it had not been for a large infusion of Saudi capital. The recent sub prime mortgage meltdown and credit crunch once again shows commercial and investment banks are horrible at managing economic risk.

When banks fail, the ultimate cost of failure of the banks shifts onto the taxpayer. The Federal Deposit Insurance Corporation (FDIC) backs failed banks. The taxpayer stands behind the FDIC. The Savings and Loan crisis alone will cost the American taxpayer in excess of $250 billion.

Lesson Three. Through massive lobbying in the early 1980s, the banking and finance industry in the United States has become extremely deregulated, de-supervised, and subsidized by the American taxpayer in numerous ways, both domestically and abroad. All protections which were put in place to protect the American consumer during the 1930s with the Glass–Steagall Act to protect and insulate them from the avarice of banks has largely been removed with the assistance of people like Alan Greenspan, Robert Rubin, Sanford Weill, Senator Joseph Biden, and former Senator Phil Gramm. The crowning piece of legislation, which brought deregulation to its zenith, was the repeal of Glass–Steagall with the passage of the Gramm-Leach-Bliley Act of 1999.

A case in point regards the new powers of banks. According to the Better Business Bureau, out of the one thousand industries they track, credit card companies and banks were the number one generator of consumer complaints across the country in 2004. Yet, due to deregulation, which began in 1978,[4] there is no longer a legal limit as to the amount of interest, which can be charged on a loan in this country. None. A state may have legal limits as to what the maximum amount of interest can be charged on a loan, but banks can export high rates from usury friendly states like South Dakota, Delaware, Arizona, Virginia, Utah, and New Hampshire. Usury or the practice of charging exorbitant amounts of interest on a loan is now perfectly legal through credit cards such as Visa, MasterCard, American Express, Discover, and through payday and refund-anticipation tax loans. Credit cards, which are usury in every sense of the word when commercial banks borrow from the Fed at forty-year lows, are now the most profitable lines of business for the banking industry with over $30 billion in annual profits alone for Citigroup, Bank of America, Capital One, and numerous others. In addition, the new bankruptcy law passed in 2005 titled "The Banking Abuse and Consumer Protection Act of 2005" was an early Christmas present for the banking industry, yet harmful to consumers. The new law makes it extremely difficult to discharge usury debt, creates a debtor's prison without walls, and

---

[4] In 1978, with *Marquette National Bank v. First Omaha Services Corporation,* the Supreme Court ruled that you could export the interest rate from where a credit or loan was issued. This opened the door for interstate banking with credit cards. In 1979, South Dakota became the first state to repeal usury laws, Citibank became the first to set up shop in South Dakota, and high interest cards were born. Other states such as Delaware, Virginia, Arizona, Utah, and New Hampshire, followed. Former Governor Pierre DuPont used this to recruit banks to Delaware. Banks, notably MBNA, JPMorgan, Chase, Morgan Stanley (Discover), American Express, Providian, and Capital One, jumped in.

makes the idea of a fresh start in bankruptcy a sham. A more appropriate name for the bill could have been, "The Consumer Abuse and Bank Protection Act," "The Creditor Strikes Back," or "Darth Vader Interest Overtakes Main Street."

Another example of the banks' newfound powers is the rebirth of *tying*. Tying, which is the practice of tying commercial loans by banks to win follow on investment banking, which sells either stocks or bonds to the public, was outlawed and prohibited in 1933. In the 1930s, Congress found that tying was a major contributor to over speculation, which ultimately helped bring about the Crash of 1929. The practice of tying brought companies with shaky balance sheets public, and when the companies collapsed, naïve investors—not Wall Street—were caught holding the bag. Congress forced the separation of commercial and investment banking industries largely because of the tying conflict of interest. With the passage of the Gramm-Leach-Bliley Act of 1999, tying is legal. The imaginary Chinese Wall that separated commercial and investment banking is gone forever. People ask what is so bad about the repeal of tying. The author replies with two words—Enron and WorldCom.

Banks, through Herculean lobbying efforts, have sought and been successful in centralizing regulatory powers at the federal level, which is their ultimate goal as it makes them extremely powerful. In many ways, centralization of regulation at the federal level gives banks impunity and places them beyond reproach. Normal citizens will find it virtually impossible to challenge a bank at the federal level. Moreover, with arbitration,[5] you have a better chance of winning the lottery than winning a case against a securities firm. States do not have the horsepower they used to in bringing financial crimes to the forefront. Even Eliot Spitzer realizes this. This is, unfortunately, what economist Friedrich von Hayek warned us about in *The Road to Serfdom*, his book about the powers of centralized planning against the rights of citizens and private property. The state is looking out for the welfare of large private banks instead of consumers and is doing so at a federal level. In a dysfunctional way, it has become a feudal system where the lords are the financiers (aka *The Pirates of Manhattan*) and the vassals are regular American people.

Even so, banks constantly get themselves in trouble, with not only American consumers and businesses, but also internationally. Whether we like it or not, history has proven that time and time again the Federal Reserve

---

[5] With *Shearson/American Express vs. McMahon in* 1987, it became the law of the land that standard arbitration with securities firms takes precedence over the Seventh Amendment of the Constitution. Securities disputes with securities firms are no longer adjudicated in a court of law but within the securities industry itself. In October 1987, however, the stock market lost 23 percent of its value in one day. Gretchen Morgenson, "When Winning Feels a Lot like Losing," *New York Times,* December 10, 2006.

System, the International Monetary Fund, the World Bank, and the United States Treasury have consistently bailed out banking interests with the collapse of Long-Term Capital Management hedge fund, the collapse of the Mexican peso, South American debt, and so on.[6] And now once again, the Federal Reserve and Central Banks around the world have to rescue banks once again due to the sub prime mortgage crisis.

The Life Insurance Industry Ended up Looking Good

"There is a principle which is a bar against all information, which is proof against all arguments and which cannot fail to keep a man in everlasting ignorance—that principle is contempt prior to investigation."
Herbert Spencer

When the author began to comprehend fully the inherent structural weaknesses and the imbedded conflicts of interest in the Federal Reserve System, banking, finance, academia, securities, and mutual fund sectors, which this author likes to call collectively *The Pirates of Manhattan,* the life insurance industry with all of its faults, came out smelling like roses. In a financial and economic system chock full of rascals and miscreants, the life insurance business, which is a financial industry as much as banks and mutual fund companies, is actually a business with a great deal of integrity and financial stability.

Through historical, mathematical, and economic research and analysis over a number of years, the author discovered that the best and safest products, which worked consistently for consumers without government subsidies over an extended period such as one's entire life, were the financial products that only came out of the life insurance industry because they had contractual guarantees. In fact, our entire Social Security and defined benefit pension systems grew out of the actuarial science and discipline of the life insurance industry. Banks, mutual funds, securities firms—they are no match to the life insurance industry when it comes to managing economic risk.

Common life insurance products that have worked consistently over an extended period include annuities, non-cancelable disability income insurance, participating-dividend-paying whole life insurance, and defined benefit pension plans. This book, however, will only focus on the benefits of permanent life insurance, although we will also address some of the benefits of annuities. Ironically, we will see that the nation's money center banks, at

---

[6] Kevin Phillips, *American Theocracy, the Peril and the Politics of Radical Religion, Oil, and Borrowed Money* (New York: Viking, 2006).

record rates, are investing a significant portion of their critical reserves in solid, stable high cash value life insurance.

The purpose of this book is to give the consumer meaningful and factual background information as to why they should consider taking at least a portion of their hard-earned dollars and putting them with a life insurance company *first*, instead of placing their money in a bank, mutual fund or other financial intermediary. In the final analysis, the reader must do what is best for him or herself. However, if you impartially analyze the facts this author is about to present, and if you are willing to work with a well-qualified life insurance agent and commit to a disciplined methodology of saving, as a consumer you should be more independent, and in control of your financial destiny. You should also have additional wealth creation opportunities and retirement income enhancements, take better care of your family, pay less in taxes, pay less interest costs, enjoy more benefits, and be less dependent upon the predatory national banking system.

Here is what we will see in the chapters ahead:

One. In "The Casino Age," we will look at how American society is speculating and gambling at record rates. Everyone appears to be trying to get something for nothing. The media lathers us up at the behest of Wall Street. Like casino gambling, the only consistent winners in the end are the casino owners. In the Casino Age, the ultimate winners are the bankers, the speculators, and the media, which get out their pompoms every day to keep the party going.

Speculating and gambling have always been a part of the American culture, but it is hard to remember when speculation and gambling were so prevalent throughout American society. In the new millennium, "The Casino Age" has many, many similarities to the 1920s prior to the Great Crash of 1929.

Two. In the chapter, "Deregulation, De-supervision, and Plenty of Subsidies," we will give a broad overview of the history of deregulation in financial services, particularly in the banking and security industries over the past twenty-five years. We will also review the Wild West of unregulated international banking.

Three. In the chapter, "Never Met a Man Who Made His Millions in Mutual Funds," we will see that the business of mutual funds is definitely profitable to fund companies, fund managers and brokers who service the mutual funds business, yet rarely profitable to the average American consumer. The mutual funds business has had a long tainted history in America. In the 1920s, the mutual funds business was born with investment pools and investment trusts, which were highly leveraged. In the 1928-29 period, United Founders, which raised $686 million, collapsed to $0.50 a share during the 1929 Crash. Goldman Sachs Trading Corporation, another early mutual funds example, launched its Shenandoah Corporation and Blue Ridge Trusts. Both were engaged in dubious practices. Initially, Goldman Sachs Trading sold for $104 per share. It collapsed to $1.75 a share in 1929.

In the 1970s, Bernie Cornfeld raised $2.5 billion in a sham mutual fund called Investors Overseas Services, which he ran out of Switzerland. Eventually that fund imploded. Robert Vesco, a confidant of Richard Nixon, worked for Bernie Cornfeld. Vesco later fled to the Caribbean and became a fugitive. Also during the 1970s, the Mates and Enterprise funds, two large mutual funds, also imploded.

In the late 1980s and early 1990s, mutual funds funded by big buyers of junk bonds created by Michael Milken and others suffered big losses when the junk bond market collapsed. The mutual fund business in Japan, another one-time highflying business in the early 1990s, lost as much as 90% of its values with bad stock market turns. In addition, more recently, we witnessed that the mutual fund business in America is a smorgasbord of conflicts of interest and corruption and a business designed to compensate the owners, managers and suppliers of mutual funds rather than the investors.

Yet today, more money than ever is going into mutual funds—account totals exceed $10.5 trillion. Mutual funds, lacking guarantees and an extended proven track record in overall investment returns, are still the investment of choice for about 400,000 corporate sponsors in defined contribution 401(k) and 403(b) retirement plans. For the investor, however, the average return on an actively managed stock mutual fund, which is where a majority of the money is, is only around 2.5 percent. There is a whole lot of sizzle in the mutual fund business, but not a lot of steak.

Four. "Life Insurance and the Human Life Value Concept." The concept of life insurance and protecting the economic value of a human life in the event of a premature death is an economic concept which has been with us for centuries. However, conventional wisdom in America, most often promoted by financial gurus who have spent little time examining the economic value of a human life or understanding the mechanics of great permanent life insurance products, constantly promotes the idea of insuring needs and goals versus economic replacement value. Furthermore, it condescendingly tells the public to purchase the cheapest term life insurance it can find.

However, major economists such as John Maynard Keynes, Friedrich von Hayek, Richard von Strigl, Solomon Huebner, and Jesus Huerta De Soto have supported the human life value concept in regards to life insurance purchases, and the value of permanent life insurance as a means of savings and capital formation. Research reveals that Americans probably did a better job of insuring the economic value of their human lives in 1950 than they are in 2004. Research also reveals that Americans are behind other cultures in purchasing life insurance; the Japanese, the Swiss and numerous other cultures are ahead of Americans.

However, the vast majority of people agree that the value of a human life is the greatest economic value of them all. The court system affirms the economic value of a life, particularly in the wrongful death financial awards. Lastly, the idea of the economic value of a human life was unequivocally reaffirmed with the payment of close to $6 billion in life insurance benefits to victims' beneficiaries of the 9/11 World Trade Center tragedy.

Five. "Bank-Owned Life Insurance." This chapter will show, beyond the shadow of a doubt, that the nation's large money center banks, which probably know as much about economics and money as anybody, purchase more permanent life insurance than any other segment of the economy. High cash value permanent life insurance is a cornerstone of a bank and an integral part of a bank's Tier One[7] capital, which is the most important asset of any bank. Through the author's research in 2004, 2005, 2006, and 2007, you will understand that banks purchase colossal amounts of permanent life insurance. Five of the six largest banks in the world—Citigroup, JPMorgan Chase, HSBC Holdings, Bank of America, and the Royal Bank of Scotland (through Citizens Banks)—all own significant amounts of high cash value permanent life insurance. Over four thousand banks own permanent life insurance products. Purchases by this group are definitely on the upswing.

Six. "Corporate-Owned Life Insurance." Although there is, to the best of the author's knowledge, no SEC requirement that life insurance cash values and benefits be disclosed on a company's balance sheet, we will see how permanent life insurance is used as an instrument of corporate finance, executive compensation, and retirement planning. Permanent life insurance, particularly dividend-paying participating whole life, has been consistently used as an instrument of corporate finance and compensation since the 1950s. From proxy statement disclosures, the author will verify the use of cash value permanent life insurance, annuities, and the actuarial discipline of the life insurance business in corporate compensation.

Seven. "Life Insurance is Something Good for the Consumer" lays out, in an analytical fashion, the reasons why permanent life insurance, particularly high cash value dividend-paying permanent life insurance is one of the best financial products anyone can own, why it should be at the heart of most financial plans today, and why it should be purchased before stocks, bonds, 401(k)s, mutual funds and so on. As good as permanent life insurance is for banks and corporations, it is the author's conviction that it is even more valuable for the consumer and their family's economic foundation. Due to

---

[7] Tier One Capital—also classified as core capital or risk-based capital. Tier One Capital supports all lending activity to the public and includes common stock and retained earnings. Tier One is considered a bank's most important asset.

intense competition within the life insurance industry, quality permanent life insurance products can be purchased today on an extremely favorable basis. Old wives' tales about permanent life insurance not being a good deal for the consumer are simply unfounded and not true. The Federal Trade Commission report on life insurance done in 1979 is woefully out of date and should be put in the paper shredder once and for all.

Money must reside somewhere. When viewed in light of all the alternatives, permanent cash value life insurance is perhaps the safest and most economically efficient holding tanks for cash savings within America today. Our nation's banks have already figured this out, Dear Reader.

Eight. "Practical Everyday Applications of Permanent Life Insurance." After a summation of the benefits of permanent life insurance, we will also review some of the practical everyday applications of permanent life insurance for today's consumers. Topics to include: Pension Maximization, Reverse Mortgages, Permanent Life Insurance in Qualified Retirement Plans, Life Insurance to Fund Health and Welfare Plans, and Life Insurance as a Methodology to Fund Estate Taxes and Settlement Costs.

Survival of the Fittest

In this Darwinian survival-of-the-fittest society of ours, with economic turbulent times most likely in the years ahead, those who have patient accessible capital set aside will benefit the most from opportunities as they present themselves. With discipline, patience, and concentration of effort, high cash value permanent life insurance can be one of the consumer's best friends in private capital formation.

Average Americans save so little. This is not entirely their fault. Inflation has significantly eroded consumer purchasing power caused by the Federal Reserve System, fractional reserve banking system and a federal government that continues to spend way beyond its means. Excessive taxes, mostly levied against lower and middle classes through heightened Social Security taxes, have confiscated wealth from regular Americans to subsidize rich tax breaks and maintain the American empire.[8] According to a report done by the International Monetary Fund in September 2005, the Japanese save as much as 30 percent of their income; the Italians, the Germans, and Canadians save as much as 20 percent; and even the British save between 10 and 15 percent of their annual incomes. However, in the United States, in 2006, the annual savings rate was a negative 1.7 percent.

---

[8] In 1983, at the prompting of Alan Greenspan, Congress raised Social Security taxes before any real Social Security problem existed. Instead, funds were used to shore up government deficits and subsidize tax breaks for the rich. Ravi Batra, *Greenspans's Fraud: How Two Decades of His Policies Undermined the Global Economy* (New York: Palgrave Macmillan, 2005). Kevin Phillips, *Wealth & Democracy* (New York: Broadway Books, 2002).

Those who save now will have the greatest opportunities in the years ahead. Those who save through life insurance will be the most efficient savers of them all.

Life Insurance Professionals: The Heroes and the Underdogs

Life insurance professionals, particularly high-end ones, are some of the best financial advisors in America today. Unfortunately, due to preconceived notions of the American public, and through evangelical jihads coming from pop culture—financial gurus with little economic grounding—life insurance agents have been flagged with an undeserved bad rap. Nothing could be farther from the truth.

When one takes an impartial view of economic history in America and studies it, one will find that Wall Street, the banking industry and speculation manias ignited by the Federal Reserve's expansion and contraction of the money supply—not life insurance companies or life insurance agents—have inflicted immense economic pain on American consumers and the country. Like an out-of-control eighteen-wheeler truck in a Mad Max movie, the interests of financiers have run over the interests of the country and the average American consumer.

Banks, the Federal Reserve System, and Wall Street have constantly sought, lobbied for, and received government support, sanctions, tax subsidies, and outright bailouts from the American taxpayer. The life insurance industry, on the other hand, has remained strong and independent throughout American history. Yes, the life insurance product has definite tax advantages to it, but the industry as a whole has not abused the gifts it has been given.

It was the life insurance industry and the life insurance agent, not Wall Street nor the banks, which maintained their strength and kept their promises during the Great Depression. It was the life insurance industry, the life insurance professional and the actuarial discipline, which engineered the whole country's pension system, not Wall Street. It was the life insurance industry, and the life insurance agent, who developed the original forms of financial planning known as *programming*. Financial planning, as we know it today, came out of the life insurance industry, not Wall Street.

Yes, there are problems with the life insurance industry—inherent in all sectors of the economy. The author will be the first to admit, some of the larger life companies tend to act like self-perpetuating oligarchies. Some of the newer stockholder-owned life companies are acting like self-absorbed Wall Street broker–dealers. However, concerning actual malfeasance and outright plunder of Americans' savings and the debauchment of the currency, the banking and securities industries beat out the life insurance companies and agents by a country mile, and then some.

Let's add some real world perspective. Life insurance companies own over 50 percent of securities broker–dealers in the country, but only seven percent of consumer complaints come out of the life insurance business. These consumer complaints are not only small in number, but are miniscule in comparison to the billions of confiscated wealth from the banking, securities, and mutual fund businesses. We will list some of the complaints, which are public information, at the conclusion of the chapter, "Never Met a Man Who Made His Millions in Mutual Funds."

This author maintains that instead of dealing with the Internet, an 800 number, or some cold financial institution, people are still better off dealing with well-seasoned highly knowledgeable financial professionals. More often than not, high-end life insurance agents are the some of the best financial planners and professionals within America. From this author's experience, life insurance agents are some of the kindest, most generous, hard working, entrepreneurial, knowledgeable, and spiritual people he has ever met concerning issues of finance and overall economics.

Russ Alan Prince, one of the country's leading authorities on working with the wealthy, says in his book, *Winning the War for the Wealthy*, about life insurance agents:

> *"Talented insurance agents are the dominant financial professionals in the upscale markets. Other top financial and legal professionals also work with upscale clients, doing an exceptional job and prospering, but when they are compared with the very best producers in the insurance industry, the insurance agents dominate. Without question, there are sensational stockbrokers, attorneys, accountants and bankers, but the "best of the best" among these professionals are no match for the "best of the best" of the insurance industry.*
>
> *This conclusion is based on more than a decade of empirical research on the upscale markets and the distribution systems of professional and financial services to these markets. There is no group of professionals more gifted, dedicated, client-focused, and innovative than high-end insurance agents."*

Let us begin. Welcome to the Casino Age.

"The city boiled with money. Rents and Property values have never been higher, and in the garment industry it was widely held that fashion had never been so fashionable... The future was a casino, and everyone was gambling, and everyone expected to win."

Salman Rushdie, *Fury*
Writing about Pre 9/11 Manhattan

"Markets can remain irrational longer than you can remain solvent."

John Maynard Keynes

"My personal belief is that Enron stock is an incredible bargain at current prices, and we will look back a couple years from now and see the great opportunity we currently have."

Kenneth Lay, *former Enron CEO*
A few months before Enron's collapse

"Anybody who plays the stock market not as an insider is like a man buying cows in the moonlight."
Daniel Drew, *19th Century Speculator*

WELCOME TO THE CASINO AGE

"Were I to characterize the United States it would be by the appellation of the land speculations."
William Priest, English traveler, 1796

"The whole crisis came solely about our extravagant and vicious system of paper usury and bank credits, exciting people to wild speculation and gambling in stocks."
President James Buchanan, 1856

"I can calculate the motions of heavenly bodies, but not the madness of people."
Sir Isaac Newton, on the speculative mania of the South Sea Bubble

"The only thing our great financial institutions overlooked during the years of the boom was the installation of a roulette wheel for the convenience of depositors."
Heywood Broun, journalist 1930s

"The fate of the world economy is now totally dependent on the stock market, whose growth is dependent upon about 50 stocks, half of which have never reported any earnings."
Paul Volcker, 1999, former Federal Reserve Chairman

"Speculative manias gather speed through expansion of money and credit or perhaps, in some case, get started because of initial expansion of money and credit. One can look back at particular manias followed by crashes or panics and see what went wrong. The tulip mania, part of speculative excitement over many objects was fattened on personal credit."
Charles Kindleberger, Manias, Panics and Crashes

A major reason why permanent life insurance is not purchased as much as it should be is that the American public has rekindled its dysfunctional love affair with speculation. Hard work, innovation, and balanced growth made the American capitalistic system great but now it all seems to be about trading and speculating in currencies.

The Federal Reserve System in 2004 said that the huge amount of household debt within America should not be a concern. They must be crazy. Patience, thrift, discipline, concentration of effort, and love of family have been tossed out the window in favor of profit maximization and speculation.

Although there is a growing distrust in the government, trust in the money mavens and the Federal Reserve System remains strong. People are still buying things they do not understand at record rates. Moreover, despite the September 11, 2001, tragedy, which should have been a wake-up call for all of us about the perils of a premature death, Americans are purchasing less life insurance than ever. According to Thompson Financial, roughly 70

1

percent of parents between the ages of eighteen and thirty-nine do not even have a will for their children in the event of a premature death.

Welcome to the Casino Age, my friends. Enron and WorldCom, two of the greatest and most stunning speculative frauds on Wall Street since 1929, have failed to leave any lasting impression on the American psyche in regards to the dangers of reckless speculation, gambling, and too much debt. Anyone who opposes the speculation mania in mutual funds and the deregulation in banking or questions the unregulated world of hedge funds or private equity deals is shoved aside in favor of an outright worship of mammon and the divinity of the speculative trade.

The Founding Fathers not only warned us about the dangers of private banks but also of the dangers of hyper-speculation engineered by banks.

You do not need to look any further than Enron. The banks who participated in Enron's debacle were the Who's Who of Wall Street: Citibank, GE Capital, J.P. Morgan, Chase Bank, Merrill Lynch, Credit Suisse, First Boston, and Deutsche Bank. Banks, as well as other advisors such as lawyers and accountants who were making as much as $1 million a week, were making enormous fees off Enron. None of these advisors said "no" to Enron's wrongdoings, and they were knowing participants in Enron's shenanigans. Merrill Lynch pushed the envelope as far as anybody, in a blatantly illegal transaction; Merrill bought three Nigerian barges from Enron to take them off Enron's books.

Populists a century ago worried about speculation and considered Wall Street a self-absorbed money trust. Millions of people—from prairie farmers to urban workers to small business owners—considered Wall Street an entity that sucked the lifeblood out of a nation through its love of speculation.

Hero worship of financiers who gamble and speculate with money of others has gone mainstream. The battle cry is for more privatization and trickle-down economics. Government and state pension funds of firefighters, teachers, nurses, and other government employees fund in large part private equity deals and hedge funds, which are the latest secretive Wall Street creations that greatly benefit speculative insiders.

Feats of cooking the books, insider trading, looting the company through stock options and total disregard of the public interest are commonplace. Ostentatious displays of wealth by bankers, mutual fund owners, hedge fund managers, and corporate CEOs are served up daily as regular fare. Instead of the worship of money being questioned as a sign of spiritual sickness, it is, in most instances when covered by the press, trumpeted as a virtue.

Politicians and financiers have dubbed the massive gambling in stocks a *shareholder nation*. Upon closer inspection of the concentrated wealth within today's society, it is more like a *sharecropper nation*. As

2

Warren Buffett commented in his 2003 Berkshire Hathaway annual report, "If class warfare is being waged in America, my class is clearly winning."

Speculation, from legalized gambling to the purchase of mutual funds, saturates America today. This level of speculation would be impossible without massive deregulation and de-supervision of the financial service industry. Speculation has led to a world of unrealistic assumptions in investment returns. Many people believe that they can get 15 percent compound annual returns in the stock market. A study that Merrill Lynch once conducted revealed that investors expected something like a 23 percent rate of return in the market.

When the majority of pension plans was invested in bonds, they worked well as the investment returns were realistic. Companies such as United Airlines got themselves in trouble when they abandoned bond investments and chased market returns. The only people who profited were the managers (around twenty-seven) who managed United Airlines pension finances.

General Motors (GM) assumes a high return of about 10 percent on investments in its pension portfolio. Yet in 2001, GM actually lost 5.6 percent. In 2005, GM managed to achieve a 12.47 percent return. However, when you lose 5.6 percent in one year, you need to double the rate of return to 11.2 percent in the next year just to break even. Those companies with the greatest access to the best advisors money can buy are vulnerable in the investment loss department. Some companies do well; others do not.

The author was to meet William (Bill) Strauss, owner of FutureMetrics (www.futuremetrics.net). Bill Strauss is an economist. His company among other things tracks the estimated annual returns of many of the larger pension plans in corporate America. Over the past five years, you can clearly see the problem with unrealistic expectations in the stock market by reviewing the data from FutureMetrics' latest survey, *2006 Annual Pension Best and Worst Investment Performance Report*. Please keep in mind, that although these numbers are estimates, they are as accurate as you are going to get. Many companies use an assumed base interest rate of 7.2 percent minimum on their pension plan assets, with an expected rate between 9 and 10 percent.

Company	5-Year Rolling Average Rate of Return-*Best*	Company	5-Year Rolling Average Rate of Return-*Worst*
Rogers Corp.	11.66%	Matthews Intl Corp.	-5.83%
Brown Shoe	11.24%	Bank of New York	-2.92%
AMR Corp.-DE	10.18%	AFLAC	-2.66%
Valero Energy Corp	9.81%	Intel Corp.	-2.36%
Snap-On Inc.	9.55%	Fuller (HB) Co.	-2.06%
Eastman Kodak	9.43%	Ikon Office	-1.31%
Loews Corp.	9.20%	Harley-Davidson	-0.98%
CNA Financial	9.16%	Hewlett-Packard	-0.84%
Occidental Petrol	8.85%	Lehman Brothers	-0.52%
Berkshire Hathaway	8.61%	UnumProvident	-0.17%

Professional investors such as Berkshire Hathaway can do well on their pension investments, but what surprised the author was that white shoe institutions such as the Bank of New York and Lehman Brothers, supposed sages of the market, found themselves in negative territory.

Mutual funds will be covered in greater depth in the pages ahead, but in 2006, *Forbes* magazine did a blended yield of the entire mutual fund family[9]. Yes, mutual fund companies can have highflying funds (which are great for advertising), but there are usually many dogs in the fund family too. When you look at the overall performance of the *mutual fund company,* you have to wonder why we put so much faith in these entities. Not only are the aggregate returns for the fund family not that great, but when you have your money in a mutual fund your principal investment is also at risk. In many instances, you would get a higher rate of return with a life insurance company where your principal investment is guaranteed.

Keep in mind, that a mutual fund company like Janus, which was heavily involved in the late trading mutual fund scandal and was hammered with over $100 million in various fines, maintained an 18 percent pre-tax profit margin for the company in 2005. It is still a lucrative business for the company, but for the overall aggregate rate of return, the results are quite different. We are talking billions of dollars in U. S. domestic stock funds.

---

[9] John Chamberlain, "Family Counseling, Who's Better—Fidelity or Janus," *Forbes,* September 18, 2006, 86.

Fund Family	Weighted Annual 6-Year Return	Equity Assets 7/31/06 ($BIL)	Fund Family	Weighted Annual 6-Year Return	Equity Assets 7/31/06 ($BIL)
Royce	13.4%	$22.3	Scudder	0.8%	$27.1
Lord Abbott	6.7%	$41.5	Wells Fargo	0.2%	$21.2
Franklin Tem	5.6%	$61.1	Allianz	-0.2%	$27.7
AmericanFnd	5.1%	$386.3	FidelityAdv	-0.7%	$47.1
Davis	4.8%	$40.2	VanKampen	-1.4%	$38.9
T.RowePrice	4.4%	$127.8	Ameriprise	-1.4%	$31.9
Hartford	4.4%	$24.5	Amer.Cent	-1.9%	$56.7
JP Morgan	3.8%	$28.9	Putnam	-2.7%	$52.5
Pioneer	3.4%	$21.2	AIM	-3.1%	$42.5
Vanguard	3.0%	$532.7	MFS	-3.8%	$38.6
MerrillLynch	2.8%	$27.6	Columbia	-4.4%	$55.7
Fidelity	1.5%	$444.7	Janus	-5.2%	$49.0

Speculation in a world without rules hurts all of us. Reckless speculation has played a major role in soaring energy prices. Deregulation allows unregulated hedge fund speculators to make massive energy and commodity trades in the over-the-counter electronic markets without any oversight.[10] Insane as it may be, the bet-the-entire-farm wagers can drive the cost of a gallon of gasoline up fifty cents a gallon in a week.

Enron: The Poster Child for Deregulation and Speculation in the Casino Age

Enron's unregulated bets imploded California's electricity markets and eventually brought the entire company down. If there were ever a poster child for the pitfalls of deregulation and overspeculation in the Casino Age, it was Enron. Enron turned a reliable power industry into a casino.

Enron was the number one contributor to George W. Bush in his first election. It was once the seventh largest company in the United States. Ken

---

[10] In 1993, Wendy Gramm, wife of powerful banking Senator Phil Gramm (R-Texas), was Chairman of the Commodities Futures Trading Commission. Before she left office, she signed an order to exempt most private over-the-counter derivative contracts from securities regulation. This one act benefited Enron immensely. Wendy Gramm would go on to become a director of Enron, and her husband Phil became a great cheerleader for Enron. When it was suggested to Alan Greenspan that a study—a mere study— be done in regards to reviewing the exemption of these over-the-counter derivatives, Greenspan severely opposed it. Roger Lowenstein, *The Origins of the Crash, The Great Bubble and Its Undoing*, (New York: The Penguin Press, 2004).

Lay, the company's chairman, was an apostle of deregulation and pushed deregulation as magic in Washington. Jeff Skilling, Enron's president was known as a compulsive gambler and he would take Enron employees on dangerous extreme trips.

Enron courted other disciples of deregulation such as George H.W. Bush and Alan Greenspan, former Chairman of the Federal Reserve. Enron liked Greenspan and his deregulation views so much that they gave him the Enron Prize for Distinguished Public Service. Enron managed to have Wendy Gramm, wife of former Senator Phil Gramm, another Texas legislator who was an apostle of deregulation, to have Enron's trading activities in over-the-counter commodity and energy trades exempt from regulation. She eventually became a director at the company. In addition, through lobbying efforts of Kenneth Lay and Jeff Skilling, Enron was able to obtain *mark to market accounting*. This is truly bizarre. With mark to market accounting, a company can book profits on the day of the order and report them as profits ten years out for Wall Street—a true smoke and mirrors accounting trick.

Enron was and still is the poster child for speculation. Not only was Enron trading in energy, it began trading in broadband and weather futures. Ken Lay was the company's biggest cheerleader for Enron stock. The market believed him, as the share price went up 50 percent in 1999 and 90 percent in 2000. It became a company fixated on its stock price instead of its core business.

Insiders profited by the billions as they pumped the stock in public, and dumped the stock in private. Enron made much of its income in trading, and like all gamblers, the company lost over $90 million in five days. With its deregulation powers in California, Enron traders exploited every loophole in the electric markets and drove energy prices sky-high by shutting down power plants and causing blackouts and a state of emergency.

Nevertheless, it was a house of cards and it eventually collapsed. Enron's dance in the Casino Age left a wake of destruction. Deregulation in California energy cost around $30 billion; the value of Enron, estimated at $70 billion, evaporated. Two billion dollars in retirement/401(k) money was also lost and employees were put in a lock up so that they could not even sell their stock. An estimated 20,000 jobs were lost.

Regardless, there always seem to be connections between politicians and banks, and banks always make money—even in the wake of destruction. Senator Phil Gramm defended Enron as it pushed Pacific Gas & Electric into bankruptcy by saying in the *San Francisco Chronicle* that California was "suffering from its own feckless policies and from environmental extremism."

UBS Paine Webber administered the employee stock option program for Enron. In the bankruptcy court, Enron selected UBS Warburg as the buyer of Enron's wholesale energy trading business. Ten months later, the state of California awarded UBS Warburg the contract to arrange for a ratepayer bailout of the failed California electric company, and the fees UBS would earn in that transaction would later exceed $60 million. In the same week, UBS Warburg hired Phil Gramm.

In September 2006, a hedge fund called Amaranth Advisors out of Greenwich, Connecticut, lost $6 billion in one week making poor bets on the price of natural gas. This would never have happened if Enron had not plowed the field for deregulation, which exempted trades in commodities such as natural gas.

As in the collapse of Enron, a Wall Street Who's Who of Banks was in some way, shape, or form associated with Amaranth. According to Mara Der Hovanesian, a writer from *Business Week* the long tentacles of Wall Street did business with Amaranth.[11] Goldman Sachs was a hedge funds investor and an energy-trading partner. JPMorgan served as a futures clearing bank and was an acquirer of Amaranth's energy-trading portfolio. Citigroup was a commodities trading partner and a potential acquirer of Amaranth's operations. Merrill Lynch was a prime broker for Amaranth. Bank of America was a corporate lender. Credit Suisse was another fund of hedge funds investor. Morgan Stanley, too, was a hedge funds investor and a natural gas trading partner. Deutsche Bank, like the others, was a notable hedge funds investor.

Amaranth, as Enron, also had impressive investors. The San Diego County defined benefit plan, a retirement plan already up to its neck in shenanigans, had $175 million with Amaranth; anticipated losses of about $87 million and decided, while Amaranth was imploding, to put another $40 million into another hedge fund, High Bridge Capital Management. Minnesota Mining and Manufacturing (3M) had an undisclosed amount with Amaranth. Indirectly, through various hedge funds, investors included the New Jersey Division of Investment, the Commonwealth of Pennsylvania Retirement System, the Philadelphia Employees Retirement System, and the Santa Barbara California County Employees Retirement System.

Banks once again, had little more knowledge than the rest of us. They have survived but, as Enron, much of the money connecting Amaranth and its investors has vaporized.

In the Casino Age, there always seems to be a deep connection between Wall Street, the federal government, and speculation. Look no further than the giant investment bank of Goldman Sachs, which operates like a gigantic hedge fund.

---

[11] Mara Der Hovanesian, "Amaranth's Loss, Wall Street's Gain," *Business Week,* October 9, 2006, 78.

7

Goldman Sachs: An Investment Bank on Steroids and Inside Connections

Investment banks like to do business with public corporations and private equity deals, but throughout history, they have actively sought to do business with governments. Banks love government business because a government's ability to tax guarantees payment of their huge fees. Individuals and corporations can go into bankruptcy, but governments do not go bankrupt for the most part. Most large banks do business with local, state, federal, and international governments. Whether building a new airport or electric facility, privatizing a highway, or just raising a revenue bond, you will inevitably find commercial and investment bank connections. Banks cherish inside connections in the federal government as it gives them another competitive advantage in the world of finance.

Goldman Sachs is the premier investment bank in the United States and the highest paid, most connected investment bank in the world.

Business is booming at Goldman. It paid itself $11 billion in Christmas bonuses in 2005 and a whopping $16.5 billion in 2006. About 287 partners made an average of $7 million in compensation at Goldman in 2006. CEO Lloyd Blankfein made $52 million in 2006. The average employee at Goldman Sachs in 2006, in an age where a majority of people are finding it difficult to make ends meet, averaged $622,000 in compensation.[12]

Goldman Sachs is a poster child for speculation in the Casino Age as it generates around 68% of its revenue in trading securities. It is also the high water mark in inside connections with Washington.[13] According to the Center for Responsive Politics www.opensecrets.org, Goldman Sachs is a top corporate political donor. Other top banking donors include Citigroup, American Bankers Association, J. P. Morgan Chase, Morgan Stanley, Bank of America, Merrill Lynch, MBNA, and Credit Suisse.

Robert Rubin, a true cheerleader and apostle of banking deregulation, was a former Goldman Sachs banker before he became Secretary of the Treasury under Bill Clinton. While Treasury Secretary, Rubin supported Alan Greenspan of the Federal Reserve, Senator Phil Gramm and Sandy Weill of Citigroup in their efforts to bring about major banking deregulation which ultimately took place. Rubin, prior to being Treasury Secretary, was Chairman to the National Economic Council. Rubin is now a top executive at Citigroup.

---

[12] Andrew Ross Sorkin, "Goldman's Season to Reward and Shock," *New York Times,* December 17, 2006. Not only is Goldman's pay outrageous, it is estimated that although Wall Street only employs about 5 percent of New York City's workers, it takes home more than 20 percent of its pay.
[13] Neil Weinberg, "Goldman Sachs: Too Big? Too Powerful? Too Bad!" *Forbes,* January 2007.

Henry Paulson is former CEO of Goldman Sachs and made $45 million with Goldman in 2005.[14] He has a net worth in excess of a half billion dollars. Paulson is now Secretary of the Treasury and he has openly supported bankers who seek to gut the Sarbanes-Oxley bill of 2002, which sought to bring transparency to corporate malfeasance with public companies. Paulson, as other Wall Street alumni, claims that investment banking is overregulated and that is why they are losing business to stock markets in London and Hong Kong.

John Thain, another top Goldman Sachs banker, now runs the for-profit New York Stock Exchange (NYSE), which was recently the not-for-profit exchange when Richard Grasso received his record $180 million dollar retirement package that caused a national scandal and is still in the courts. Thain has been also involved with the Federal Reserve Bank on an international level.

Joshua Bolten, another former Goldman Sachs banker, is now George W. Bush's White House Chief of Staff.

Stephen Friedman, another Goldman Sachs alumnus, was Chairman of the President's Foreign Intelligence Advisory Board and Chairman of the National Economic Council until 2005.

Jon Corzine, a former Goldman Sachs banker who spent over $60 million to be elected as a U.S. Senator, is now the Governor of New Jersey.

Jim Cramer, the best-selling author who is perhaps Wall Street's most visible advocate and cheerleader for hyper-speculation through rapid trading in and out of stocks through his show *Mad Money* on CNBC, is also a former Goldman Sachs employee.

Edward Lampert is one of the highest paid hedge fund managers in the world. Lampert made $425 million running the unregulated hedge fund, ESL Investments, in 2005. He is also a Goldman alumnus.

John Whitehead is another Goldman Sachs prodigy. Whitehead was Chairman of the Lower Manhattan Development Corporation, Chairman of the Federal Reserve Bank in New York and a Deputy Secretary of State.

Other Government Connections in Banking and Wall Street

John Snow, the recent Secretary of the Treasury and Dan Quayle, former vice president, both work for the highly secretive private equity firm, Cerberus Capital Management.

George H.W. Bush, former president, has been involved in the mammoth private equity firm, the Carlyle Group, for years and served as an advisor to Carlyle until 2003. George W. Bush was on the board of directors

---

[14] Duff McDonald, "Please Sir, I Want Some More, How Goldman Sachs Is Carving Up Its $11 Billion Money Pie," *New York Magazine,* November 2005.

of one of the companies the Carlyle Group handled years ago. Don Rumsfeld was involved with Carlyle until 2005. Arthur Levitt, former Chairman of the Securities and Exchange Commission, is a senior advisor to the Carlyle Group. James Baker III, former Secretary of State under George H.W. Bush, served Carlyle until 2005. Richard Darman, former Director of the U.S. Office of Management and Budget under George H.W. Bush, has been a senior advisor to the Carlyle Group since 1993. William Kennard, former Chairman of the Federal Communications Commission under Bill Clinton, is a managing director of Carlyle Group's media division.

Deregulation, inside connections, and speculation have dismantled virtually every piece of apparatus, which was put in place to protect the American consumer. With deregulation, Wall Street can vastly improve its profits and legitimize its speculative excesses with our money.

In the Casino Age, Wall Street, mutual funds and other speculators turn their noses up at forms of high cash value life insurance, or any stable savings instruments for that matter, because it is not money that can be used again and again in their casino. In the final analysis, whole life insurance competes with Wall Street for the savings dollar, and if there is one thing a financier or banker hates, it is competition.

The media, instead of looking at core causes of why Americans save so little or expose the tragedies of speculation, sidestep the speculation and gambling issue, giving the consumer the world's economic history in sixty seconds or less. Instead of letting the truth be the guide, attention-deficit media move on to the next talking head money manager or the next commercial.

Various financial institutions, with the assistance of slick Madison Avenue advertising, have successfully brainwashed the consumer into believing there is no difference between saving and investing. The two concepts are quite different, but as far as the financial institutions and the media are concerned, they are one and the same. The only way to save, according to them, is to put it all in the markets.

Instead of empirically looking at the beauty of permanent whole life insurance as a savings and economic workhorse, the media has abandoned common sense and love of family and replaced it with a high-stakes celebrity poker game. Through incessant promotion and advertising funded mostly by the nation's banks, mutual fund companies, large broker-dealers, and other participants of the Casino Age, the media have systematically de-sensitized an entire nation about the real dangers of speculation and an American Empire built on debt. Instead of questioning the outright foolishness of the total embracement of gambling and speculation, the cable television shows recommend buying on the dip, staying in the market for the long haul, and waiting for the next economic enlightenment.

Speculation and gambling have always been a part of the American psyche. Speculation in securities and real estate is nothing new either, but it is hard to remember a time when speculation has been such a domineering force with so little public resistance. Speculation in the Casino Age is so pervasive that it borders on mental illness. Grandiose thinking, delusional unrealistic expectations, and tragic addictive behaviors are everywhere. Speculation is a serious social problem, but instead of the media sounding the warning bells, they zoom in for a close up of another overpaid executive or self-aggrandizing investment banker clanging the opening bell of the New York Stock Exchange. Instead of recommending caution, the media says, "don't worry, have some more." In a way, it is like encouraging a recovering alcoholic to drink a bottle of gin.

Speculation in the Casino Age is everywhere—the stock market, mutual funds, hedge funds, Internet gambling, state lotteries, casinos, high stakes celebrity poker, slot machines, thoroughbred horses, off-track betting, harness racing, greyhound dogs, puts, calls, options, commodities, mountains of derivatives, Deal or No Deal, Who Wants to Be a Millionaire, and on and on it goes.

Casino gambling is a $50 billion business. Nationally, Americans spend over $650 billion a year on legalized gambling. In 2000, over 34 million people visited Las Vegas. Over 127 million visited casinos nationwide. It was in this year that Americans spent more on gambling than they spent on all other sports and entertainment. From 1976 to 1998, there has been a forty-fold increase in gambling overall. Forty-eight of the fifty states now allow some type of gambling. Thirty-eight have lotteries. Thirty-three states have Indian casinos. All told, there are about nine hundred casinos in America.[15]

Speculation games of pure chance such as state lottery games, where the government always wins and the consumer inevitably loses, are embraced as proven methodologies to raise taxes. Not that they are that much better, but at least games such as blackjack, slot machines and the like return over 90 percent of their payout to the gambler. For state lotteries, where we spend $53 billion annually to include scratch tickets, the returns range from 40 to 60 percent.

One of the most bizarre manifestations of speculation in the Casino Age was when a retired Rear Admiral John Poindexter, who gained notoriety during the Iran-Contra scandal, announced that the Defense Advanced Research Projects Agency (DARPA) would run a futures market in terrorism. People would actually be able to speculate on death and destruction

---

[15] Edward Winslow, *Blind Faith, Our Misplaced Trust in the Stock Market and Smarter Safer Ways to Invest* (San Francisco: Berrett-Koehler, 2003).

11

throughout the globe. Only elites from government, business, and academia would be allowed to place bets. Bets and trades were to be limited to $100.[16]

The insane part of all of this was the delusional belief in the power of the market, the power of the speculative trade. Speculating became hyper-rationalizations, and people started believing that the stock market was the supreme conveyor of the truth. Everyone who listened to Wall Street wisdom could create work-free wealth by jumping on the speculation bandwagon.

Internet gambling is another new addiction this country could do without, as it, too, has proven to be highly addictive. As it stands now, Internet gambling is now illegal in this country, yet much of the seed money to capitalize Internet casinos came from the white shoes of Wall Street. Merrill Lynch, Goldman Sachs, Fidelity, and Morgan Stanley have all flouted laws and invested hundreds of millions of dollars in online casinos and betting parlors.[17] They have used funds to set up shop in London and other offshore sites. A major portion of these online casinos' revenue came from Americans incomes.

Casinos. Everyone wants a casino. As if a casino ever cured, or will cure, the ills of society. About one in every twenty Americans has a gambling problem. Statistics show that five percent of the people who buy lottery tickets purchase 51 percent of the total tickets and as a nation, we spend over $52 billion in lottery and scratch tickets alone.

Gambling and other vices, which complement casino gambling, create more ills within a society. Studies have shown that within a 50- to 250-mile radius of a casino, alcohol, drug abuse, bankruptcy, and prostitution are common problems that go along with our embracement of speculation.

Recently, this author read in horror that developers were trying to break the ground for a casino in Gettysburg, three miles from one of the major battlefields of the Civil War. Gettysburg is a symbol of the American struggle; putting in a casino there would be a sacrilege and desecration of sacred ground. Interestingly, Morgan Stanley is an $80 million dollar backer.

It is a speculate-till-you-drop economy. Cable television shows like *Fast Money* and Jim Cramer's *Mad Money* proliferate. *Mad Money,* a show that is pure speculation and gambling in stocks, gets holy water legitimacy thrown on the show by having remote broadcasts from Boston College and Georgetown University. Everywhere we turn; there is yet another electronic billboard, talk show, print advertising campaign, or investment guru talking about where the stock market is going to go, but no one really knows.

---

[16] For a wonderful overview of the history of speculation in America, Steve Fraser, *Every Man a Speculator* (New York: Harper Collins, 2005).

[17] Even though internet gambling was illegal in this country, Wall Street firms backed outfits in London and other offshore sites. Matt Richtel, "Wall Street Bets on Gambling on the Web: Investment Industry that Is Illegal in the U. S.," *New York Times,* December 25, 2005.

Now we have hedge funds. Hedge fund operators run without any regulation in the Casino Age, making billions by speculating on currencies, stocks, the price of gasoline, natural gas—you name it. Although we have not had any domino collapse of hedge funds as of yet, we did see a granddaddy of a collapse in 1998 with Long-Term Capital Management. In 2005, Bayou Partners blew up about $400 million, and in September of 2006, we saw the giant hedge fund Amaranth Advisors lose $6 billion in one week.

Credit Derivatives and Credit Swaps: Extreme Speculation

For those of you on the lookout for the next potential financial catastrophe, keep your eye on the business of credit derivatives and credit swaps. Hedge funds love to sell credit swaps, which is a type of insurance on a bond that protects principal and interest payments. The hedge fund selling the credit swap collects a premium on the bond. If the bond does not go into default, the hedge fund manager looks like a financial Einstein. However, if the bond defaults or goes sideways, the seller of the credit swap must make good on the so-called insurance. Because these hedge funds are so leveraged, a domino collapse would cause an economic meltdown. The capital losses are incomprehensible.

According to an article in *Forbes,* entitled "A Dangerous Game" by Daniel Fisher,[18] the aggregate amount of loans, bonds, and other debt covered by credit swaps is now pushing $26 trillion, a staggering sum, and twice the annual output of the United States. The article states that hedge funds now account for 58 percent of these types of derivatives (credit swaps).

Corporate defaults are currently low, so the temptation to write credit swaps must be overwhelming. However, if the corporate bonds go into default…there are no words to describe the after effects.

In the article, Fisher says that fourteen dealers, including JPMorgan Chase, Citigroup, Bank of America, and Goldman Sachs, dominate the credit derivative business. JPMorgan's aggregate exposure is $3.6 trillion, three times its assets and thirty-three times its total capital. Fisher says that regulators have no reason to worry—yet. *Haven't we heard that one before?*

Big banks require hedge funds to back up their swaps with cash. However, banks can only make rough guesses as to the value of the swaps and the value of the collateral on hand at the hedge funds. What type of security does that offer? Not a lot. Hedge funds are unregulated.

Frightening still, is that defined benefit pension assets, which are supposed to be invested in extremely safe and prudent investments, are now

---

[18] Derivative contracts could pose an economic meltdown, at the very *least*, a systemic threat to the economy. Daniel Fisher, "A Dangerous Game: Hedge Funds Have Gotten Rich from Credit Derivatives. Will They Blow Up?" *Forbes,* October 16, 2006.

rapidly entering into the unregulated hedge fund world of 2 and 20. The *2* in the equation is the base management fee that the hedge fund receives regardless of investment performance, and *20* means the 20 percent of the profits the hedge fund manager retains as a cut for speculating with other people's retirement money.

The Reappearing Ghosts of the 1920s

When one takes an impartial historical look at stock market speculation, one finds the idea of a ten-, twenty-, or thirty-year bull, or continually rising, stock market absolute lunacy. It is fantasy, an apparition, and a figment of the imagination. Nevertheless, through enormous advertising campaigns, Herculean public relations and media complicity, the American public is being serenaded once again by the Piped Pipers of Wall Street, much like it was during the 1920s. We are being told, once again, as in the 1920s, that we can make money without working for it.

The economic and social parallels between today and the 1920s are eerie to say the least. In the 1920s, there was a vast expansion of the money supply by the Federal Reserve System, which facilitated the Crash of 1929. Later a severe contraction or reduction of the money supply undoubtedly contributed to the Great Depression.

In October 1987, the stock market lost 23 percent of its value in one day. Today, this Fed has vastly expanded the money supply to keep the party going. By bringing down long-term interest rates to forty-year lows, the Federal Reserve System has flooded the market with cheap money and ignited a real estate speculation mania as well. Moreover, as the new Fed Chief Ben Bernanke takes the helm, we are seeing the beginning of a contraction of the money supply, which inevitably must go up to make American public debt more appetizing to foreign investors.

In the 1920s, we saw massive stock speculation on margin instigated by large non-regulated securities and banking industries. Today, we see colossal leveraged speculation in hedge funds and private equity deals brought to you again by deregulated securities and banking industries.

In the 1920s, we saw the birth of consumer credit in the "buy now, pay later" type of thinking. Today we see the borrowing of money at an unprecedented pace. People are using their homes like ATMs. The government borrows between $1.5 to $3 billion a day from Japan and China to keep the empire moving.

In the 1920s, we saw massive speculation in Florida real estate and then a collapse in values. Today, we have witnessed massive speculation in all real estate and a beginning of the decline in values. People are very

14

overleveraged. Banks and subprime lenders are waist deep in delinquent payments—not a good sign.

In the 1920s, we saw the growth of the investment trust or the investment company, which became the new vehicle for small savers who wanted to invest in the stock market. The amount of investment trusts, which is where today's mutual fund was born, increased by the hundreds before 1929, and they would become even more dangerous with leverage or borrowed money. People lost their life savings with the Crash. Today, a majority of savings, retirement savings in particular, is going into stock-based mutual funds and consumers lost $5 trillion by 2002. Do people have any more protection than they did in the 1920s? No, and they are probably more at risk with greater debts. Nevertheless, over 8,000 mutual funds compete for people's savings.

In the 1920s, Calvin Coolidge, ran his administration on the belief that business was the base of America's prosperity and that government should not interfere. Today, George Bush and much of Congress increasingly seeks to deregulate industries, de-supervise them, and give public tax dollars to subsidize private industries.

In the 1920s, the country was showing signs of trouble. Steel production was declining. Construction was slowing down. Larger sections of the population were getting poorer and poorer. Easy credit made it easier for people to get deeper and deeper into debt. Popular magazines promised the insider track to easy money.

Today, America is once again showing early warning signs of impending disaster. Jobs are outsourced to the Far East. General Motors and Ford are in the intensive care unit. Our military spending is like a runaway freight train as we drain our treasury to maintain hundreds of outposts around the world. No longer can an average family survive on just one income; husbands and wives are both working harder and harder and seeing their paychecks purchase less and less. Bankruptcies are at an all-time high, even among the senior portion of the population. In addition, like the 1920s, get-rich quick schemes proliferate from our most visible types of media—television and print.

While average citizens today struggle to make ends meet as they did in the 1920s, speculators and bankers, as their counterparts in the 1920s, have incomes, which are hard to fathom.[19] In the 1920s, Thomas Lamont was a financial leader in the United States and a banker with the white shoe Morgan

---

[19] Banker, Wall Street, and hedge fund compensation recently is hard for most people even to fathom. Some hedge fund managers, such as T. Boone Pickens, made $1.5 billion in 2005. Many others earned hundreds of millions. Richard Fairbank, of Capital One credit cards, in total compensation, exceeded $250 million in 2005.

Bank. Lamont said five days prior to the stock market crash, "The future appears brilliant. Our securities are the most desirable in the world."

Today, another banker has been thrust into one of the most powerful positions in the American republic. Henry "Hank" Paulson is the new Treasury Secretary of the United States. Paulson was the former CEO of Goldman Sachs and has a net worth somewhere between one-half and three-quarters of a billion dollars. In a commencement address at Harvard in 2006, Paulson's remarks echoed those of Lamont in 1929 when he said, "(he) has never seen a better global economy."

Sure, it is a great economy if you are a speculator, a banker, in the media business, a government employee, or someone else supporting the American empire. It is not a great economy if you are looking at the price of gas, have to pay for healthcare out of your own pocket, watch food prices rise, pay taxes, trying to figure out a way to pay for college, and so on. Moreover, this, Mr. Paulson, is the vast majority of us.

Permanent Life Insurance: A Green Oasis in a Scorched Earth World of Finance

In the midst of the Casino Age, permanent life insurance, primarily high cash value whole life, is one of the safest and most versatile reservoirs for savings. In a way, dividend-paying permanent life insurance is a Swiss Army knife of financial products. Tragically, the media and other financial gurus continue to downplay the positive aspects of whole life. In fact, there is somewhat of a financial jihad against permanent life insurance.[20] Term life insurance is consistently pushed as the only way to go for the American consumer.

This book will empirically prove that those with superlative financial resources such as banks, corporations, and high net worth people, purchase permanent cash value life insurance by the tractor-trailer load. Term life insurance, although valuable coverage, is, in the final analysis, all cost to the consumer and the most profitable to a life insurance company.

According to a Penn State University study done in 1993, about one in ten term life policies survives the period for which it was written. The study also revealed that the average life span for a term life policy before it was terminated or converted was less than two years. Seventy-two percent of term life policies are either terminated or converted within the first three years.

---

[20] The author's research revealed that numerous "financial experts" had documented prejudices against permanent life insurance products and life insurance agents and put these prejudices in writing. Some include Suze Orman, Jane Bryant Quinn, Dave Ramsey, Elizabeth Warren of Harvard, and economist and author Burton Malkiel of Princeton University.

16

Yet the most glaring statistic was that only about 1 percent of all term life policies sold resulted in a death claim. An in-house study performed by Northwestern Mutual Life reported somewhat similar findings.

To understand better the economy and the strength and versatility of permanent life insurance within our economy, the consumer should have a rudimentary understanding of where most savings dollars are going today. Most discretionary saving is going into mutual funds, particularly through defined contribution retirement plans such as 401(k) and 403(b) programs.

To understand better the economy and the strength and versatility of permanent life insurance, the consumer should have an understanding of the past twenty-five years of deregulation, particularly in banking. Let us proceed to the next chapter, "Deregulation, De-supervision, and Plenty of Subsidies."

DEREGULATION, DE-SUPERVISION AND PLENTY OF SUBSIDIES

"Many of our rich men have not been content with equal protection and equal benefits, but have besought us to make them richer by act of Congress."
                Andrew Jackson, veto of Second Bank charter extension, 1832

"Free trade in banking is tantamount to free trade in swindling."
                Thomas Tooke, nineteenth-century English economist

"The issue which has swept down through the centuries and which will have to be fought sooner or later is the people versus the banks...all power corrupts, absolute power corrupts absolutely."
                Lord Acton, Historian, 1887

"Deregulation became a kind of religion—it was supposed to enable people to get better products or more services competitively. But it doesn't mean wiping out all the protection of the consumers in order to respond to some kind of dogma."
                Felix G. Rohatyn, famous financier, New York Times, May 16, 2004

"The repeal of the Glass–Steagall has enabled the giant financial conglomerates like Citigroup to become involved in a great variety of different businesses which often raise serious conflicts of interest. Those involved have to be particularly sensitive to these potential conflicts and have controls in place to avoid them."
                Lewis D. Lowenfels, expert attorney, securities law New York Times, May 16, 2004

"It is a necessary part of the business of a banker to profess a conventional respectability which is more than human. Lifelong practices of this kind make them the most romantic and least realistic of men."
                John Maynard Keynes

'"Innovation and deregulation have vastly expanded credit availability to all income classes," says the Fed chief. He did not mention his own role in this democratic revolution. He is too modest. He is a Danton and Robespierre put together. The Fed chairman accomplished more than all the nation's innovators and deregulators put together. Dropping the price of credit below the inflation rate, he offered the entire world something for

18

nothing. Now everyman could get himself into financial trouble, not just kings, speculators, and financiers. He made it possible for lending institutions to extend such a long rope of credit to the common man that millions are sure to hang themselves."

Addison Wiggin and William Bonner, Empire of Debt

"Wall Street was riddled with abuses. It just wasn't one corrupt individual. It was an entire business model that was flawed. It was distressing to me how simple and outrageous it was. It was so complicated that you said, wow, at least they are smart in the way they were doing it. It was simple; it was brazen. The evidence of it was overwhelming. There is no question that the creations of "super banks" have created a conflict of interests and a web of relationships that provide the opportunity for massive abuse, and what we uncovered shows there was massive abuse."

Elliot Spitzer, The Wall Street Fix, PBS Television, May 8, 2003

"Self-regulation by an industry tends to usually to be self-serving and often inefficient. There is a danger that government commissions, set up ...originally to regulate an industry, will in fact end up as a tool of that industry, becoming more concerned to protect it from competition than to protect the customer from the absence of competition...The SEC must itself be under constant congressional scrutiny lest it lessen rather than increase the protection the consumer receives from vigorous competition.

Paul Samuelson, Nobel Laureate economist, 1967 Senate Commission on Banking and Currency Hearing on Mutual Fund Legislation, 90th Congress, 368-69

Looking back over the landscape of American finance between 1940 and 1980, it is evident that this period was one of the best economic runs the United States has ever seen. Whereas today, according to the World Institute for Development Economics Research of the United Nations, the top ten percent of the population in America now owns 70 percent of the country's wealth compared with France at 61 percent of the wealth, 56 percent in the United Kingdom, 44 percent in Germany, and 39 percent in Japan.

Between 1940 and 1980, well-paying jobs, reasonable costs for healthcare, loans, real estate, food, and affordable energy costs were more attainable. It was also a time when it was possible to have one breadwinner, typically the male, support an entire household. Leisure time was not a luxury. We were once the world's greatest creditor. Now we are the world's greatest debtor.

This period was also one of the only times in American history when the interests of banking and securities industries were one of the last priorities of the American economic agenda. The hangover of overspeculation, the Stock Market Crash of 1929, the Great Depression, and the related pain and suffering of these events were still burned into the American psyche. Americans, as a whole, had a great mistrust for all things involved with banking in general and Wall Street in particular. With their track record, who could blame them?

Major legislation was put in place to protect the consumer from the conflicts of interest in the banking and securities industries, which caused the economic calamity of the 1930s.

Some of the laws passed were:

* First, in 1933, the Glass–Steagall Act was enacted to separate the commercial and investment banking interests. Congress had decided that the collusion in those two industries was a major contributor to the Crash of 1929 and the Great Depression.

* Second, in 1933, we saw the introduction of the Securities Act of 1933, which brought the registration process to the securities business. This included registration of mutual funds. The act created the Securities and Exchange Commission (SEC).

* Third, in 1934, the Securities Exchange Act was passed. This authorized the SEC to provide fair and equitable securities markets.

* The introduction of the Investment Company Act came in 1940, which set the structure and regulatory framework for investment advisors and the mutual fund industry.

* Last, in 1956, the Bank Holding Company Act (BHC) was adopted, placing multiple bank holding companies under federal supervision. This act also stipulated that the non-banking activities must be closely related to the business of banking.

However, Americans seem to have short memories. In fact, during the 1980s, we became the United States of Amnesia. All the pain and suffering that the banking and securities industries had caused in prior years seemed to vanish from the minds of American consumers who were busy funding the Wall Street casino.

Since the early 1980s, deregulation in banking and other financial services has been sold to the American public as a financial nirvana and economic rapture. Lobbyists, public relations firms, congressional leaders, the Federal Reserve, large banks, and securities firms promised more services, lower costs of financial products, job creation, and a more vibrant economy with the deregulation of financial services.

What America got with deregulation were fewer services, reduced banking hours, excessive service fees (which have gone up as much as 400 percent), legalized predatory interest rates, regressive bankruptcy laws, more volatility in the stock market, shorter boom and bust business cycles, heightened corruption, excessive executive compensation, blatant conflicts of interest, less transparency, debauchment of the currency, job exportation, less competition for larger banks, more taxpayer subsidies, and a stagnant, less stable, economy which has hit the middle and lower classes particularly hard.

Deregulation has given birth to a new era of the *überbank* or super bank and has resulted in the unfathomable concentration of economic power within America's banking industry. There is little, if any, formidable competition to prevent these super banks from abusing their power. This abuse of power with financial service deregulation was demonstrated with the collapse of Enron and WorldCom, the high technology meltdown, usury interest rates, a plethora of mutual fund scandals, new bankruptcy legislation that favored the banks over the public, unregulated hedge funds, and now a subprime mortgage industry, which is imploding.

Increasingly, new super banks appear to be operating as a monopolistic economic cartel like The Organization of the Petroleum Exporting Countries or OPEC. In addition, with the Federal Reserve System in their corner, super banks appear untouchable. Large financial institutions, the first to wave the flag of patriotism and jingoism in gargantuan advertising and public relations campaigns are offshoring many jobs. Large banks such as Bank of America and mutual fund companies like Fidelity are embracing offshoring of jobs to ensure profitability.

Deregulation, de-supervision and plenty of subsidies have created an economy, which favors those at the top of the economic ladder—with financial firms at the top of the monetary food chain. And when one impartially examines the world of finance, they will see that financiers do not manufacture anything but debt, economic risk and excessive compensation (roughly 21 percent of all wages in New York City are from the securities business but they only comprise about 4.7 percent of the work force).

Deregulation was packaged in a pretty prom dress and given the public relations name *financial services modernization.* In reality, bank and securities deregulation is a Trojan horse for super banks to get into your pocketbook in every conceivable way.

Deregulation Did not Happen Overnight

A main purpose of this book is give the consumer ample evidence that shows we live in a shark-invested financial services economy and that permanent life insurance is a safe and secure financial oasis for your savings.

To understand all of the sharks swimming in the economic oceans, the reader should have a good understanding of deregulation.

Deregulation did not happen overnight. Where we are today is the result of thirty plus years of concentrated lobbying by banks and securities industries, and to a small extent, the insurance industries. The author would like to summarize the important developments in deregulation, which brought us to our current situation. Later, we will discuss in detail the major components of deregulation; namely:

*   The Garn–St. Germain Act and the Savings and Loan Disaster
*   Repeal of Usury Laws: Darth Vader Interest Takes Over Main Street
*   Arbitration for Broker–dealers: Self-Regulation on Steroids
*   The Repeal of Glass–Steagall
*   The Birth of the 2005 Bankruptcy Abuse and Consumer Protection Act
*   International Banking: No Regulations, No Supervision, and a Ton of Subsidies
*   Banker and Manager Compensation in a World of Deregulation
*   Summing Up Deregulation, De-supervision, and Plenty of Subsidies
*   How Deregulation Marches on.

A Brief History of Financial Deregulation in America

In 1950, President Harry S. Truman signed the Revenue Act of 1950. Buried deep within this law is the section of the tax code, which gave birth to the stock option as a form of executive compensation. Although stock options have been with us since 1950, they did not become a major form of compensation until the 1980s, mainly because stocks and their value were going nowhere.

As stock prices levitated, stock options became a major form of employee and executive compensation, particularly within the high tech arena. However, they were not without a cost. The existence of options gives an executive or other insider the opportunity to loot a company legally. In essence, stock options are just a legal method of transferring wealth from the shareholders of a company to senior managers and other key people. It is estimated that stock options dilute as much as 30 percent of a company's value.

Continuing down the historic path of deregulation brings us to August 1971, when President Nixon took the United States off the gold standard. From that date on, the country could no longer redeem its international debts in gold. In 1933, President Roosevelt took the country off the gold standard domestically. Individuals and corporations could no longer demand payment in gold.

Nixon was forced to take the country off the gold standard as war debts from Vietnam continued to pile up, and Middle Eastern countries, in the midst of the first of many oil crises, demanded payments for oil with gold bullion, which drained gold reserves. With no "gold standard" for international debts, the Federal Reserve System and the federal government can create paper money at will, which leads to a long road of inflation. Since 1971, the US dollar has lost at least 80 percent of its value.

Later in 1975, a Mayday in the securities industry occurred when the SEC deregulated fixed commissions charged on securities transactions. For years, high fixed commissions had been the mother's milk of income for the securities industry. With the era of high stock commissions coming to an end, securities firms and major investment companies found themselves scrambling for income that was more lucrative.

The US Supreme Court handed out the ruling of the Marquette National Bank vs. First Omaha Service Corporation case in 1978. The court held that banks and credit card companies could charge their customers the highest rate allowed in their home states—not the customers' states of residence. This ruling created the foundation for high interest credit cards.

Traveling on, in 1979, South Dakota became the first state to repeal usury laws. As a result, there was no longer a legal limit for the interest rate on a loan. Whatever the market could bear became the law of the land. Citibank was the first bank to set up shop in South Dakota in 1981 to exploit laws. Governor Pierre DuPont of Delaware had his state join the bandwagon, luring credit companies from banks such as MBNA, JPMorgan Chase, Morgan Stanley (Discover), and HSBC Bank. Virginia followed, with Capital One quickly setting up shop there. Utah finally chimed in and picked up American Express; Arizona followed with Bank of America; and Providian set up shop in the author's home state of New Hampshire. The most profitable segment of the entire banking industry is credit cards. Usury interest becomes the sweet spot for banking profits.

The following year, the Depository Institutions Deregulation and Monetary Control Act of 1980 was passed. This act provided universal requirements for all financial institutions and was the first step to removing restrictions on competition for deposits. In 1980, the Comptroller of the Currency and the Federal Reserve also authorized banks to establish securities subsidiaries allowing them to combine the sale of securities with investment advisory services. The banks were back in the securities business. The Glass–Steagall Act was crumbling. The dismantling of the apparatus, which protected and insulated the consumer from banks, had begun.

23

Usury went mainstream in 1981, when Citibank set up its first high rate interest card in South Dakota. The company started charging 20 percent interest rates on its credit cards. In its home state of New York, Citibank would have been limited to 12 percent. Predatory lending becomes a major business component of white shoe banks.

A year later, in 1982, the Garn–St. Germain Depository Institutions Act was signed authorizing financial instruments such as money market accounts. This act vastly expanded the lending powers of thrift banks. Ironically, this piece of legislation led to the Savings and Loan fiasco.

Entering our historical account of deregulation is Bank of America. With its purchase of discount securities broker Charles Schwab in 1983, the company entered the securities business. Schwab, however, bought back the business in 1987. Although they are not in the middle of the dance floor of the securities business, banks are showing their faces in the industry and proving they are in the dance for the long haul.

More traction for the banks in the securities business occurred in 1987 with the Federal Reserve ruling an interpretation of Section 20 of Glass–Steagall. The Fed, with the assistance of Alan Greenspan, essentially allowed capitalized affiliates of commercial bank holding companies to engage in a variety of securities transactions on a limited basis. The same year, the case of *Shearson/American Express Inc. vs. McMahon* came into the spotlight. With this legal case, it was upheld by the United States Supreme Court that standard arbitration clauses signed when opening up an account with a securities firm takes precedence over the Seventh Amendment of the United States Constitution. So much for due process. Disputes with securities firms and other broker–dealers were no longer adjudicated in a court of law, but within the securities industry with arbitration. It was a grand slam victory for the securities firms and a major setback for the consumer. In October 1987, the stock market lost 23 percent of its value in one day.

The enactment of the Financial Institutions Reform, Recovery and Enforcement Act followed several years later in 1989, providing massive government funds to bail out insolvent savings and loan institutions with the assistance of the Resolution Trust Corporation. Over twenty-nine hundred banks failed. Taxpayers picked up the tab—witnessing the greatest collapse of banks since the Great Depression.

Another piece of the Glass–Steagall Act was tossed out the window when, in 1990, JPMorgan was permitted to underwrite securities. Ghosts of the 1920s and the 1930s began to reappear in Technicolor™.

The downward cycle plunged into an abyss when Wendy Gramm, Chairman of the Commodity Futures Trading Commission and wife of banking Senator Phil Gramm of Texas, signed an order to exempt most

24

private derivative contracts from regulation right before leaving office.[21] For companies like Enron, who by this time had generated a major portion of its income from trading derivatives in electricity, it was like hitting the lottery. Enron appreciated Gramm's help so much that it later appointed her a director of the company. The company later used this exemption to speculate in electricity and exploit the weaknesses of newly deregulated electricity markets. Its actions eventually brought the state of California to its knees. Even though consumers paid $30 billion in extra electric utility fees, Enron became a Wall Street darling. A house of cards, Enron collapsed under the rising scandal.

Interstate banking was permitted in the U. S. with the passing of the Riegle–Niel Interstate Banking and Branching Efficiency Act of 1994. This led to a mad rush of consolidation, mergers, and acquisitions.

The Supreme Court ruled in 1995 in the case of *NationsBank vs. Variable Annuity Life Insurance Company* that annuities were not a form of insurance under the National Bank Act of 1956. What did banks do? They began to sell annuities to depositors in a big way. It was just another piece of the Glass–Steagall Act being stripped away.

Another piece of legislation to reduce litigation against major broker–dealers, securities firms, banks and other financial entities was the Private Securities Litigation Reform Act of 1995. This was pushed through Congress as part of Newt Gingrich's Contract with America. In the middle of the heightened speculative era of the 1990s, this act shielded executives and accounting firms from making dubious financial projections. James D. Cox, professor in corporate law at Duke University said, "It was the ultimate in special interest legislation."[22]

The Supreme Court, in 1996, in the case *Smiley vs. Citibank* ruled that credit card fees were indeed the same as interest charges on credit cards. This led to a new era of unlimited fees and penalties. For credit card companies, fee income went up 100 percent.

Several other notable events took place in 1996. The first was that the Supreme Court, in the *Barnett Bank* case allowed banks to sell insurance nationwide. In addition, Section 20 of the Glass–Steagall Act was amended to allow commercial bank affiliates to underwrite up to 25 percent of previously ineligible securities in either equity or debt. Banks, even though the Glass–Steagall Act is still on the books, are now engaged actively and openly in insurance and securities underwriting.

---

[21] Roger Lowenstein, *The Origins of the Crash, the Great Bubble and Its Undoing* (New York: Penguin Press, 2004), p.96.

[22] William Wolman and Anne Colamosca, *The Great 401(k) Hoax* (Cambridge, MA:Perseus Publishing, 2002), 62.

Additional framework was put into effect in 1997 to eliminate the barriers that discriminated against foreign-owned firms. The General Agreement on Trade Services was a piece of legislation that set the groundwork for companies like the United Bank of Switzerland (UBS) to acquire securities firms such as Paine Webber.

A super bank was born in 1998, when Citibank and Travelers merged to form Citigroup. The new company created the largest financial conglomeration of all time, the largest coming together of banking, insurance and securities interests—when legislation still on the books said it was illegal to do so. Essentially Sandy Weill of Travelers and John Reed of Citibank thought Congress was not moving fast enough—to heck with it, let's do it on our own. Moreover, they pulled this off with the blessings of the President of the United States, Bill Clinton, the Chairman of the Federal Reserve System, Alan Greenspan, and the Secretary of the Treasury, Robert Rubin. When it was all over, what happened? Robert Rubin, the secretary of the treasury, became the vice chairman of Citigroup.

Shortly thereafter, in 1999, the Gramm–Leach–Bliley Act was passed—completely repealing the former Glass–Steagall Act. Gramm–Leach–Bliley allowed banks, insurance companies, and securities firms to affiliate with each other and sell one another's products. It was probably the most heavily lobbied and most expensive piece of legislation ever. A non-partisan research group, the Center for Responsive Politics, reported that in 1997 and 1998, banking, insurance, and securities industries gave $58 million to federal political candidates, donated $87 million in soft money to political parties, and spent an additional $163 million in additional lobbying expenses. An all-star cast, namely Alan Greenspan of the Federal Reserve, Representative Jim Leach of Iowa, Senator Phil Gramm of Texas, Robert Rubin, Secretary of the Treasury and Sandy Weill of Citigroup, as his new firm would have to be unwound if the repeal of Glass–Steagall did not go through, supported the repeal of Glass–Steagall. Citigroup even hired Jesse Jackson[23] to increase its public relations efforts. The practice of tying commercial loans to follow on profitable securities underwriting, which was a prohibited practice for more than sixty-five years, was now allowed.

In 2004, the Office of the Comptroller of the Currency (OCC) exercised its supervisory muscles by making itself the exclusive authority on national banking issues, which was one of the major goals banks wanted out of the passage of Gramm–Leach–Bliley. In a case that had its origins at the state level in California, the OCC used its preemption rights to fine Providian Bank over $300 million for its abusive lending practices involving credit cards. This is a clear victory for big national banks as they can now only be

---

[23] Charles Gasparino, *Blood on the Street: the Sensational Story of How Wall Street Analysts Duped a Generation of Investors* (New York: Free Press, 2005) 110.

challenged at the federal level. The Better Business Bureau in 2004 reports that in the over one thousand industries it tracks, the number one type of complaint they receive is consumer complaints with banks and credit card companies.

The year 2005 gave rise to the Bankruptcy Abuse Prevention and Consumer Protection Act. The new law increased some protection for IRA accounts, but it clearly ruled in favor of banks that portrayed themselves as being "the victims" in bankruptcy courts, when debtors seek to have high interest rate credit cards discharged. Congress, who racks up annual deficit bills of $500-$600 billion annually, obviously felt pity towards the banking industry by passing this regressive bill.

In 2006, there was a flurry of activity contributing to deregulation. The Supreme Court, in March 2006, in *Merrill Lynch vs. Dabit* ruled in an 8-0 decision to block class action lawsuits filed by stockholders who contend they were tricked into holding onto declining company shares. The decision, however, did not block lawsuits filed by individuals, but rather suits filed on behalf of large groups of people. The ruling made it much harder for individuals to join forces to file high stakes fraud cases.

The next big event of 2006, which should have made major headlines passed by mostly unnoticed—a report released by the Federal Reserve System explaining that data on the total money supply within circulation is no longer important. They killed the M3, which shows the entire growth in the money supply and a key measure of inflation.

The SEC also failed to enact rules in 2006 requiring the registration of hedge funds, which now number around eight thousand and manage more than $1.3 trillion of assets. They continue to operate as unregulated entities with much volatility as they often borrow significant amounts of money in highly speculative bets. No meaningful data exists on hedge funds.

A piece of legislation passed by Congress in 2006, the Pension Protection Act, became a bonanza for the mutual fund industry. The Investment Company Institute (ICI) and mutual fund giant Fidelity successfully lobbied for automatic enrollment with defined contribution retirement plans such as 401(k) and 403(b) plans. The act virtually guaranteed the mutual fund business additional trillions of dollars in assets and billions in fees.

Not long after, the New York Stock Exchange and the National Association of Securities Dealers merged into one regulatory authority. The result? Less regulation. Attorney General William Galvin of Massachusetts was greatly disappointed and stated that it was one less cop on the beat to protect the consumers from securities crimes.

Finally in 2006, the Committee on Capital Markets Regulation was formed. No new legislation has been passed, however. This committee includes financiers, academics, and attorneys who have been given the task to

27

unwind and gut the Sarbanes-Oxley Act of 2002, which was put in place to bring greater accountability to the boards of public corporation and make companies more accountable to their shareholders.

Both Henry Paulson, secretary of the treasury, and Sanford Weill, former chairman of Citigroup, endorse the committee. In fact, in October 2006, Weill on *CSPAN* television from Dallas, Texas, comments that consumers will be well served by the Committee on Capital Markets. Weill also said that the Federal Reserve should be more of a regulator in financial markets. Weill fails to mention that the country's commercial banks own the Federal Reserve System.

Garn–St. Germain and the Savings and Loan Disaster

"My friends, there is good news and bad news. The good news is that the full faith and credit of the FDIC and the U. S. government stand behind your money in your bank. The bad news for you, my fellow taxpayers, is you stand behind the U. S. government."
L. William Seidman, former head of the Federal Deposit Insurance Corp. (FDIC)

In 1982, The Garn–St. Germain bill allowed the savings and loan industry to diversify their portfolios out of local mortgages. It also allowed it to invest in junk bonds, speculative real estate ventures or any other opportunities that tickled bank directors' fancies, such as *their own personal projects*. With Garn–St. Germain, savings and loan institutions could also sell off their non-performing loans so they would be immediately charged against profits.

Garn–St. Germain also gave savings and loan institutions carte blanche insurance for depositors in case of bank failure. Each account was now insured up to $100 thousand per account regardless of the financial status of the bank. The deregulation of the industry allowed some savings and loan institutions to operate essentially without any capital requirement.[24] At one time, about five hundred insolvent banks were allowed to operate in the hope of being brought back to life. The word *savings* should have been omitted entirely from the term *savings and loan*.

William Black, in his authoritative book about the collapse of the savings and loan industry, *The Best Way to Rob a Bank Is to Own One,* gives us a ringside seat to the debacle. Black was intimately involved as a regulator/attorney overseeing the entire collapse. He writes:

---

[24] William K. Black, *The Best Way to Rob a Bank Is to Own One* (Austin: University of Texas Press, 2005), 31.

I have explained that according to economic theory, deregulating an industry that is massively and pervasively insolvent and has deposit insurance guarantees disaster. Pratt designed the Bank Board's deregulation and the deregulatory Garn–St. Germain Act of 1982. Pratt and Roger Mehle, an assistant secretary of the treasury, drafted the legislation.

Pratt's deregulation was doomed from the outset because he used the worst possible model of deregulation, Texas, to guide his efforts. He gave Texas an award in recognition of serving as his model. Texas-chartered S&Ls caused by far the worse losses during the debacle…

Pratt made it possible for one man to own an S&L. Pratt eliminated the Bank Board rules that prevented an individual from owning more than 15 percent of the stock and that required there be at least 400 shareholders. Second, Pratt relaxed conflict-of-interest rules that restricted officers and directors from using their positions for personal gain…

The third key fact of deregulation was Pratt's further weakening of the net worth requirement…He did so in two ways. The obvious change was reducing the net-worth requirement to 3 percent of total liabilities. That is a ludicrously low level of capital. A typical manufacturing company in the 1970s would have fifteen times as much capital. An S&L with a 3 percent capital is a few bad loans away from failure…

An S&L's capital requirement could be far less than the nominal requirement because it could, for example, meet the 3 percent requirement by showing that its capital represented 3 percent average liabilities over the last five years. The next footnote provides an example that illustrates the point; but the perverse bottom line was that the faster you grew, the lower your effective percentage of capital requirement…By lowering the nominal requirement to 3 percent and continuing five year averaging, Pratt knew he was essentially eliminating the capital requirement, and that came on top of pervasive accounting abuses.

The combination of very low nominal capital requirements and five year averaging meant that the faster growing control frauds could grow by roughly $1 billion for every additional $1 million of "capital" they could report. This thousand-to-one leverage opportunity was one of the keys to the astonishing growth that made control frauds ideal for Ponzi schemes and imposed horrific damages on taxpayers. Every $1 million in fraudulent accounting income could put the taxpayer at risk by an additional $1 billion. (pp. 28-32).

One of the main points of Black's book is that the American public has failed to remember the numerous problems brought about by bank deregulation. With bank deregulation, we also witnessed a new type of white-collar crime which William Black calls *control fraud*. [25]

Control Fraud

Control fraud was the orchestrated conspiracy and manipulation of accounting and other important financial information to make a bank look healthy. Control fraud was a symphony of financial deception that bank insiders, accountants, law firms, lobbyists, and other highly paid consultants used to manipulate the financial health of a bank.

By Black's accounts, three hundred of the failed S&Ls were involved in control fraud with over one thousand bank insiders being convicted on felony charges. Control fraud will ultimately cost the American taxpayer over $250 billion when it is all said and done.

Charles Keating, the infamous banker of Lincoln Savings and Loan, used control fraud to bring about one of the largest bank failures in the S&L disaster. Keating was a textbook case of banker deception. He had friends in very high places, which he used to his advantage. They came to be known as the Keating Five. The Keating Five was a group of five U. S. Senators (Alan Cranston, Dennis DeConcini, John Glenn, John McCain, and Donald W. Riegle, Jr.) who pressured the Bank Board for leniency on behalf of Charles Keating.

Keating also had high paid consultants like Alan Greenspan. [26] William Black also discusses in his book the naivety of consultants such as Greenspan and other financial authorities in ferreting out the real financial problems of a shaky S&L bank.

Keating's control fraud could have taught us the lessons we needed to learn to avoid the ongoing wave of control fraud. Consider Greenspan's, Benston's and Fischel's evaluations of Lincoln Savings. Greenspan said that it "posed no foreseeable risk" to the FSLIC (Mayer 1990, appendix C, U.S. House Banking Committee 19893:603-606). Benston said Lincoln Savings should serve as a model for the industry. Fischel proved it was the best S&L in the nation. Three of the nation's top financial experts took the worst corporation in the nation (perhaps the worst in the world) and pronounced it superb. That is the measure of how successful control frauds are in deceiving

---

[25] Ibid, pp. 1-16.

[26] Edward Chancellor, *Devil Take the Hindmost: A History of Financial Speculation* (New York: Penguin Group, 2000), 276. In a letter dated February 13, 1985, where Greenspan was paid $40,000 for writing two letters and testifying, Greenspan maintained that Keating's management had turned Lincoln into a "strong financial institution" and would not pose any foreseeable risk to the federal insurer.

experts who do not understand fraud mechanisms and assume CEOs cannot be crooks. (p.246)

Repeal of Usury Laws: Darth Vader Interest Overtakes Main Street

"The modern theory of the perpetuation of debt has drenched the earth with blood and crushed its inhabitants under the burdens every accumulating."
Thomas Jefferson

"Man was lost if he went to a usurer, for the interest ran faster than a tiger upon him."
Pearl S. Buck, The First Wife

"Rapacious usury, which, although more than once condemned by the Church, is nevertheless under a different form of but with the same guilt, still practiced by avaricious and grasping men, so that a small number of very rich men have been able to lay upon the masses of the poor a yoke a little better than slavery itself."
Pope Leo XIII, 1890s

"Steal a little and they throw you in jail. Steal a lot and they make you a king."
Bob Dylan

Usury is the practice of either an individual or a financial institution charging excessive rates of interest on a loan. Beginning in 1978, with the Supreme Court's ruling in *Marquette National Bank of Minneapolis v. First of Omaha Services Corp. et al,* it became the law of the land that a bank could export the interest rates from one state to another. One may live in a state like Minnesota, which limits interest rates to 18 percent, but still be charged any rate of interest on a credit card from a bank domiciled in a state like South Dakota or Delaware.

In 1979, in order to lure business, South Dakota became the first state to repeal usury laws. In 1981, Citibank became the first bank to set up its credit card business in South Dakota. Other states that followed were Arizona, Utah, Virginia, and New Hampshire. This gave new life to the predatory lending industry in America.

In his book about the Federal Reserve System, *Secrets of the Temple,* author William Greider describes how the concept of usury took off like wildfire in the 1980s.

31

When usury became legal, of course some lenders would demand more than a fair return. In Washington, D. C. Pearl S. Merriwether was desperate for a loan. Disabled and out of work at sixty-two, she was unable to pay her gas and telephone bills and so she turned to First American Mortgage Corporation. First American provided her a one-year $25,000 mortgage with an effective rate of 142 percent. This was now legal. First American reported that over a two-year period, it lent more than $2 million at interest rates ranging from 100 to 150 percent.

As state legislatures followed Congress by repealing usury limits on consumer loans, other desperate or ill-informed borrowers would pay more, too. In Flagstaff, Arizona, a Navajo family named Kearns borrowed from Ideasource, Inc. at 127 percent interest. In Richmond, Virginia, an elderly couple, Charles and Gertrude Taylor, borrowing $5,325, was charged 39 points, or $2,100, in order to make the transaction. In South Carolina, car dealers charged up to 150 percent interest. Some of these victims, either gullible or desperate, lost their homes to lenders—much the same way the French peasants lost their small plots of land to the avarice rentier in the sixteenth century. (p.176).

With the blessings of complacent federal and state governments, interest and cumulative finance charges on revolving lines of credit for credit cards and other types of revolving and installment debt escalated. Interest rates of 30, 40, 50, and 150 percent or higher became perfectly legal. Because of the legalization of usury, credit cards such as Visa and MasterCard have become the "sweet spot" for bank profits and the most profitable lines of business for financial giants Citigroup, Bank of America, Capital One, and numerous others.

In step with excessive interest rates, other forms of usury have also been exploited. In banker language, it is called *subprime lending*. However, for most people it is known as *predatory lending*. Predatory lending services are marketed to and directed at low-income people, elderly households, neighborhoods of immigrants, communities of color, and those people who may be down on their luck. What is alarming is the exponential growth of predatory lending. Because of deregulation, predatory loans or new forms of usury are commonly seen in the following areas.

One. *Car title loans.* These loans put at risk an asset essential to the well-being of a family. If a borrower defaults on a small loan secured by the title of the auto, the lender can confiscate the vehicle.

Two. *Predatory mortgage lending.* People, who do not otherwise qualify for traditional mortgage lending, are targeted with subprime loan offers through heavy telemarketing and advertising. The largest subprime mortgage lender, Ameriquest of Orange County, California, was a sponsor of the 2005 Rolling Stones tour. In 2006, Ameriquest agreed to a $325 million national settlement because of its predatory lending practices. Predatory mortgage lending tactics include the sale of mortgages with prepayment penalties, hidden fees, undisclosed interest rates, falsification of loan applications, overvalued appraisals and high pressure sales tactics to get people to refinance, and so on. In 2007, subprime mortgage lending companies are dropping like flies, as consumers cannot afford the excessive interest rates charged on subprime loans. Over forty-seven subprime lenders have gone out of business. Some of the largest subprime mortgage lenders are being shut down. They include New Century, Fremont General, Ameriquest, OwnIt, and ResMAE. Since there is so much profit in subprime lending, big banks, including Wells Fargo, HSBC Household Finance, Option One (H&R Block), WMC (subsidiary of GE Money), Washington Mutual, CitiFinancial, First Franklin (acquired by Merrill Lynch), GMAC, BNC (Lehman Brothers subsidiary), Decision One (owned by HSBC) and OwnIt (was partially owned by Merrill Lynch and Bank of America) have been involved. Even a new website charts this new subprime mortgage debacle called "The Mortgage Lender Implode-O-Meter." You can visit it at www.ml-implode.com.

Three. *Refund anticipation loans or RALs.* These loans are short-term usurious loans secured by the anticipated taxpayer refund credit. According to the Consumer Federation of America, consumers paid an estimated $1.6 billion in RAL fees in 2004, based on IRS data, with an estimated 12.3 million taxpayers using RALs. RALs are extremely expensive bank loans, which last about seven to fourteen days until the actual IRS refund pays the loan. In reality, with electronic filing, consumers that have a bank account can get the refund within two weeks.

RALs cost between $29 and $129 in origination fees. Tax preparers and their bank partners can also tack on an additional $25 to $40 for processing the instant refund. The annual interest rate on a RAL can be from a low of around 40 percent to a high of about 700 percent. When you add in administrative fees, actual loan rates on RALs can effectively range from 70 to over 1,800 percent!

California Attorney General Bill Lockyer sued H&R Block for unfair business practices and predatory lending related to RALs. This was just one of several suits. In 2005, Block agreed to pay $62.5 million to settle class action claims in regards to violating consumer protection laws in four states.

H&R Block not only markets RALs, but it also owns a subprime mortgage company called Option One (see above), which primarily markets itself to minorities. Recently, the Office of Thrift Supervision approved H&R Block for a savings bank charter, despite alleged reports of underpaying its own taxes and misstatements of earnings with the Securities and Exchange Commission.

Four. *Payday loans.* Payday loans are short-term cash loans that are financed against a borrower's personal check held for future deposits or electronic access to a bank account. Payday loans range in size from $100 to $1000, depending upon state legal maximums. The average loan term is about two weeks. Loans cost an average of 470 percent annual interest rate. Finance charge ranges can run as high as $30 to borrow $100. As a result, with finance charges, a two-week payday loan can have interest rates anywhere from 390 to 780 percent.

Payday loans increasingly seek to take advantage of our military personnel. According to information reported by the Associated Press in September 2006, approximately 225,000 service members, or roughly 17 percent of all military personnel, use payday loans. The Pentagon accuses payday lenders of surrounding military bases as exploiting troops.

There is a proposal in Congress to limit interest rates on payday loans to 36 percent to loans charged to soldiers. Yet a Congressman, Geoff Davis (R-KY) opposes a rate cap on high interest rate payday loans to soldiers. One of Davis's top campaign donors was CNG Financial of Mason, Ohio, owner of national payday lender Check 'n Go.

Consumer Federation of America's web site *Payday Loan Consumer Information* at www.paydayloaninfo.org provides a wealth of information.

Five. *Student loans.* Some student loans charge up to 17 percent interest annually. Senator Edward Kennedy of Massachusetts stated that it "time to chase the money lenders out of the temple," in regards to high priced student loans offered by non-governmental educational lenders.

Arbitration for Broker–dealers: Self-Regulation on Steroids

Arbitration is the process whereby a third party outside a court of law settles a dispute between two or more parties relating to securities claims or other financial wrongdoing. Individual investors have never had much luck going after Wall Street for its shenanigans. With arbitration, the odds of winning a favorable settlement against a securities firm are grim. In actuality, you have better odds of winning the lottery or drowning in a cistern.

Consider an arbitration case reported by Gretchen Morgenson, December 10, 2006, in the *New York Times*, titled "When Winning Feels a Lot Like Losing." In this case, Ms. Morgenson reports that Mabel Strobel invested $1 million—her entire life savings—with Morgan Stanley in 1998. Her broker put the 79-year-old woman's funds into technology stocks and Morgan Stanley mutual funds. Her portfolio, which was 99 percent invested in stocks, was subsequently clobbered in the market. Strobel lost $300 thousand in value by 2002.

Therefore, she went ahead and filed an arbitration case against Morgan Stanley and her broker, claiming that her money had been invested inappropriately. In 2004, an arbitration panel found that Morgan Stanley was liable for Ms. Strobel's losses and gave Ms. Strobel an award of $5,000 in compensatory damages. They also charged her $10,350 in arbitration fees. Therefore, although Ms. Strobel won the case, she was charged $5,350 more in legal fees. Morgan Stanley, according to the article, only had to pay $6,900 in arbitration forum fees.

Ms. Strobel has not given up and has filed a motion in federal court to vacate the arbitration award. However, since 1987, arbitration has been the methodology of resolving securities disputes and, as of right now, the case is tied up in the courts. Given Ms. Strobel's age of 86, it behooves Morgan Stanley to keep the case open.

Like the National Association of Securities Dealers (NASD) and the New York Stock Exchange (NYSE), arbitration is another form of self-regulation, which is stacked in favor of the securities industry. Appointed insiders settle adjudication of the securities wrongdoing. In addition, as we witnessed in recent history, the self-regulatory agencies proved to be useless in ferreting out the numerous securities crimes, which took place in the 1990s and in the new millennium. Virtually all innovative and investigative policing of the securities business originated at the state level with people like Eliot Spitzer.

With the Supreme Court case *Shearson/American Express Inc. v. McMahon*, it became the law of the land that standard arbitration clauses which one signs when one sets up an account with securities firm takes precedence over the Seventh Amendment of the Constitution.[27] If you lose a significant amount of money and you feel you have been deceived or cheated, you gave up your rights to have your case heard by a judge and jury by signing the arbitration paperwork.

In addition, the SEC, which is the citizens' watchdog for securities crimes, is filled with securities industries insiders not likely to prosecute their friends in the business. Consider that Arthur Leavitt started out in the securities business with Sandy Weill and ended up running the SEC. William Donaldson, co-founder of the investment bank Donaldson, Lufkin & Jenrette, ended up running the SEC for a bit. Paul Roye, who oversaw the mutual fund business while at the SEC, worked as a lawyer for the mutual fund business prior to the SEC. After leaving the SEC in a wake of mutual fund scandals, Roye went to Capital Research in Los Angeles, owner of mutual fund giant American Funds. Andrew "Buddy" Donohue is now the new Director of the

---

[27] Gary Weiss, *Wall Street Versus America* (New York: Penguin Group, 2006). Weiss gives us the tale of Rand Groves, a sad story about how one individual tried to go against giant Merrill Lynch for investment losses, and even with tremendous persistence, lost. Weiss clearly points out how Americans have little, if any, protection against Wall Street interests.

Division of Investment Management at the SEC, which oversees the mutual fund business. Previously, Donohue was general counsel for Merrill Lynch Investment Managers. Prior to that, "Buddy" worked for Oppenheimer Funds, Inc. Donohue has been on the board of governors of the industry trade group, the Investment Company Institute (ICI) for a number of years and made numerous contributions to their political action committee, ICI PAC.

In addition, in March 2006, in *Merrill Lynch vs. Dabit,* the Supreme Court, in an 8-0 decision, blocked state class action suits by stockholders who contend they were tricked into holding onto declining shares of a company such as WorldCom and Enron. With the existing arbitration ruling in 1987, the Dabit ruling was a major victory for Merrill Lynch and other investment banks. It does not bode well for investors or for representatives of securities firms, which are trying to take investment firms to court at the state level. New lobbying such as the Committee on Capital Markets Regulations mentioned later in this chapter is trying to whittle away at securities laws even more.

Neither Admit nor Deny Any Wrongdoing: the Fines Do not Justify the Crimes

> *"A man with a briefcase can steal more money than a hundred men with guns."*
>
> *Don Corleone, The Godfather*

If arbitration and the recent 2006 Supreme Court ruling were not bad enough, the matter of prosecuting and convicting insiders within the securities industries is almost impossible. The nature of the securities industry is that it is *self-regulatory* which means the industry polices and regulates itself, particularly as related to the NASD and the NYSE. In the final analysis, the consumer must look out for himself.

For instance, consider Andrew Fastow, the former Chief Financial Officer of Enron. Fastow was definitely one of the key architects behind Enron's collapse. Yet Fastow only received six years of jail time for his part in the conspiracy where tens of billions were lost. Conversely, this author was watching television recently and a young African American was doing thirty-two years for drug trafficking.

You might be wondering whatever happened to those crooks involved in prior big time white-collar securities and banking crimes. They are doing quite well, actually. In the book, *Blind Faith*, Edward Winslow gives us an update on some of the most notorious securities and banking crooks of the 1980s, including Ivan Boesky, Michael Milken, and Charles Keating.

36

"In the past when executives went beyond the legal loopholes and committed fraud, we found that white-collar villains were in a class by themselves. The average jail sentence for corporate criminals in the S&L scandal of the 1980s was three years—twenty-nine months less than someone convicted for a first drug offense. And what about the three leading avatars of corporate greed during the 1980s—Michael Milken, Ivan Boesky, and Charles Keating? Keating spent less than five years in prison. Boesky spent two years behind bars and paid $100 million. Milken was sprung in less than two years, though he paid more than a $1 billion in fines and settlements. But that's not to say he is in a financial squeeze. In 2002, Milken was reportedly worth a cool $800 million. Boesky won $20 million, a house worth $2 million and $200,000 a year for life in a divorce settlement. Keating is "tanned and fit" and "cutting a social swath" in Phoenix." (p. 65.)

According to the *Forbes* 2006 edition of the four hundred richest people in America, Michael Milken is now worth $2.1 billion. For all the fines, penalties, and sanctions levied against the banking, securities, and mutual fund industries, this author cannot think of one industry figure who is doing major jail time. In the case of Enron, Citigroup alone spent $2 billion to settle with investors in a class-action lawsuit. Lehman Brothers and Bank of America combined spent $491.5 million to settle litigation claims with Enron. In the case of WorldCom, Citigroup paid $2.65 billion and Bank of America paid $460.5 million to settle class-action lawsuit claims.

In the next chapter, you will see some hefty fines levied against banks and mutual fund companies, but by various estimates, the total fines levied against the financial services industry were much less—only around 5 percent of gross profits. Moreover, the fines, even when they are imposed, are levied against the financial institution, which costs the shareholders more money than it does the individuals who actually did the crimes. Secondly, many times fines are tax-deductible to the corporations, leaving taxpayers indirectly subsidizing this malfeasance. Worse still, even when fines are levied, a good portion of the awards often goes directly to state treasuries and education programs, which have nothing to do with the investor's loss.

Although Bernie Ebbers will probably never see the light of day for running WorldCom into the ground, Sandy Weill and Jack Grubman are not in jail for their roles in violating Glass–Steagall or in inflating WorldCom stock. As a practical matter, it is difficult to prosecute and convict individuals of securities crimes because criminal intent must be proven. Further in-depth consideration will be given to white-collar crime in the next chapter, "Never Met a Man Who Made His Millions in Mutual Funds."

Repeal of the Glass–Steagall Act Paves the Way for the Passage of the Gramm-Leach-Bliley Act of 1999

"It was an incredible scene, but I saw it played through twice. Once was during a period of time when Al D'Amato chaired the [Senate] Banking Committee—and was not successful in getting the repeal of Glass–Steagall— where hundreds of lobbyists descended upon the Congress, were in the hallways morning, day, and night. Lobbyists for the insurance companies, for the investment banks, for the commercial banks, pulling for their own parochial interests.

Then when Phil Gramm became chairman of the banking committee, the same group came down, only they were now supplemented by lobbyists for the derivatives industry, for other new products that they had developed, and for the stock exchanges and the options exchanges. They were buttonholing senators and congressman, morning, day, and night."
Arthur Levitt, The Wall Street Fix, PBS, May 2003

"He was certainly for it. The Federal Reserve Board, in fact, had been for repeal repeatedly through the 1990s…I think [Greenspan] played a substantial role, in the sense that were he against it, it could not have happened. He could not have stopped the market from encroaching over boundaries—those were sort of natural market events. But he could've stopped—at least slowed it down and, I think, probably stopped—the friendlier regulatory environment."
Alan Binder, Professor of Economics, Princeton, The Wall Street Fix, PBS, May 2003

"Part of [Weill's] deal with the Federal Reserve was to get rid of all those Glass–Steagall violations in the new Citigroup within two years. Otherwise, he would have been faced with a divestiture of a company which had been just been put together, because of an old law which is still on the books. So it clearly behooved him, and many other people in the financial services industry who wanted to accomplish essentially the same sort of thing in the future to push to get Glass–Steagall repealed…

So they pushed hard?

Pushed very hard…They pushed so hard that the legislation, HR-10, House Resolution 10, which became the Financial Services Modernization Act, was referred to as 'the Citi-Travelers Act' on Capital Hill…

Did the Fed's approval of the Citibank-Travelers merger really give impetus to Congress to pass the act?

Yes. Without the Fed's approval, Congress would have probably dragged their feet...But once the Fed gave its imprimatur, it was only a matter of time before it would fall. Part of this had to do with the general halo effect around Alan Greenspan on Wall Street at the time..."
Charles Geisst, Professor of Finance, Manhattan College,
The Wall Street Fix, PBS, May 2003

"The repeal of Glass–Steagall was a big deal. It enabled kind of colossal combinations that just weren't envisioned before, where you brought the savvy of an investment banking house like Salomon Smith Barney together with Citibank. Citibank could loan an enormous amount of money. So when you put those two things together, it's kind of an unbeatable combination. Saying you can investment bank them and commercial bank them at the same time, it's a very powerful combination."
Scott Cleland, CEO Precursor Group, The Wall Street Fix, PBS, May 2003

The securities and banking industries won the Super Bowl of deregulation with the repeal of the Glass–Steagall Act of 1933. Roger Lowenstein, in his book, *Origins of the Crash,* says this about deregulation, the repeal of the Glass–Steagall Act, and Alan Greenspan's support of less regulation.

"The private banks that dominated the derivatives business industry fiercely lobbied against regulation, and their success demonstrated the too easy conduit that often existed between Washington and those it regulated. In 1993, just before Clinton took office, Wendy Gramm, the departing chair of the Commodity Futures Trading Commission and the wife of the Texas senator, signed an order exempting most private derivative contracts from regulation. The industry's appreciation may be judged from the fact that a few months later, Gramm was named a director of Enron, a big trader of energy derivatives...

However, Greenspan repeatedly sided with private bankers to inhibit controls and even to suppress disclosure. In the spring of 1998, when a successor to Gramm at the Commodity Futures Trading Commission proposed a study—a mere study—to revisit the question of whether to regulate derivatives, Greenspan, along with Rubin, quashed the idea. Remarkably, even after the hedge fund Long-Term Capital Management imploded at the end of the summer, prompting a rare Fed intervention and stunning markets (thus demonstrating that disclosure had been inadequate), Greenspan called for lessened regulation." (pp. 96-97).

Joseph E. Stiglitz is the 2001 winner of the Nobel Peace Prize in Economics and a former key economic advisor to President Bill Clinton. Stiglitz said this about irresponsible bank lending with the repeal of Glass–Steagall in his book, *The Roaring Nineties:*

"The consequences predicted by the critics of Glass–Steagall repeal only began to come to light as the corporate and banking scandals emerged. Most notable were Enron's banks continuing to provide credit even as its prospects looked increasingly murky. Even if Enron was down, it was not out: so long as there were prospects for more big deals, issuing new securities, it made sense to continue to lend the company more money. And Enron's banks continued to lend to it even as its appalling problems began to surface. In the succession of corporate and financial scandals that followed Enron, numerous other cases came to light in which banks continued to lend almost to the day of bankruptcy; they knew, or should have known, of the risk, but the lure of the mega-profits from new deals, should the firm weather the storm, made the lending attractive nevertheless. (In some cases, lending was motivated more by fear that bankruptcy would expose some of the banks' dubious deals and expose them to recriminations for touting the company's stock, so they hoped against hope maybe, with the loan, the company would somehow manage to survive).
Under the old regime, investors at least had some assurance that if a firm was in trouble, it would have trouble borrowing money. (p.161).

In his edge-of-the-chair book, *Blood on the Street: The Sensational Inside Story of How Wall Street Analysts Duped a Generation of Investors*, Charles Gasparino writes about how Citigroup openly violated Glass–Steagall laws, which were still on the books:

"The new financial model brought tremendous profits to Wall Street. Citigroup, the ultimate supermarket combining Travelers Group and its Salomon Smith Barney investment bank with Citicorp, the world's largest bank, became one of the market's most profitable companies...
The glaring problem, of course, was that the firm would have been illegal as the still formidable law that prevented combinations of investment banking and commercial banking, known as Glass–Steagall Act, remained in effect. Influenced, no doubt, by millions of dollars in campaign contributions to Wall Street-friendly politicians, Glass–Steagall had been whittled down during the 1990s, but not totally eliminated. That is, until Weill and Citigroup got into the act. With the help of friends in Washington, including his new No. 2 executive, former Goldman Sachs CEO and Treasury Secretary Robert Rubin, as well as Jesse Jackson, the civil rights leader turned Weill lobbyist,

Weill rolled over what remained of Glass-Steagall Act, prodding Congress to repeal the law, and ensuring Citigroup's survival.

Citigroup didn't exactly wait for Congress to give it the green light before making its mark on Wall Street. Not long after the merger, commercial bankers and investment bankers began sharing clients. Companies complained that the firm linked its commercial lending business to bond underwriting; companies that hired Citigroup to sell a bond deal would be approved for a commercial loan. One document labeled "AT&T Debt Financing/June 16 2000" listed for AT&T the amazing array of services the firm offered, from Jack Grubman's research, to Eduardo Mestre's investment—banking expertise, to Citigroup's ability to lend cash, and even the advice and counsel of the firm's ultimate rainmaker, Weill himself. Another Citigroup memo virtually bragged about the intricate and lucrative web of relationships that Citigroup offered another big customer, WorldCom. "Citigroup is one of the closest financial institutions to [WorldCom]," the memo says. "Citibank is one of Wcom's leading international banks, providing loans, trade, cash management and FX services to Wcom International subsidiaries…SSB is clearly the lead investment bank of Wcom." (pp. 108-110).

With the repeal of the Glass–Steagall Act, the banks and securities businesses regained control of all the power they lost in the 1930s. With the ink barely dry, one has to wonder about the wisdom of the repeal of Glass–Steagall. From 1933 to 1999 that act served this country well. In the 1930s, Congress had found that the practice of tying commercial loans to shaky companies to gain follow-on stock and bond offerings was a major contributor to the overspeculation in the 1920s, which ultimately led to the Crash of 1929, and the Great Depression.

Congress knew that banks put their clients in a headlock for follow-on securities underwriting with the practice of tying. As a result, investment banking and commercial banking were separated at the hip in America for very good reasons. Glass–Steagall was designed to insulate bank depositors from the risks involved when a bank deals in securities and has a greater potential to collapse. With the repeal of Glass–Steagall, this insulation no longer exists.

If there was ever a wrecking ball that went crashing through consumer protection, it was the complete repeal of the Glass–Steagall Act with the passage of the Gramm-Leach-Bliley Act of 1999. The newer act also made it increasingly difficult, if not downright impossible, to challenge or sue broker–dealers or national banking institutions in state courts. Some of the major points of the Gramm-Leach-Bliley Act are as follows (comments are in italics):

41

Sections of the 1933 Glass–Steagall Act mandating the separation of commercial and investment banking were repealed. *Illegal becomes legal. Chinese Wall doctrine gets thrown out the window. Tying, the process of tying a commercial loan to an investment banking deal is now legal again. Enron and WorldCom collapsed in part because of tying.*

The Bank Holding Act of 1956 was eliminated, prohibiting banks from underwriting insurance. *Banks remind the author of the farmer; he does not want all the land, just all of the land next to his. Various banks such as Citizen's/Royal Bank of Scotland have already found themselves in trouble selling variable annuities to older people. Citigroup has a very dysfunctional approach to underwriting life insurance. Its subsidiary, Primerica, only recommends term life to its customers, whereas Citibank buys billions of high cash value life insurance for its own account. JPMorgan Chase plays the same tune with Chase Insurance and its own account.*

The Federal Reserve Board was erected as the *primary* regulator of financial holding companies. *A private corporation, the Federal Reserve Board has more power than the United States government.*

Financial holding companies were permitted to conduct activities that are *"complementary"* to banking. *Complementary to banking is such a wide term that you could steer the Titanic through it and have a few football fields to spare.*

The non-financial activities of firms predominantly engaged in financial activities were grandfathered for at least ten years. *Cannot exactly figure this one out, but it sure sounds dangerous and has enough ambiguity and hot air to float a balloon across the Grand Canyon.*

The Treasury Department and the Federal Reserve were given the right to veto each other's decisions on new financial powers. *The Federal Reserve, a private corporation, can veto the United States Treasury.*

Sharing of customer account numbers with third-party marketing firms was prohibited and financial institutions were required to establish privacy policies and disclose them once a year. *A total joke. If one reads these disclosure agreements, and no one does, the law gives these new super banks the power to cross-sell a consumer to death within their own group of companies and makes information available to just about everyone. This is a HUGE PROBLEM in financial services and means that as long as you disclose the problem, it is ok. Disclosure becomes absolution of any wrongdoing.*

States were prohibited from interfering with insurance sales by national banks. *Banks want to have everything challenged in federal court, not state courts. Kenneth Lewis, CEO of Bank of America, on PBS public television show, "Meet the CEO" from Howard University in Washington, DC, clearly maintained that he only wants one regulator with which to deal, and thus states lose their powers prosecuting national banks. With the Office of the Comptroller of the Currency finding against Providian Bank in 2004, federal government flexes its muscle and minimizes states' involvement. Not good.*

The Comptroller of the Currency was stripped of the legal advantage in court disputes with state insurance regulators over state laws enacted after September 3, 1999. *From the author's research and experience, consumers have always been more protected by state insurance regulators than they have been by federal regulators. This insertion into the repeal of Glass–Steagall is more window dressing than it is anything else.*

The Birth of the 2005 Bankruptcy Abuse and Consumer Protection Act

> *"Any city, however small is in fact divided into two, one for the poor, the other for the rich, they are at war with one another."*
> Plato, The Republic

> *"If class warfare in America is being waged in America, my class is clearly winning."*
> Warren Buffett, Annual Report, Berkshire Hathaway

> *"The way to stop financial joy-riding is to arrest the chauffeur, not the automobile."*
> Woodrow Wilson

After banks and credit card companies spent close to $100 million in lobbying, the United States Congress and George W. Bush gave them an early Christmas present in 2005. This new law, the 2005 Bankruptcy Abuse and Consumer Protection Act, which should have been called *"The Visa and MasterCard Relief Bill: The Creditor Strikes Back"* proves that banks are not only greedy, but their greed is insatiable.

The American Bankers Association and credit card companies, such as Bank of America, Citigroup, American Express, Capital One, and JPMorgan Chase, heavily supported passage of the new bankruptcy bill. Credit cards are some of the most profitable portions of their entire business model. It is estimated that the top ten issuers of credit cards have about a 90 percent share of the revolving credit card market.

However, credit cards are a game of deception. They send out teaser rates of zero percent interest, but if people are late (on any payment), a credit card company can take out its hammer with a universal default and boost the rates up to 30 percent (when banks are borrowing from the Federal Reserve at forty-year lows). Credit card companies create microscopic contracts, which hardly anyone takes time to read. In fact, a professor in contract law would probably have trouble figuring out the terms and conditions of a bank credit

43

card. In addition, with all credit cards, because they are *revolving lines of credit*, the banks can change their contracts with borrowers virtually at will (about fifteen days).

The status quo with credit card lending is already bad in America. With the birth and passage of the new bankruptcy bill, it just got worse.

The Birth of the New Bankruptcy Bill

The original conception of the new bankruptcy bill was likely conceived in the mind of one Charles Cawley[28], who, with his partner Al Lerner, became the founder of MBNA—infamous for their credit card programs. MBNA was a pioneer in the affinity credit card market, where groups with common backgrounds or affinities are solicited. Affinity cards try to give the consumer a sense of "belonging." It is a dysfunctional way to stand out in this economic world. This author knows this as MBNA has such a pitch within one of his industry's trade groups.

The first successful affinity credit card was pitched to Georgetown University. By using Georgetown's name, the university would share revenue with MBNA.[29] The rest as we say is history. Usury affinity credit cards with touchy-feely characteristics are now attached to airlines, colleges, clubs; you name it. They are everywhere.

Excessive profits are made in credit cards. The last year Charles Cawley worked for MBNA he made over $52 million. Al Lerner died in 2002 leaving his family as one of the richest in the world. According to Forbes magazine, in 2006 Norma Lerner, his widow, daughter Nancy and son, Randolph were each worth $1.5 billion. Randolph now owns the Cleveland Browns and is in negotiation to buy the Birmingham, England, soccer club Aston Villa for $120 million.

MBNA was sold to Bank of America in 2005 for $35 billion in cash and stock. When MBNA was headquartered in Delaware, it was one of the largest employers in that state—one of the first to repeal usury laws.

MBNA had been the number one donor to Senator Joseph R. Biden (D-DE). It is perhaps no surprise that Senator Biden was a constant advocate of MBNA[30] and was the original spokesperson for the new bankruptcy bill, which became law October 17, 2005. MBNA was also the second largest contributor to George W. Bush. Only Enron gave more. MBNA was also a large employer in the state of Maine. Charles Cawley made his summer residence in Camden, Maine, and had friends such as George H.W. Bush who

---

[28] Lowell Bergman and Patrick McGeehan, "Expired: How A Credit King Was Cut Off," *New York Times,* March 7, 2004.
[29] Ibid.
[30] Ibid.

had summer homes there also. Charles Cawley liked George H.W. Bush so much that he donated $1 million to his presidential library and gave $300 thousand to George H.W. and Barbara Bush to attend events sponsored by Cawley in Maine.[31]

In selling their story to Congress, bankers with their lobbyists, jingoism and massive public relations campaigns, portrayed themselves as the abused victims in the bankruptcy court. Bankers scolded individuals for discharging their credit card balances in the bankruptcy court. The condescension against people going bankrupt came from high places. Alan Greenspan, in fact, said, "Personal bankruptcies are soaring because Americans have lost their shame."[32]

Although there are serious gaps in research as to why people go bankrupt, this author's research in the subject area revealed that few people go bankrupt to take advantage of the banking system. For the vast majority, going to bankruptcy court is the last thing people want to do. Interestingly, bankruptcy seems to be more of a middle-class phenomenon. Bankruptcy is a complex issue and is cumulatively a composite manifestation of many financial problems such as large medical bills, disabilities, small business failure, drastic changes in income, unfortunate circumstances, and divorce. In effect, there seems to be a high correlation between the filing of a divorce and subsequent filing for bankruptcy.

When families or individuals have a financial meltdown and approach bankruptcy, they often have illnesses and no additional financial resources. Bankrupt parties are usually incapable of retaining the proper legal counsel, which may help prevent further damage. Credit collection firms hound individuals and families. Verbal abuse and intimidation from collection firms are commonplace. Credit card balances, second mortgages, and collection lawsuits overwhelm people approaching bankruptcy. As they approach the courthouse to file, people are emotionally spent and exhausted. They want the torture to stop.

The National Association of Consumer Bankruptcy Attorneys says that 79 percent of the people who have filed for bankruptcy since October 2005 were in debt due to circumstances beyond their control. David Himmelstein of Harvard Medical School and well-known attorney Elizabeth Warren of Harvard Law claim in their 2003 study *Illness and Injury as Contributors to Bankruptcy* that 54.5 percent of bankruptcies were due to illness or injury. Major medical bills seem to be the straw that broke the camel's back. Himmelstein and Warren accurately point out that high medical

---

[31] Ibid.

[32] As cited in Kelly Edmiston, "A New Perspective On Rising Non-Business Bankruptcy Filing Rates: Analyzing the Factors," The Kansas City Federal Reserve Bank, www.kansascityfed.org , 2006.

45

bills usually mean the disability of a debtor. In addition, with all disabilities, additional costs are incurred at a time when a consumer can least afford them.

Information that comes out of the banking industry seems to contradict bankers' claims that they are being abused in the bankruptcy court. A report authored by Fed economist Kelly Edmiston and published by the Kansas City Federal Reserve, titled *A New Perspective in 2006 on Rising NonBusiness Bankruptcy Filing Rates: Analyzing Regional Factors,* points out several findings, which contradict bankers' contentions that they are being willfully abused:

- Bankruptcies are being filed more by older people than younger people (banks claim that young people were abusing the system)
- Legalized gambling and pathological gambling problems seem to exist within a 50 to 250 mile range of a gambling casino. Although it is difficult to make a correlation between gambling and bankruptcy, ample evidence suggests there are serious societal problems with gambling such as prostitution, alcohol, and drug abuse and compulsive behavior, which are factors that can lead to bankruptcy.
- Divorce seems to trigger bankruptcy more often, due to a substantial, immediate, and unanticipated reduction in income for all parties.
- As much as 19 percent of all bankruptcy filings are connected to self-employed people. The failure rate of new businesses in America is about 70 to 80 percent.

Bankruptcy also has a ripple effect, creating problems for years to come. The bankruptcy remains on a credit report for a decade. Employers screen job applicants using credit reports. The cost of purchasing a car, as well as housing, goes up substantially. Furthermore, many debts cannot be discharged in bankruptcy. Taxes, student loans, alimony, child support, and other court orders remain payable.

This support of the Bankruptcy Abuse Prevention and Consumer Protection Act is the ultimate example of hypocrisy from wealthy congressional politicians who drag the entire country down with their cataclysmic deficit spending of up to $500-$600 billion per year or more. In the rarified cloistered economic world in which they live, the lack of compassion these politicians have as to why people do go bankrupt is appalling.

Congressman Ron Paul (R-TX), in his press release dated March 13, 2006, "How Government Debt Grows," discusses how our politicians spend taxpayers' money:

Raising the government debt ceiling is nothing new. Congress raised it many times over the past 15 years, despite the supposed "surpluses" of the Clinton years. Those single-year surpluses were based on accounting tricks that treated Social Security funds as general revenues. In reality, the federal government ran deficits throughout the 1990s, and the federal debt grew steadily...

When the government borrows money, the actual borrowers—big spending administrations and politicians—never have to pay it back. Remember, administrations come and go, members of Congress become highly paid lobbyists, and bureaucrats retire with safe pensions. The benefits of deficit spending are enjoyed immediately by politicians, who trade pork for votes and enjoy adulation for promising to cure every social ill. The bills always come due later, however. Nobody ever looks back and says, 'Congressman So-and-so got us into this mess when he voted for all the spending 20 years ago.'

For government, the federal budget is essentially a credit card with no spending limit, billed to somebody else. We hardly should be surprised that Congress racks up huge amounts of debt! By contrast, responsible people restrain their borrowing because they will have to pay it back sometime. It's time for American taxpayers to understand that every dollar will have to be repaid. We should have the courage to face our grandchildren knowing that we have done all we can to end the government spending spree.

The Actual Bankruptcy Bill

The Bankruptcy Abuse Prevention and Consumer Protection Act hurts low-income people, single parents, minorities, the recently divorced, the elderly, entrepreneurs, and those just down on their luck. Under the new bankruptcy law, citizens will become indentured servants to the credit card companies. It becomes increasingly difficult to file a Chapter 7 bankruptcy, and most people will have to opt for a Chapter 13 bankruptcy. This requires a debtor to file a financial plan to pay back what they owe.

Those going bankrupt incur significantly higher legal bills. Most attorneys are doubling or tripling their legal fees as the new law creates additional liability. As a result, many lawyers are exiting the bankruptcy business altogether.

The new law requires that citizens undergo mandatory credit counseling. However, there are no uniform federal licensing requirements for credit counseling. Only about seventeen states require licenses. Credit card counseling services are known for making constant phone calls and harassment. Some credit counselors have been known to offer ways to restructure your debt, which ends up being more expensive. Unfortunately, like many things in finance, there can be tremendous conflicts of interest.

47

Some consumers may think they are getting help or an advocate, when the credit counselor may have direct ties to the creditors themselves.

Many credit counselors claim to be not-for-profit. This too can be a game of deception. Some not-for-profit credit counselors siphon off income as consulting fees to for-profit entities. Another tactic is for owners of the credit counseling companies to take huge salaries. This not-for-profit smoke and mirrors game has been so abused in the credit counseling business that in 2006, the Internal Revenue Service revoked the not-for-profit status of several large credit-counseling companies.

Americans seem to be the only true victims to stem from the passage of the Bankruptcy Abuse Protection and Consumers Protection Act. It only protects banks and other financial institutions. The law did increase protection for IRAs up to $1 million, but it is incomprehensible to believe that someone who had that kind of money in an IRA would be going bankrupt (other than O.J. Simpson).

With the new law, the consumer will need to become less dependent on the banks for private capital formation. As we will see later in the book, life insurance, particularly dividend-paying high cash value life insurance is the ideal alternative to a bank.

Additional Subsidy: Mutual Fund Industry Gets Automatic Enrollment with Pension Protection Act of 2006

Extra deregulation points were scored by the mutual fund industry with the passage of the Pension Protection Act of 2006, which grants employers permission to enroll employees automatically into their 401(k) programs, which are for the most part funded with mutual funds. We will see in the next chapter, "Never Met a Man Who Made His Millions in Mutual Funds," that few people really make money in mutual funds, other than the owners or fund managers.

International Banking: No Regulations, No Supervision, and Lots of Subsidies

American banks operate on a huge scale internationally whether directly or indirectly through the quasi non-commercial World Bank or the International Monetary Fund (IMF). To understand truly the total subsidy that banks receive in the American economy, the consumer should have some background as to how banks operate in the international sphere; after all, we are in a global economy. It will also give the reader a glimpse of our poor image in world affairs.

International bankers have inflicted much pain and suffering on the people to whom they lend and to the American taxpayer who ends up bailing the banks out. You see, old powerful government officials never seem to fade away. They just seem to end up in the international banking business and working out of the opulent headquarters of the World Bank in Washington, D.C.

Robert McNamara, a former secretary of defense and one of the primary architects of the Vietnam War, was, at one point, running the World Bank. John Perkins, in his book, *Confessions of an Economic Hit Man* says this about McNamara running the World Bank.

"I see now that Robert McNamara's greatest and most sinister contribution to history was to jockey the World Bank into becoming an agent of global empire on a scale never before witnessed. He also set a precedent. His ability to bridge the gaps between the primary components of the corporatocracy would be fine-tuned by his successors. For instance, George Schultz was secretary of the treasury and chairman of the Council on Economic Policy under Nixon, served as Bechtel president, and then became secretary of state under Reagan. Caspar Weinberger was a Bechtel vice president and general counsel and later secretary of defense under Reagan. Richard Helms was Johnson's CIA director and then became ambassador to Iran under Nixon. Richard Cheney served as secretary of defense under George H. W. Bush, as Halliburton president, and as U. S. vice president to George W. Bush. Even a president of the United States, George H.W. Bush, began as founder of Zapata Petroleum Corp, served as an ambassador to the U. N. under presidents Nixon and Ford, and was Ford's CIA director." (p. 91)

Paul Wolfowitz, the primary architect of the Iraq war, is now the head honcho. When Wolfowitz went to work at the World Bank, he brought along with him Karl Jackson whom he knew from the Defense Department. Kevin Kellems joined as well. He was an advisor to Wolfowitz when he served as Secretary of Defense. At one time, Kellems was a former spokesman to Dick Cheney.

Wolfowitz also recruited Robin Cleveland, who was a senior budget official under George W. Bush and helped arrange the large war budgets for fighting in Iraq and Afghanistan. Senator Richard Lugar a (R-IN) maintains that the World Bank is a focal point of major corruption. Lugar claims that between 1946 and 2004 approximately $26 to $130 billion in money lent by the World Bank has been misused or siphoned off. Jeffrey Winters, a professor at Northwestern University, says his research suggests that due to corruption the World Bank has wasted about $100 billion. If other multilateral banks are added to the list[33], the total corruption pot rises to $200 billion.[34]

Far too often, international quasi-governmental banks, which originate on the idea of encouraging economic development and reducing poverty, are derailed by corruption. Corruption exists not only with the recipients of the loans, but from within the bank itself. According to *U.S. News & World Report,* the corruption is enormous.[35] Problems such as kickbacks, bribery, embezzlement, collusive bidding practices, and other dishonest practices skim off up to 20 percent of the $20 billion the bank disburses each year.

In the international sphere, banks operate in a Wild West environment and foreign banks can dominate a banking system within a country. For instance, in Mexico, 80 percent of banking interests are outside owned and Citigroup, through its Banamex Bank is a major presence there. International banks operate largely unfettered and when they get into trouble (as they often do), U. S. banks often call in the Federal Reserve, the International Monetary Fund, the World Bank, and the United States Treasury to bail them out.

Between 1982 and 1992, to avoid a domino affect on U. S. banks due to debt crisis in Mexico, Argentina, and Brazil, the Federal Reserve and the United States Treasury created relief packages to prop up bad loans U.S. banks made. To subsidize American banking interests further, the United States Treasury had to come to the aid of the sliding Mexico peso to protect interests of investors who were heavily involved in high-yield Mexican debt.[36]

Congressman Ron Paul, in a press release dated September 27, 2004, talks about how banking and corporate interests are inevitably backed and subsidized by the American taxpayer.

A recent report by the congressional Joint Economic Committee on which I serve highlights the reckless manner in which one organization, the International Monetary Fund, wastes your money around the world.

The IMF provides a perfect illustration of both the folly of foreign aid and the real motivations behind it. The IMF touts itself as a bank of sorts, although it makes "loans" that no rational bank would consider—mostly to shaky governments with weak economies and unstable currencies. The IMF has little incentive to operate profitably like a private bank, since its funding comes mostly from our credulous US Congress that demands little

---

[33] Emad Mekay, "Poorest Pay for the World Bank Corruption-US Senator," *Inter Press Service,* May 14, 2004. www.commondreams.org.
[34] Ibid.
[35] Edward T. Pound, "Senator Bashes World Bank Corruption," *U. S. News & World Report,* March 26, 2006.
[36] Kevin Phillips, *Wealth and Democracy* (New York: Broadway Books, 2002).

accountability. As a result, it is free to make high-risk loans at below-market interest rates.

The real purpose of the IMF is to channel tax dollars to politically connected companies. The huge multinational banks and corporations in particular love the IMF, as both used IMF funds—taxpayer funds—to bail themselves out from billions in losses after the Asian financial crisis. Big corporations obtain lucrative contracts for a wide variety of construction projects and IMF loans. It's a familiar game in Washington, where corporate welfare is disguised as compassion for the poor.

John Perkins, best-selling author of the book, *Confessions of an Economic Hit Man,* summarizes the power U. S. banks and corporations have over other countries. As an economic hit man (EHM), Perkins writes:

That is what EHMs do best: build a global empire. We are an elite group of men and women who utilize international financial organizations to foment conditions that make other nations subservient to the corporatorcracy running our biggest corporations, our governments and our banks. Like our counterparts in the Mafia, EHMs provide favors. These take the form of loans to develop infrastructure—electric generating plants, highways, ports, airports, or industrial parks. A condition of such loans is that engineering and construction companies from our own country must build these projects. In essence, most of the money never leaves the United States; it is simply transferred from banking offices in Washington to engineering offices in New York, Houston or San Francisco.

Despite the fact that the money is returned almost immediately to corporations that our members of the corporatocracy (the creditor), the recipient country is required to pay it all back, principal plus interest. If an EHM is completely successful, the loans are so large that the debtor is forced to default on its payments after a few years. When this happens, then like the Mafia we demand our pound of flesh. (p. xx)

The power of bank lending, which is directly subsidized by the American taxpayer due to deposit insurance, the Federal Reserve System, favorable laws, and numerous documented bailouts, can be reckless and wreak havoc on a country. Perkins discusses the case of Ecuador.

My contemporaries and I, and our modern corporate equivalents, had managed to bring it (Ecuador) to virtual bankruptcy. We loaned it billions and billions of dollars so it could hire our engineering and construction firms to build projects that would help the richest families. As a result, in those three decades, the official poverty rate grew from 50 to 70 percent, under-or-unemployment increased 15 to 70 percent, public debt from $240 million to

51

*$16 billion, and the share of national resources allocated to the poorest
citizens declined from 20 percent to 6 percent. Today, Ecuador must devote
nearly 50 percent of its national budget simply to paying off its debts—instead
of helping millions of its citizens who are officially classified as dangerously
impoverished.*

*The situation in Ecuador clearly demonstrates that this was not the
result of a conspiracy; it was a process that had occurred during both
Democratic and Republican administrations, a process that had involved all
the major multinational banks, many corporations, and foreign aid missions
from a multitude of countries. The United States played the lead role, but we
had not acted alone. (pp. 239-240).*

Joseph Stiglitz was the 2001 recipient of the Nobel Prize in
Economics. In his book, *Globalizations and Its Discontents,* Stiglitz explains
some of the problems he encountered when he was chief economist of the
World Bank. He writes about the no regulation and no supervision world of
international banking:

*Instead, we have a system which might be called global governance
without global government, one which a few institutions—the World Bank, the
IMF, the WTO—and a few players—the finance, commerce and trade
ministries, closely linked to certain financial and commercial interests—
dominate the scene, but in which many of those affected by their decisions are
left almost voiceless. (pp. 21-22)*

Stiglitz tells us about the power of the IMF and other banking
institutions over a small country like Ethiopia. Per capita income in Ethiopia
is around $110 annually. It is a country where two million people have died
due to drought and famine. Despite being a third world country, Ethiopia had
good prospects for growth and low inflation. However, the country needed
funds for further growth. The IMF wanted Ethiopia to deregulate its banking
system using inappropriate and inconsiderate Western standards. Stiglitz
further writes about the power of Western banks and the IMF over small
countries:

*Ethiopia's entire banking system (measured, for instance, by the size
of its assets) is somewhat smaller that that of Bethesda, Maryland, a suburb
on the outskirts of Washington with a population of 55,277. The IMF wanted
Ethiopia not only to open up its financial markets to Western competition but
also wanted to divide its largest bank into several pieces. In a world in which
U. S. mega financial institutions like Citibank and Travelers or
Manufacturers Hanover and Chemical say they have to merge to compete
effectively; a bank the size of North East Bethesda National Bank really has*

no way to compete against a global giant like Citibank. When global financial institutions enter a country, they squelch the domestic competition. And as they attract depositors away from the local banks in a country like Ethiopia, the may be far more attentive and generous when it comes to making loans to large multinational corporations than they will to providing credit to small businesses and farmers...

Ethiopia resisted the IMF's demands that it "open" its banking system, for good reason. It had seen what had happened when one of its East African neighbors gave in to IMF demands. The IMF had insisted on financial market liberalization, believing that competition among banks would lead to lower interest rates. The results were disastrous: the move was followed by the very rapid growth of local and indigenous commercial banks, at a time when the banking legislation and bank supervision were inadequate, with predictable results—fourteen banking failures in Kenya in 1993 and 1994 alone. In the end, interest rates increased, not decreased...

There was clear evidence that the IMF was wrong about financial market liberalization and Ethiopia's macroeconomic position, but the IMF had to have its way. It seemingly would not listen to others, no matter how well informed, no matter how disinterested. Matters of substance became subsidiary to matters of process. Whether it made sense for Ethiopia to repay the loan was less important than the fact that it failed to consult the IMF: Financial market liberalization—how best this should be done in a country at Ethiopia's stage of development—was a matter of substance and experts could have asked for their opinion. (pp. 30-31).

In the book, *The Debt Threat*, Noreena Hertz writes about crazy U. S. banking escapades in foreign lands:

A loan is said to have been granted to Costa Rica in 1973 on the basis of a single Time article. Chase Manhattan and many other banks tried to lend to countries that were already in default to them: when Chase offered Bolivia a new loan in 1976, for example, it did so in complete disregard of the fact that it was a creditor on another loan for which Bolivia was already in default. Mexico was offered additional loans even though it had already committed 65.5 percent of its export revenues to paying debt service charges, which indicated a preexisting level of commitment that was already extremely high and extremely difficult to service. And many bankers making the loans just didn't know what they were doing. As one of the bank executives involved in the negotiations said at the time, "I am far from alone in my youth and inexperience. The world of international banking is now full of aggressive, bright hopelessly inexperienced 29-year-old vice presidents with wardrobes from Brooks Brothers (and) MBAs from Wharton or Stanford..."

By 1976, Citibank was earning 72 percent of its income abroad; Bank of America, 40 percent; Chase, 78 percent; First Boston, 68 percent; Morgan Guaranty, 53 percent; and Manufacturers Hanover, 56 percent. (pp. 33-34).

The financial carnage precipitated by American banks doing business abroad was inevitable. Many countries, like homeowners today, had taken out variable interest rate loans. Early in the 1980s, initial variable rate commercial loans were as low as 0.5 percent. As we know, interest rates in the 1980s went double digit. International loans of 13.1 percent or more became commonplace. Debt payments in countries like Argentina tripled. Loans, which once made sense, saw their payments go through the roof.

Unable to pay these loans, developing countries were forced to take on new loans just to pay the interest due. Many times the loan proceeds, if they came from an entity like the IMF, were used to pay back interest payments to the banks in the United States. Capital within the countries dwindled away.

The World Bank and the IMF came to the rescue, not so much to chastise the banks for lending out money at such a high rate, but really just to save the banks. Billions went down the drain in packages that did not work. Latin America got deeper and deeper into debt. More countries ceased making interest payments to American banks.

In the end, the name of the game was *bailout*. Once again, the American taxpayer ended up subsidizing troubled American banks. Realizing that countries were having a hard time remaining solvent, never mind going bankrupt, Treasury Secretary Nicolas Brady came up with a plan—a 20 percent debt forgiveness and securitization of the remaining debt into bonds, which were partially underwritten by the United States Treasury.
Problem bank loans, which were essentially illiquid assets, with the help of the United States Treasury became tradable bonds. Now these bonds trade in the trillions.

Bankers' Exceptions in Regulation

Banks have enjoyed favorable exceptions in government regulations to enhance their profit agendas. Under the Securities Exchange Act of 1934, a notable exception was given to banks to exempt themselves as broker–dealers in the securities business, even though bank trust departments solicited wealth management business from very wealthy individuals and families for decades. The trust business was considered incidental to banking. Because of these favorable exceptions, banks have been able to avoid the scrutiny and compliance issues, which other broker–dealers, insurance companies, and advisors have had to comply with for years.

When the Gramm-Leach-Bliley Act of 1999 repealed the Glass–Steagall Act entirely, it also repealed banks' exception for registering as a broker–dealer. Banks, in the new era of bank deregulation, would obviously be soliciting all of their depositors and prospects for securities purchases, insurance planning, additional loans, wealth management and so on.

According to the SEC release #2005-130, September 9, 2005, banks were able to extend compliance dates further in regards to broker–dealer registration until at least September 30, 2006. With the latest release, #2006-169, on September 29, 2006, the exemption for banks was extended to January 15, 2007. Even though banks pressed for deregulation to lessen competition, they, due to their power, have been able to live under another set of standards, which other competitors have had to comply with for years.

Hedge Funds: Exempt from Regulation

Hedge funds, those eight thousand or so private investment partnerships that control somewhere around $1.3 trillion, are exempt from regulation. Recent efforts by the SEC to have hedge funds at least register at the federal level went down in flames. For now, hedge funds only have to register as investment advisors if the state requires it.

Wall Street has a true love affair with hedge funds anyway. By various estimates, hedge funds now constitute up to 50 percent of commission income in trading, so Wall Street does not want to regulate a potential problem child who is making them a lot of money. Roughly 20 percent of corporate and public pensions in the United States now use hedge funds along with stocks and bonds. University endowments and foundations use more than 12 percent of assets in hedge funds.

A hedge fund can be a house of cards. The collapse of Long-Term Capital Management of Greenwich, Connecticut almost brought the world banking system down with it when it lost 92 percent of its capital. The defunct hedge fund run had to be rescued by Alan Greenspan and the Federal Reserve System.

In the summer of 2006, a hedge fund called Bayou Partners blew up in Connecticut leaving investors in the neighborhood of $400 million short. In September 2006, Amaranth Advisors closed its doors after it lost $6.2 billion on bets in natural gas. Public pension money from San Diego was in that fund. They lost in the vicinity of $175 million.

Archeus Capital, another hedge fund based in Manhattan that had $3 billion in assets in 2005, announced it was closing its doors and blamed its closing on administrative problems. In addition, in November 2006, the SEC filed charges #2006-189 against Vipers Founders Fund, a defunct hedge fund in the hands of Edward Ehee of Oakland, California. The SEC alleged that Ehee was raising money for a hedge fund that no longer existed with fictitious claims that the fund had $18 million in assets and made 10 percent annual returns. Evidently, it was a classic Ponzi scheme, as Ehee used new money raised to pay off prior investors and siphoned off money for car payments, mortgages, vacations, and personal bank accounts.

Hedge funds can be extremely volatile. They often borrow obscene amounts of money to make leveraged bets in stocks and bonds, which could blow the roof off a house. Hedge funds are an extremely lucrative business for their managers in an unregulated environment. They charge management fees that would make a mutual fund manager blush and have their clients enter into one-sided agreements.

You will see in the next chapter, "Never Met a Man Who Made His Millions in Mutual Funds," that unregulated hedge funds were waist deep in the market timing, late-trading mutual fund scandals as well. Eddie Stern of Canary Capital Partners," Izzy" Englander of Millennium Partners, Gary Pilgrim, and Veras Capital Master Fund recently paid $38 million in fines and disgorgements for market timing and late-trading violations with 810 mutual funds. It also included a cast of characters from the mutual fund business—Bank of America Nations Funds, Janus, PIMCO, and Strong Funds.

Will there be another Long-Term Capital Management? Probably, but for now, hedge funds are not held accountable. CAVEAT EMPTOR.

Banker and Manager Compensation in a World of Deregulation

"I don't believe people should go home with an empty pail. This guy Grasso saved the world. We couldn't pay him anything close to what he was worth."
Kenneth Langone,
The Man Behind Richard Grasso's $180 Million PayDay,
New York Times, March 14, 2004
Grasso was running the not-for-profit New York Stock Exchange (NYSE). Langone, an investment banker, made millions with initial funding for Home Depot. He is worth about $1 billion according to Forbes magazine in 2006.

"At the level of pay that those of you who run banks get, why the hell do you need bonuses to do the right thing?...Do we really have to bribe you to do your jobs? I don't get it. Think of what you are telling the average worker, that you are the most important people in the system and at the top, your salary isn't enough, you need extra incentive to do your jobs right."
Rep. Barney Frank (D-Massachusetts),
December 1, 2004
New York Plaza Hotel,
warning bankers at the American Banker Association awards meeting about bankers pressing for more deregulation.

"One of the things about my lifestyle is that I don't want to know what anything costs."

New York banker John Castle
who spent $500 thousand
chartering jets to fly his horse
Spot to a veterinary specialist
Wall Street Journal, April 8,1999

"Everybody here is overpaid, knows they are overpaid and determined to
continue to be overpaid."

Julian Robertson,
Wall Street investment manager
who made over $500 million in 1997.
Washington Post, January 31, 1998

"It's already on fire, but it is going to get even hotter."
Dolly Lenz, real estate broker,
NY Daily News, February 25, 2006
Lenz was commenting on how
Wall Streeters are using record
bonuses to buy high priced
Manhattan real estate.

"Where are the c-c-c customer's yachts?"
Henry Clews, Fifty Years on Wall Street,
commenting on being shown a squadron
of broker yachts in New York harbor.

Deregulation and de-supervision have awarded bankers, mutual fund managers, hedge fund managers, private equity managers, and assorted financiers Olympian paydays. The more this author dug into the overall compensation of financiers, the more disgusting it got.[37]

Hedge Fund Compensation

The top hedge fund managers run unregulated investment funds for wealthy investors and institutional investors such as pension funds and

---

[37] In a recent article written by Bill Buford, "The Taming of a Chef," in *The New Yorker,* April 2, 2007, he mentioned how bankers and hedge fund managers are not concerned with budgets when it comes to executive meals, which often cost in the tens of thousands. Six bankers in London spent sixty-three thousand dollars on one sitting for food and wine and tried to expense it to business.

college endowments. Their compensation makes bankers look like paupers. According to Institutional Investor's *Alpha* Magazine, the average take-home pay for the top twenty-five hedge fund managers in 2004 was over $250 million. This was up from $207 million in 2003, and was more than double that of $110 million in 2002. From *Alpha:*

Manager	Fund Managed	Total Compensation 2005
James Simons	Renaissance Technologies Corporation	$1,500,000,000
T. Boone Pickens	BP Capital Management	$1,400,000,000
George Soros	Soros Fund Management	$ 840,000,000
Steven Cohen	SAC Capital Advisors	$ 550,000,000
Paul Tudor Jones	Tudor Investment Corp. .	$ 500,000,000
Edward Lampert	ESL Investments	$ 425,000,000
Bruce Kovner	Caxton Associates	$ 400,000,000
David Tepper	Appalosa Management	$ 400,000,000
David Shaw	D.E. Shaw & Co.	$ 340,000,000
Stephen Mandel, Jr.	Lone Pine Capital	$ 275,000,000
Israel Englander	Millennium Partners	$ 230,000,000
Jeffrey Gendel	Tontine Associates	$ 215,000,000
Kenneth Griffin	Citadel Investment Group	$ 210,000,000
Timothy Barakett	Atticus Capital	$ 200,000,000
James Pallotta	Tudor Investment Corp.	$ 200,000,000
William Von Mueffling	Cantillon Capital Mgmt.	$ 200,000,000

In an industry, which is very unregulated, they make a knock-the-wind-out-of-you income. With compensation like this, hedge fund managers increasingly appear to be the new robber barons.

Banker and Other Financier Compensation

Condensed from a report performed by USA Today, here are some of the total compensation figures put together in April 2006 in regards to overall compensation of some financiers within the banking and investment banking industries. This is limited to CEOs only. Others within the banks can earn as much or even more than CEOs.

Goldman Sachs $622 Thousand Average Compensation per Employee

"Whilst bankers at Goldman Sachs will be splashing out on second homes, cars and polo ponies with their multi-million-pound bonuses, cleaners at Goldman Sachs are being squeezed by staff cutbacks."

Goldman Sachs has roughly 287 partners who make, on average, $7 million each. Surpassing the all-time high compensation pool of $11 billion in 2005, Goldman Sachs ladled out $16.5 billion in total compensation in 2006. That equals to average total compensation per employee of $622 thousand, although this compensation is not evenly spread around. Some top dogs at Goldman get as much as $50 million or more, with some high traders getting close to $100 million. The 2005 winner at Goldman Sachs was Hank Paulson, who made about $45 million at Goldman. Today he is the Treasury Secretary of the United States. Paulson's successor is Lloyd Blankfein who took home $53 million in 2006.

Any way you look at it, bankers and hedge fund managers make a ridiculous amount of money in a deregulated, de-supervised banking industry. According to a March 24, 2007, issue of *The Economist* it appears that Kenneth Lewis of Bank of America is leading the pack with total compensation of $114.4 million in 2006.[38]

Company	Executive	Total Compensation 2005 (Salary, Bonus & Stock Option Gains)
Capital One Financial	Richard D. Fairbank	$249,267,658
Lehman Brothers	R.S. Fuld, Jr.	$ 74,958,627
Morgan Stanley	John J. Mack	$ 68,187,675
Goldman Sachs Group	Henry M. Paulson, Jr.	$ 45,075,736
Merrill Lynch	E. Stanley O'Neil	$ 38,121,766
Wells Fargo	Richard M. Kovacevich	$ 28,786,617
American Express	K. I. Chenault	$ 26,539,841
Bear Stearns	James E. Cayne	$ 26,351,671
Bank of America	Kenneth D. Lewis	$ 24,125,711
PNC Financial Services	James E. Rohr	$ 23,487,787
Citigroup	Charles Prince	$ 22,927,089
Washington Mutual	Kerry K. Killinger	$ 21,968,936
U S Bancorp	Jerry A. Grundhofer	$ 19,894,765

[38] According to a recent study performed by the Corporate Research Library in Portland, Maine in 2007, executive compensation is growing immensely because of the SEC required disclosure of the present value of top executives' pension and deferred compensation agreements. Kenneth Lewis' retirement package is worth $83 million, but others such as Edward E. Whitacre, Jr. of AT&T was $158.4 million and Ray Irani of Occidental Petroleum Corp came in second at $124 million.

| Wachovia | G. Kennedy Thompson | $ 17,750,373 |

Pensions for Bankers and Other Financiers

    Many bankers receive astronomical defined benefit pensions for life, which adds to their compensation package. These special pensions far exceed the legal limits of most individuals under normal retirement rules. In 2006, the maximum qualified defined benefit pension for non-governmental employees in this country was $175 thousand annually. Most of us, perhaps 99 percent of the entire population, will never see that type of pension.

    The SEC and the OFHEO (Office of Federal Housing Enterprise Oversight) fined Fannie Mae, the largest U.S. buyer and guarantor of home mortgages, $400 million for $6 billion of accounting fraud. Senior executives overstated earnings by as much as $11 billion, so they could collect tens of millions in bonuses. For their part, former CEO Franklin D. Raines and CFO J. Timothy Howard were tossed out of Fannie Mae, a housing finance company chartered by Congress. Yet they did not walk away without exorbitant pensions. Raines and his wife receive $1.37 million annual pension as well as no cost medical, dental, and $2.5 million in life insurance for life. Howard and his wife will receive $432 thousand for life, medical benefits at retiree rates, and $1 million in life insurance benefits for life.

    Defined benefit pensions are very costly plans to fund. Interestingly, as we will see in the chapters "Bank-Owned Life Insurance" and "Corporate-Owned Life Insurance" many of these very high-end pension benefits for financiers and corporate executives are funded with high cash value permanent life insurance.

    In addition to very high base compensation, here are some of the life pensions that financiers have given themselves in a world of deregulation. This information is condensed from a study done by the *New York Times* on April 9, 2006.

Company	Executive	Estimated Annual Pension
Aflac	Daniel P. Amos	$2,266,184
American Express	Kenneth J. Chenault	$ 963,590
Bank of America	Kenneth D. Lewis	$3,501,128
Lehman Brothers	Richard S. Fuld, Jr.	$1,250,000
Mellon Financial	Martin G. McGuinn, Jr.	$1,385,000
Morgan Stanley	John J. Mack	$ 414,035
PNC Financial Services	James J. Rohr	$3,048,791
State Street	Ronald E. Logue	$1,150,000
U.S. Bancorp (USB)	Jerry A. Grundhofer	$ 575,531
Wells Fargo	Richard M. Kovacevich	$2,335,000

Summing Up the Casualties of Deregulation, De-supervision, and Plenty of Subsidies

The collateral damage of deregulation and de-supervision within the American banking and securities industry is everywhere. Deregulation and de-supervision accelerated the implosion of the savings and loan industry. This will ultimately cost the American taxpayer $250 billion or more.

Deregulation of usury laws or the practice of charging exorbitant rates of interest has become an imbedded income stream of the American financial system, and becomes a core profit center for large banks. Darth Vader interest overtakes Main Street. Deregulation, through arbitration, became the law of the land in the late 1980s. Arbitration gives consumer's little, if any, protection or recourse for justice when it comes to challenging large securities firms in courts.

The repeal of Glass–Steagall removed most of the safeguards, which protected and insulated consumers from big banks for years. Mega companies like WorldCom, Enron, Winstar, Global Crossing, and dozens of miscellaneous high tech companies flamed out and dropped like flies in the new era of deregulation. Investment firms and brokerages may be shoved around in deregulation, but investors are mugged. They lost $7 trillion in the meltdown alone.

An $11 billion dollar accounting fraud at WorldCom cost corporate shareholders and bondholders around $40 billion. Enron, once the seventh largest company in America, went down in flames as a pioneer in deregulation and lost $70 billion in market capitalization. People watched their 401(k) savings vaporize. Alan Greenspan became an apostle of deregulation and one of the ringleaders. With Robert Rubin and Sanford Weill, they got Senator Phil Gramm to sponsor a banking deregulation bill and tear Glass–Steagall down.

With the assistance of a complacent Congress, the Federal Reserve, and a printing press, Greenspan flooded the market with fiat dollars and debauched the currency. Since 1971, the dollar has lost at least 80 percent of its value.

The IMF, the World Bank, and the United States Treasury continually bail out international bankers, who consistently get over their heads in international markets. In the end, the taxpayer ends up paying the bill.

A banking industry, not happy with astronomical profits from the credit card business, manages to get the assistance of the United States Congress, punishing citizens with a draconian bankruptcy bill. The mutual fund business is reborn in the deregulated 1980s. A sector, which is paraded about as a paragon of integrity, ends up being a financial nightmare out of a Stephen King novel.

Deregulation was the economic gunboat, which bankers and the securities industry wanted and got. With deregulation, bankers became the Pirates of Lower Manhattan. As the gunboat moved throughout the waters of the American economy, financiers opened fire and invaded all the laws, which protected consumers. They made billions upon billions in fees speculating with other people's money. They went to places like Davos on Gulfstream jets and to assuage and ease their guilt for looting America, they set up private foundations to make themselves look good.

In its wake, after the banks won the battle for deregulation, the props of the gunboats chewed up companies, held citizens hostage to the agenda of banks and vaporized people's savings. The Congress passed the Sarbanes–Oxley Act in 2002 to make corporations more accountable, but now bankers are trying to take that down as well.

Deregulation Marches On

In February 2006, the New York Stock Exchange, once a not-for-profit entity, with the assistance of Goldman Sachs, merged with Archipelago Holdings, Inc. owner of the Pacific Exchange to form a new for-profit New York Stock Exchange. It was divided up into three separate entities—New York Stock Exchange LLC (NYSE LLC), NYSE Market, and NYSE Regulation, Inc., which is the self-regulatory division of the New York Stock Exchange.

In November 2006, the National Association of Securities Dealers, (NASD) announced its intention to merge its self-regulatory operations with NYSE Regulation, Inc. The argument is that this will streamline broker–dealer registration, increase efficiency, bring more consistency to securities oversight in the industry and reduce costs for broker–dealers. What the public will get is one big self-regulatory organization or one less cop on the beat to look out for securities crimes. Like most regulation, things will be more controlled at a central New York location. Wall Street and bankers' dreams of removing state oversight from the securities and banking businesses are coming close to reality.

In addition, laws, which were put into place to bring accountability to corporate America, namely the 2002 Sarbanes-Oxley, are now being challenged. Henry Paulson, former CEO of Goldman Sachs, and now Secretary of the Treasury is already blessing a new group of corporate, financial, and academic bigwigs, which claims that regulation has gone too far. The real reason perhaps is Wall Streets own hubris. They are losing investment banking deals to competitors who are more adept in London and Hong Kong.

The new committee, in a press release on September 12, 2006, called itself the Committee on Capital Markets Regulation (www.capmktsreg.org).

With the stench of Enron fading away, Wall Street and corporate America are looking for less regulation once again and looking to rewrite Sarbanes-Oxley.

Some committee members read like an "in crowd" of Wall Street and its suppliers—Kenneth Griffin, CEO of Citadel Investment Group, one of the larger hedge funds in America, made over $210 million in 2005. Samuel DiPiazza, Global CEO of PriceWaterhouseCoopers; Robert Glauber, Harvard Law School professor and former chairman and CEO of the NASD; Cathy Kinney, President and COO of the New York Stock Exchange; William Parrett, CEO of Deloitte; Robert Pozen of Massachusetts Financial Services; James Rothenberg, Chairman, Capital Research and Management; and Thomas Russo, Chief Legal Officer of Lehman Brothers.

Essentially, the Committee on Capital Markets Regulation calls for limited government oversight of private industry and would like to make it a lot tougher for individuals to sue companies and auditors for fraud. Moreover, like the Gramm-Leach-Bliley Act of 1999, the committee is trying to tie the hands of state officials in charging financial and accounting firms with crimes, and let them only use the hammer of criminal charges as a last resort.

Businesses want relief from lawsuits and fewer criminal prosecutions. The committee wants to be able to rewrite the law concerning having auditors certify that a company's financial controls are in order. They do not want any more Eliot Spitzers. The securities industry once and for all wants to route out state regulation, yet in the final analysis, the states have been the true consumer watchdogs, not the Feds.

Yet, if one sees how the Office of the Comptroller of the Currency squashed state prosecutors in the Providian bank case in 2004, it does not look good. Big banks all want preemption on a federal level so they do not have to deal with fifty different states.

You have to wonder on whose side of the aisle our new treasury secretary is. Hal Scott, chairman of the committee, had this to say in the *New York Times* when asked why no regulators were included, "We generally tried not to include regulators. We would not put people in the position who had formulated these rules in the past. They may have a lack of objectivity."

Yet Mr. Paulson, the new Secretary of the Treasury, is pushing for more deregulation and is using the Department of the Treasury to do so. He is certainly not including regulators in open discussions. On March 13, 2007, on *CSPAN* television, the Treasury Department sponsored a program on "U.S. Business Regulation" at Georgetown University in Washington D.C. In many ways, it was a rendezvous of The Pirates of Manhattan. The meeting, which was sponsored by the Treasury Department, seemed to be more about the interests of finance and the interests of New York. In attendance were Henry Paulson, treasury secretary and Goldman Sachs banker; John Thain, former Goldman Sachs banker and now president of the New York Stock Exchange; Warren Buffett, investor; Michael Bloomberg, mayor of New

York; Jeffrey Immelt, CEO of General Electric; Robert Rubin, former treasury secretary and vice-chairman, Citigroup; Jamie Dimon, CEO of JPMorgan Chase; Christopher Cox, chairman of the SEC; Paul Volcker, former chairman of the Federal Reserve; and Arthur Levitt, former chairman of the SEC.

The author found the program rather amusing and self-serving. Alan Greenspan, even though he is no longer the Fed chairman, tried his best to grab the spotlight. He claimed the regulation within the system was working fine, that banks who are lending out huge amounts of money to hedge funds know what they are doing, and there are counter weights to reduce risk. Arthur Levitt spoke up worrying about investor protection, but Robert Rubin constantly upstaged him. Rubin was comparing the United States to the United Kingdom, and he mentioned how everyone in the room has sat down with the exchequer of England for coffee. The consensus was that there was too much regulation and too much litigation from lawyers. In a way, it was disgusting. Between all of these men, there were tens of billions in wealth made in speculation of one form or another. They were doing their best to paint a horror story about attorneys' fees and unwilling to admit their part in the meltdown. To them, the economy could not be doing better.

The only one who brought some sense of sanity to this *CSPAN* broadcast was former Fed chairman Paul Volcker. He said we have to stop praising all the virtues of finance, and that no one is looking at the downsides of an economy based in financial services. Volcker maintained that the nation was too top heavy in finance; there was too much leverage and borrowing of money and virtually no saving of money. Whether we like it or not, the gap between the rich and the poor is growing greater and greater.

Now they are telling us to put all our money into mutual funds, which is a chief source of funding for this completely speculative excess. Think again. Let us proceed to the next chapter, "Never Met a Man Who Made His Millions in Mutual Funds".

NEVER MET A MAN WHO MADE HIS MILLIONS IN MUTUAL FUNDS

"Overwhelming evidence proves failure of the for-profit mutual fund industry. When the fiduciary responsibility to produce high-risk adjusted returns for investors inevitably comes into conflict with the profit motivation to provide substantial revenues for funds management companies, investor returns lose and company profits win.

Mutual fund investors consistently fail to achieve investment objectives, because the balance of power in the investment management world skews dramatically in favor of the profit-seeking investment manager. When a sophisticated provider of financial services stands toe-to-toe with a naïve consumer, the all-too-predictable conclusion resembles the results of a fight between a heavyweight champion and a ninety-pound weakling. The individual investor loses in a first-round knockout."

David F. Swenson, Unconventional Success, 2005
Swenson manages over $14 billion for Yale endowment

"The industry has lost its way. We have turned a very good profession into a business which is good for the business but not for the investor."
John Bogle, New York Times, November 2, 2003
Founder and former CEO Vanguard

"The sad truth of the matter is that over time the vast majority— approximately 80 percent—of the mutual funds underperform the overall stock market."

The Motley Fool

"Despite the hopes of those of many inside and outside the industry, the 'late trading' and 'market timing' allegations were not limited to a few bad apples involved with one distinct private investment company. Large fund complexes such as Bank One, Bank of America, Putnam, Janus, MFS Investments, Alliance and others have been named in our investigations, and you can expect more to come…

I have been outraged and dismayed by the recent discovery of late trading abuses. These instances of late trading were just not occasional, isolated or justifiable exceptional cases—such as where a customer entered a symbol incorrectly and the fund adviser sought to make a correction after hours, or where there was an inadvertent error in processing an order ticket, and the adviser then corrected it. No, the abuses we have seen were clear, systematic, repeated violations of SEC rules and of the obligations of fiduciary duty to the fund shareholders. Simply put, certain chosen investors were allowed to arbitrage a sure thing. There was no risk to the trader, but to the detriment of other shareholders.

If this were not enough, perhaps the most disturbing aspect of what has been discovered is that CEOs at some of these fund complexes were directly involved in these abuses. These CEOs showed an appalling lack of both business and personal ethics. On top of this, these CEOs' cavalier actions put their personal financial interests in front of their business' reputations. And, indeed, put the viability of their businesses at risk. As a former lawyer who spent many years of my professional life working with the fund industry, I am discouraged, to say the least."

> *Commissioner Paul S. Atkins, SEC*
> *Remarks before ABA Section of Business Law*
> *London, England, March 2, 2004*

"The scam in market timing throughout the mutual fund crisis has been that the smaller investors are seeing their returns diluted so the big investors can walk away with the profits."

> *Eliot Spitzer, August 9, 2004*

"The trouble with mutual funds is that that they are rewarded for the money they attract, not for the money they earn."

> *George Soros*

"This is a case about an investment advisor placing its interest in making a profit ahead of the interests of the mutual fund it serves."

> *SEC comment June 2005 in regards to Smith Barney Mutual funds and Citigroup Global Markets defrauding mutual fund investors for inflated transfer fees which resulted in an additional $93 million in pure profits and an additional $17 million in annual revenues for Citigroup. Citigroup Global Markets settled.*

"Fund managers are even more than kinetic than ever: their behavior makes whirling dervishes appear sedated by comparison. Indeed, the term 'institutional investor' is becoming one of those self contradictions called an oxymoron, comparable to 'jumbo shrimp' and 'lady mud wrestlers.'"

> *Warren Buffett*

"This is the same old ineffective enforcement we've seen time and time again. The SEC is more interested in protecting the securities industry than they are exposing it. It is hard to believe they have thoroughly investigated the facts in little over a week."

> *William F. Galvin, Attorney General Massachusetts*
> *commenting on Putnam Funds' quick settlement with the SEC, when managers were*
> *caught rapid trading in and out of mutual funds.*

"Over the past twenty years, you would have been better off owning the asset management companies than owning their services."

> *Don Phillips, Managing Director,*
> *Morningstar Like the Fund, Love the Company,*
> *New York Time, April 9, 2006*
> *Commenting on how it is more profitable to own a mutual fund company than to use*
> *its services.*

"I suppose if I were to give advice it would be keep out of Wall Street."

> *John D. Rockefeller*

The author has never met a man or woman who made his or her millions and millions of dollars in mutual funds. Not one. The author has seen people make millions in small businesses, stock deals, inventions, real estate, the medical field, entertainment, and professional sports, but never in mutual funds.

Dalbar, Inc., a Boston-based national research firm, in July 2003, published a report, *Quantitative Analysis of Investor Behavior,* confirming that few people actually make their millions in mutual funds. Unfortunately, mutual fund investors chase returns and barely keep in tow with inflation. On their web site, www.dalbarinc.com , some of the findings are as follows:

"Some investors are savvy (or lucky) enough to profitably time the markets—but they are the exception. Millions of investors chase returns after hearing about the markets ups and downs on the six o'clock news and a recent Dalbar study shows that most equity fund investors earn less than inflation as they try fruitlessly to buy low and sell high. Fixed income investors do a little better but still earn less than the index.

Motivated more by fear and greed than intellect, these investors chase market returns to the detriment of their pocketbooks. An update to DALBAR'S Quantitative Analysis of Investment Behavior (QAIB) study shows that since 1984, equity mutual fund shareholders have held their funds for a little over two years, and, as a result, have earned less than inflation. Investors in fixed income products do a little better but still earn far less than posted returns.

* The average equity investor earned a paltry 2.57% annually; compared to inflation of 3.14% and the 12.22% that the S&P 500 index earned annually for the last 19 years.

* The average fixed income investor earned a 4.24% annually; compared to the long-term government bond index of 11.7%"

Not surprising. John C. Bogle, founder and former CEO of Vanguard Mutual Funds, has spent his entire life in the mutual funds business. He has been a vociferous critic of the for-profit mutual funds business. In the *Wall Street Journal* (July 8, 2003), Bogle made these comments in regard to how little money people make in mutual funds:

"The bewildering array of choices among nearly 5,000 equity funds has ill served investors. The returns incurred by the average equity fund investor since 1984 have averaged just 2.7% per year, a shocking shortfall to the 9.3% return earned by the average fund. The result is that the average fund investor has earned less than one-quarter of the stock market's 12.2% annual return."

In the book, *Empire of Debt*, authors Addison Wiggin and William Bonner reaffirm and remind us that the greater fool theory is alive and well in America. Seeing the dark humor in mutual fund and stock investing, they write:

"Wall Street insists that investing is like healthcare; it is not a zero sum game either. One investor does not have to die so that another makes above market gains. We can all get rich. This is like saying we can all be above average. "Rich" is a relative term, not an absolute one...

Over time, all investors are destined to lose money (compared with the general market), for the cost of the Wall Street casino must be paid. Brokers, analysts, deal-makers, financiers, fund managers, account managers—all the financial intermediaries who make up the Wall Street industry—draw salaries and pensions as long as they draw breath. That money too, must come out of investors' pockets, so that over the long run, the average investor's real return must be lower than the actual return from the investments. And many, including most of the little guys, will actually lose money...

The typical investor in public markets has no idea what he is doing. Putting his money into a stock or a mutual fund brings him a temporary happiness. He sees himself as Kirk Kerkorian making a bid for General Motors or Warren Buffett shrewdly moving on an insurance company. "I bought Google," he tells his wife. His chest expands. He feels a crown of authority on his head and imagines his most private part growing. For he has mastered the most sacred and all-powerful rite of our time; with a single gesture he has joined the Knights Templar, the Freemasons, and the local country club. He is in. He is with it. He gets it. He is one with all the other swells who make up this wondrous modern economy. He has gone to Wall Street like Sir Galahad to Camelot.

He does not realize the misery awaiting him. Only later, much later, does he discover that he is not a hero, but just a chump—an insignificant speck of dust on Wall Street's white shoes.

The scene would be depressing if there weren't something gloriously comic in it. Wall Street is doing nothing evil; it is merely doing its job—separating fools from their money.

The root of the misconception is the nature of investing, at least, the public form of it. The idea of it is that a man can get rich without actually working. All he has to do is put his money "in the market" by handing it over to Wall Street, and through some magic never fully described, it comes back to him 10-fold. He must see his broker as Christians see Jesus at the wedding feast. He casts his dough on the water of the lower Hudson and the East River, and it comes back multiplied into really big money.

There must be some science to it, he imagines, some wisdom that investment geniuses came up with years ago that—like penicillin or quinine—is now available to him. But it is not so. Instead, the whole edifice of Wall Street is built on a hollow wish: that you can get something for nothing." (pp. 308-309)

Philip Augar is a former investment banker. In his book, *The Greed Merchants: How the Investment Banks Played the Free Market Game,* Augar says this about the codependent, dysfunctional conflicts of interest between Wall Street brokers and the mutual fund business:

"Because so many mutual shareholders started to invest close to the top of the market, the average shareholder's annual return between 1984 and 2002, according to one estimate, was a miserable 2.6 percent—far short of the S&P 500's 12 percent annual return over the same period.

Fund managers might not have wanted to draw attention to their own poor performance by seeking recovery from brokers, but they should have pushed the point: Conflicts of interest contributed to the collective failure to see the bubble for what it was.

At just the moment when the fund managers needed help, the brokers were deficient. They should have been shouting from the rooftops what they were saying to colleagues in private: sell, sell and sell...

Vested interest and influence also kept fund managers on the sidelines, for institutional investors and mutual funds in particular were connected to the brokers in all sorts of ways. The fund managers were not in a position to get very upset about laddering and spinning, because all too often they were recipients of the broker's favors. They relied on them for generous allocations of hot new issues to keep their performance up with the pack, and in return were prepared to generate lots of commission.

Mutual funds habitually gave brokers extra trading business for pushing their mutual funds through brokers' distribution networks...

Eight of the world's top twenty largest institutional investors belong to organizations that also own investment banks; they were hardly likely to sue each other. (pp. 194-195).

Contrary to the incessant downpour of slick Madison Avenue advertising and endless cavalcades of affluent fresh scrubbed couples smiling about their mutual fund purchases, mutual funds are full of risks as well as conflicts of interests. While few investors make money in mutual funds, it is a pot of gold for those who own and manage them.

In researching the mutual fund industry, this author has seen a recurring pattern of problems. These patterns are rarely, if ever, tied together cohesively in the mainstream press because the mutual fund companies and the financial institutions who own fund companies are some of the largest advertisers in America today. Every financial publication is chock-a-block full of advertisements for mutual fund companies. It is obviously in the best interests of the media not to bite the hand that feeds them. The author identified the following:

One. Mutual funds love to show past performance as an indication of how they may do in the future. While prior performance is a great advertising gimmick, it is absolutely no guarantee or indication of what to expect. Srikant Dash, a global equity index strategist at Standard & Poor's, said this in the company's semiannual report on mutual fund performance in August 2006:

"Standard & Poor's research shows that very few funds manage to consistently repeat top-half or top-quartile performance. The low count of mutual

funds that consistently maintain top-quartile rankings is a sobering reminder about the risks of chasing past performance."

There has never been a straight-line bull market of ten, twenty, or thirty years. At best, mutual fund performance is a crystal ball projection like something out of a Harry Potter movie. No one knows what the stock market will do. No one knows what interest rates will be. No one knows how tax laws will change or how much inflation will take away in purchasing power.

Two. Mutual fund mountain chart illustrations always show dividends and capital gains reinvested back into the mutual fund. These are *taxable events,* but cleverly minimized and camouflaged by mutual fund companies in microscopic footnotes. Within the fine print, one sees the disclosure *"assumes all dividends and capital gains are reinvested."* Fund returns are shown on a *pre-tax basis.* If the taxes paid were to be taken out of the impressive mountain chart illustrations, the funds would crumble and the charts would be flatter than the state of Indiana.

Roger Lowenstein, in his book, *Origins of the Crash: The Great Bubble and Its Undoing* writes about the taxes generated through excessive stock trading with mutual funds:

"It was, of course, to the detriment of investors that mutual funds traded in and out of stocks so rapidly—because the investors were stuck with the higher tax burden that resulted from short-term sales. But it was not to the detriment of mutual fund managers, because their results were reported, and generally evaluated (by Morningstar and such), on a pretax basis. This reinforced their tendency to speculate." (p. 71).

When the stock market and mutual fund performance tanks and goes into a tailspin as it did around 2001, the financial institutions replace the mutual fund mountain charts with circle pie asset allocation charts. Mutual funds, like airplanes, do not operate in a vacuum. Mutual funds must contend with pilot error, headwinds, and all types of bad weather. Like airplanes, investors in actively managed mutual funds will encounter economic headwinds such as manager costs, commissions, market risk, inflation risk, lost opportunity costs, taxes, and hyperactive quick-to-pull-the-trigger speculative traders.

Taxes always erode investment output. According to one Lipper Research study, investors paid $9.6 billion in taxes on mutual funds in 2005, a 48 percent increase from 2003. Even though capital gains rates have been lowered, mutual funds can still be hammered in the overall return, hitting the taxpayer with a sizable tax bill. The following examples illustrate this problem.

Mutual Fund Capital Gains...
(Source: Morningstar, December 31, 2000 and Navigator Asset Management)

Mutual Fund	2000 Total Return	%Capital Gains
Janus Venture	-46%	13%
Putnam Int'l New Opportunity	-38%	24%
Janus Mercury	-23%	10%
Vanguard US Growth	-20%	18%
T. Rowe Price Int'l Discovery	-16%	20%
Fidelity Contra Fund	-7%	18%

Three. The natural order of most businesses is to reduce costs as capacity grows. Yet for mutual funds, the costs have actually doubled since the 1950s largely because of excessive trading within the portfolio. In the 1950s, the average portfolio turnover rate was about 15 percent, whereas today 100 percent portfolio turnover is commonplace. Even turnover ratios of 200 percent and 300 percent are typical. Some turnovers are absolutely absurd. In 2006, *Forbes* magazine[39] reported the following turnover ratios: Gartmore US Growth Leaders, 827 percent; Prasad Growth Fund, 731 percent; Dreyfus Founders Passport-A, 729 percent; Marketocracy Masters 100, 647 percent; and Gartmore Nationwide Leaders Fund-A, 523 percent! The problem with all of this trading is that the more funds trade, the more it costs. Mutual funds pass these commission costs on to you. Furthermore, fund managers have proven to be lousy traders, so not only is trading costly, it has proven to be stupid. Yet mutual funds are not happy disclosing all of these trading costs, and most consumers never read their mutual fund statements or prospectuses.

Following are examples of various mutual fund costs. Because of these high costs, exchange traded funds, index funds, and separate account products are growing dramatically, although even index funds offer no downside protection.

---

[39] John Chamberlain,"The Outer Limits, Some of These Funds Go Way Beyond the Ordinary," *Forbes*, September 18, 2006. Even the author was shocked at this amount of trading.

71

Mutual Fund Total Costs
(*Source: Navigator Asset Management*)

Mutual Fund	Expense Ratio%	Trading Costs %	Sales Charge%	Total Cost %
Aim Constellation	1.20	.54	1.10	2.84
Alliance Balanced	1.32	2.14	.85	4.31
Berger 100	1.48	1.37	0.00	2.85
Fidelity Blue Chip	1.02	2.18	.60	3.80
Fidelity Contra	1.00	2.82	.60	4.42
Fidelity Sel. Comp.	1.69	2.27	.60	4.56
Janus Enterprise	1.23	2.32	0.00	3.55
Janus Growth/Inc	1.17	2.34	0.00	3.51
Scudder Cap Grwth	.98	2.84	0.00	2.82
Average All Funds	1.47	1.41	.66	3.53
Average No-Load Funds	1.26	2.19	0.00	3.46

Four. Mutual funds with so much portfolio turnover, cannot and do not accurately disclose holdings within the portfolio. Because there is so much activity, prospectuses are virtually meaningless. Therefore, the direction of the manager and the mutual fund itself can easily drift away from the original purpose or objective of the fund. This is what is known as *style drift.* John Bogle, in an article in the *Wall Street Journal,* June 20, 2000, entitled, "How Mutual Funds Lost Their Way," puts it this way:

"Fund managers, once long-term investors, have become short term players—speculators, if you believe that holding stocks for an average of 406 days has little to do with investing. Fund portfolio turnover, averaged about 17% annually during my first 15 years in this industry, rose to 90% last year.

The hyperactive trading atmosphere of the day is partly responsible. But the shift in control from investment committee to portfolio manager has also played a major role. For better or worse, the industry's dominant force has changed from consensus to impulse. What's more, portfolio managers turn over at a rapid rate. The average manager last just six years, and then a new broom sweeps the portfolio clean. It seems there are a few stars in the mutual-fund firmament, just many comets."

Five. Mutual funds have become too diversified. The average mutual fund today holds around 130 stocks. It is almost impossible for any one-fund manager to keep on top of that kind of activity. There are simply not enough hours in the day to do so. To make money in life one needs concentration of effort and focus. Diversification is a defensive rather than an offensive strategy. One hedge fund manager made an amusing comment, "diversification is disworsification." In reviewing hundreds of proxy statements for this book, the author found that most corporate CEOs make their millions by focusing on the *one stock* that they know the most about—the company for which they work.

Concentration of effort in investing is like light. When light is diffused, there is not much power. Concentrate light under a magnifying glass, and you can start a fire. Concentrate light even further through a laser, and you can burn through steel. Warren Buffett warned investors in 1993 in a letter saying that, "spreading your bets around a large number of stocks is likely to hurt your results and increase your risk." Warren Buffett does not believe in excessive trading. When someone once asked Buffett what his favorite holding period for an investment was, he said, "Forever." Academic research also suggests that mutual funds concentrated in one area perform better than their over-diversified brethren do.

Six. Investors are blindly entering into very complex one-sided financial arrangements. In 2006, the Securities Investor Protection Corporation tested a group of 635 self-proclaimed investors.[40] Eighty-three percent of the test takers failed on investment basics while 80 percent mistakenly believed that they were insured against investment fraud losses. When four out of five Americans think there is an agency to protect them against fraud, we have an obvious problem in investor naivety.

Another survey performed in September 2005, by the Opinion Research Corporation for the Consumer Federation of America (CFA)[41] confirms investor naivety:

- Only one-third of mutual fund owners considered cost or mutual fund volatility to be important
- Only 40 percent considered the fund's risks to be important
- Most investors are concerned with the fund company's reputation and the past performance of other funds
- Only 28 percent of investors, who relied on advisors to help them with their mutual fund selections, did any research themselves
- Only 37 percent of investors considered a prospectus to be important

---

[40] "Most Americans Don't Know Investment Basics," *Financial Advisor Magazine,* January 2006.
[41] Ibid.

Seven. Selection of funds has become a game of chance. Fund investors bear the selection risk. Picking the right actively managed mutual fund is similar to looking for a needle in a haystack, as there are more that 8,700 funds from which to choose. The odds are better if you play roulette. Just take the example of Ford Motor Company mutual fund options for their 401(k) plan. Ford offers over thirty different funds from eleven different companies.

Eight. Mutual fund investors front 100 percent of the money and retain 100 percent of the risk. Fund managers put up little capital (it only takes $100 thousand to start a mutual fund) and are virtually guaranteed a very high income and compensation package if they garner enough money under management.

However, mutual funds do implode and go into a tailspin. Consider in 2001, Merrill Lynch Mid Cap Growth lost 36.6 percent, its Premier Growth lost 52.6 percent, its Focused Twenty Fund became unfocused and lost 70.1 percent, Fundamental Growth lost 19.4 percent, and Global Growth lost 26 percent.

Many funds disappear and merge with other funds. Merrill Lynch set up a mutual fund called the Internet Strategies Fund. With a much-hyped beginning, the fund was launched in the spring of 2000, only to close down a short time later in 2001. Investors incurred losses of nearly $900 million while Merrill Lynch earned $45 million on fees.

Morgan Stanley once operated the Asian Equity Fund with $350 million under its umbrella, but that fund also closed in 2003. Over the past decade, in total, around 1,900 funds disappeared.[42]

Nine. Johnny-One-Note-Planning is prevalent. Every day, the industry, through spending hundreds of millions of dollars, largely influences our perceptions in regards to mutual funds. Through blitzkrieg waves of advertising, we become brainwashed into believing that mutual funds are a sure-footed path for creating wealth like the Yellow Brick Road out of *The Wizard of Oz*.

Advertising does work. Business at fund companies like Fidelity is booming. Consider that in 1999 and 2000, billions poured into technology mutual funds as the NASDAQ approached 5,000. Estimates are that about 80 percent of funds went into technology, but later investors lost between 60 and 80 percent of their money, in large part due to Johnny-One-Note-Planning in the media. Americans bought high and sold low.[43]

In reality, fund investing is like walking directly into the path of a tornado. Knowing the risks, financial gurus still pump up mutual funds and speculation in stocks as the Holy Grail of wealth creation. In the book, *Making the Most of Your Money,* Jane Bryant Quinn says this:

---

[42] Barton Biggs, *Hedge Hogging* (Hoboken, NJ: John Wiley & Sons, Inc., 2006).
[43] Ibid.

74

"I love mutual funds because they're so easy as well as so smart. Anyone can learn enough to buy a good one. What other investment can make that claim?" (p. 502)

On page 582, Ms. Quinn continues:

"Over the long term, stocks beat the tar out of other financial investments. If you have not noticed my preference for stock-owning mutual funds, you have been using this book as a doorstop."

Comrade-in-arms Suze Orman says in the *Nine Steps to Financial Freedom*:

"The price of admission to the world of money is lower and than you think and, especially with the onset of mutual funds, the easiest and safest way to create your own fortune, and here is what they talk about it inside...No load funds can be purchased without the help of an advisor—no middleman, no commissions, no hidden costs, just smooth sailing to greater and greater wealth over time." (pp. 209-210)

Ponzi once said, "If a man focuses on just one thing, he might as well be blind." As in the 1920s, today, virtually each and every financial magazine and television show is crammed full of mutual fund advertisements, get-rich-now schemes and scorecards highlighting the hottest funds. The media rarely question the follies of mutual fund investing. In fact, *CNBC* salutes the mutual fund business as a place of worship in programs such as *Fast Money*.

To further serenade the American public and win advertising dollars, newspapers and magazines such as the *Wall Street Journal, Barrons,* the *New York Times, Money, Forbes,* and *Fortune* have special sections to salute the mutual fund industry. There is a codependent love affair with the media and Wall Street. Gary Weiss, in his book, *Wall Street Versus America,* writes:

"The media's love affair with power and money is scrupulously apolitical. The financial media are equal opportunity deifiers, putting the left-leaning mogul George Soros on a pedestal, downplaying his missteps, with just as much devotion as they do to his far more numerous conservative brethren. The common denominator is not ideology but color—Intaglio Green, the color of the cloth-pulp concoction that is Wall Street's only moral compass, only purpose and allegiance. Intaglio Green knows no ideology, no political party, no religion or race." (pp. xxviii-xxix)

Moreover, as long as the media disperse investment advice content, which is "considered broad and general," it is exempt from registering as an investment advisor. In addition, that requirement only applies to public airways. Cable television is exempt from any standards.

Ten. As mutual funds attract too much money, they become overweight. The larger funds lose their nimbleness and become as easy to turn around in markets as an aircraft carrier.

Eleven. A consistent problem associated with the mutual fund business and all of stock market investing for that matter is its *unrealistic expectations.*[44] Large institutional investors, with all the professional assistance one could possibly ask for, do not perform. Just consider the unrealistic expectations United Airlines had in funding its defined benefit pension program. Its overly optimistic delusional expectations of what it could generate in stock market returns on its pension plan helped send the company into bankruptcy.

Twelve. No mutual fund "police" exist, and frankly, at around 8,700 or more mutual funds, there are too many funds to keep in check. There are only several dozen people within the SEC monitoring the entire mutual fund industry, which manages trillions of dollars, and employs thousands of people. In a Government Accountability Office (GAO) April 2005 report, *Mutual Fund Trading Abuses,* some of the problems related to the SEC monitoring the industry are discussed:

> *"SEC has taken several steps to strengthen its mutual fund oversight program and the operations of mutual fund companies over the past 2 years, but it is too soon to assess the effectiveness of several key initiatives…To improve its capacity to anticipate, identify, and manage emerging risks and market trends in the securities industry, SEC has created a new office that reports directly to the agency's chairman. However, it is too soon to assess the effectiveness of the new office as it had only 5 of 15 planned employees as of February 2005 and was still defining its role within the agency…Moreover, SEC has not developed a plan to ensure that agency staff receive and can review the annual compliance reports on an ongoing basis. Without such a plan, SEC cannot ensure that it has taken full advantage of opportunities to enhance its mutual fund oversight program and detect potential violations on a timely basis."* (pp. 5-6).

There you have it. In 2005, the SEC was only preparing to hire fifteen people to monitor a major financial industry. Remember, folks, the whole exposure of the mutual fund scandal came about from the state level with Eliot Spitzer, not the federal government. Furthermore, the SEC, which is supposedly looking out for the consumer interest, is in bed with the securities business and the mutual fund industry.[45]

---

[44] Ibid.

[45] For many years, those who regulate the securities and mutual fund business end up working for it. Professor John P. Freeman of the University of South Carolina documented this before Congress in January 2004. Edward Siedle, "The Irrelevant SEC—In Bed with the Industry It Is Supposed to Regulate, It Needs a Shake Up," *Forbes,* November 27, 2006, 40. Siedle is a former attorney with the SEC.

Take for example, former SEC chairman William Donaldson who was also the co-founder of the investment bank Donaldson, Lufkin & Jenrette. Paul Roye worked as a lawyer for the mutual fund business before moving over to the SEC to oversee mutual funds. As a top SEC official, Paul Roye seemed to be a bit annoyed about having to monitor problems in the mutual fund business. While with the SEC, Roye revealed indifference in regards to *"revenue sharing"* which in reality is a *"kickback"* from the mutual fund firms to the brokers who peddled their funds.

In the book, *Wall Street Versus America,* Gary Weiss says the following:

> *"Roye made it very clear that the SEC had no canine in this particular fight. He approached the subject of fees, expenses, and revenue-sharing arrangements with kind of a bored indifference, such as you might find in a bartender who has witnessed too many fistfights. Roye was not even willing to pay lip service to the notion that such payments were problematic. The words "conflicts of interest" were nowhere to be found in his analysis of the payments (except for a footnote saying that those conflicts were addressed). Roye devoted most of his assessment to a dry legal analysis that made the payments seem about as insignificant as the loose change that falls out of your pocket when you sit on a sofa." (p. 97).*

When Roye left the SEC after the mutual fund scandals, he went to work for Capital Research of Los Angeles, owner of American Funds and one of the largest mutual fund companies in America. Paul Haaga, Roye's former law boss, was the biggest lobbyist for the mutual fund business when he was the head of the mutual fund trade group, the Investment Company Institute (ICI). Haaga left ICI, and now works at Capital Research with his old associate Paul Roye.[46] Today Andrew "Buddy" Donohue oversees the unit at the SEC which, polices the mutual fund business. Yet Donohue a lawyer, worked for Merrill Lynch and Oppenheimer Mutual Funds. He was also a consistent political contributor to the Investment Company Institute [ICI] Political Action Committee. Donohue was also in the board of governors of ICI in 2004 and 2005.

Thirteen. The idea that independent directors are guardians looking out for mutual fund shareholder interests is a bit farfetched. Companies that had a majority of independent directors such as MFS, Nations Funds, Strong Funds, Alliance Capital, Putnam, and Pilgrim Baxter were involved in late trading and market timing scandals—no-risk profits to the traders, yet clearly detrimental to the shareholders.[47]

---

[46] Ibid.
[47] Gary Weiss, *Wall Street Versus America: The Rampant Greed and Dishonesty That Imperils Your Investments* (New York: Penguin Group, 2006). Mr. Weiss is a former writer for *Business Week* and gives the reader an inside view of Wall Street.

Fourteen. Pay-to-play dollars, kickbacks, and other "revenue sharing" arrangements between mutual funds and the broker–dealers who sell them hurt the consumer. Mutual fund companies are charged by brokerage firms for the privilege of being put on a preferred list. In exchange for revenue sharing payments (a kickback in any business other than the securities business), mutual fund families have special access to a firm's sales force to push the sale of certain funds and variable annuities.

David Swensen, in his well-researched book, *Unconventional Success* points out that even the supposedly squeaky-clean mutual fund companies such as American Funds/Capital Group are involved in the revenue sharing kickback arrangements in a big way. American Funds had arranged for approximately $100 million in stock brokerage commissions to brokers who specifically sold their funds. The fund company had about fifty revenue sharing agreements with banks, financial advisors, investment banks, insurance companies, and industrial firms.

Many financial institutions were involved in kickback arrangements. Some of them included Smith Barney, Morgan Stanley, PNC Bank, American Funds (Capital Group), Fidelity, AIM/Invesco, Massachusetts Financial Services (MFS), PIMCO Funds, Franklin Templeton, Edward D. Jones, Putnam Investment Management, Hartford Financial, and American Express now known as Ameriprise Financial Services, Inc.[48]

Swensen, in his book, writes about Edward D. Jones, one of the nation's largest distributors of mutual funds. He points out that Jones received $80 million in 2002 and $90 million in 2003 in additional fees to push seven mutual fund families. This obviously compromises a broker or planner's supposed independence. In fact, Swensen goes on to mention that about 90 to 95 percent of Jones' sales came from those seven fund families.

Even though this behavior is repugnant, the only thing the SEC asks for is disclosure of the revenue sharing. In many other businesses, kickbacks would mean jail time. In the fund business and with many securities wrongdoings, *disclosure is absolution.* Instead of making direct cash payments to compensate Wall Street, there was the business of *directed commissions*, another twisted way in which Wall Street compensates itself. Essentially mutual fund companies pay inflated commissions to get money into brokerage firms' hands to distribute funds.

Fifteen. Incestuous relationships are all too common. Mutual fund companies, because they control so much in liquid savings and because they often have deep business relationships with major companies, often look the other way in protecting the shareholders for whom they are supposed to be

---

[48] David F. Swensen, *Unconventional Success: A Fundamental Approach to Personal Investment* (New York: Simon & Schuster, 2005). Swensen is regarded as one of the most consistent top investors in America.

looking out. Mutual fund companies are watching out for themselves rather than the investors they are supposedly serving.

Gretchen Morgenson, in an article in the *New York Times* on September 10, 2006, titled, "How to Find a Fund's True Colors," said this:

> *"While funds are supposed to be protecting their shareholders, the sorry fact is that they often have lucrative relationships with companies whose shares they own on behalf of their clients. These cushy ties can be jeopardized if a fund votes against management's proposals or directors"*

Morgenson goes on to review the case of Pfizer, the pharmaceutical giant and its executive compensation policy. A case in question was the overall compensation package for Hank McKinnell, the former CEO who ran Pfizer from 2001 to 2006. During his time at Pfizer, McKinnell received $65 million in pay and an $83 million pension benefit while the company lost close to half of its value.

Some fund companies, such as Putnam, which owns a good deal of Pfizer, were against the overall amount of compensation that went to McKinnell. Other fund companies, such as Barclays Global Investors, Dodge & Cox, Fidelity, and Northern Trust went along with the package, even as some of the largest shareholders at Pfizer had.

According to Morgenson, Fidelity manages several funds in Pfizer's retirement plans. Likewise, Barclays earned $2.65 million and Dodge & Cox earned $1.65 million as investment advisors to Pfizer's pension plan in 2004. Northern Trust also earned close to $2 million as a trustee to Pfizer's pension plan in 2004.

Later in the article, Morgenson summarizes:

> *"In other words, no pay for performance disconnect—not even an $83 million pension dispensed to a chief executive who presided over the destruction of billions of dollars in shareholder value—is egregious enough to halt Northern Trust's rubber stamp for corporate directors.*
> *It is thanks to this kind of large-shareholder passivity that we have seen the biggest transfer of wealth from owners to managers in the history of corporate America. And it is this kind of inertia that allows continued corporate wrongdoing. The fact is, too many fund companies have supported practices that betray shareholders but benefit corporate executives as well as the funds themselves. Only fund shareholders can stop them."*

A Whole Lot of Money Tied up in Mutual Funds

In 2006, the Investment Company Institute (ICI)[49], a mutual fund trade group, reported that about $10.013 trillion reside in mutual funds, and about 55 million households and 96 million shareholders own mutual funds. Trillions of dollars is an astronomical amount to be tied up in one industry, when various sources figure the total assets within the national economy is in the neighborhood of about $44 trillion. Moreover, the majority of mutual fund shareholders have moderate incomes. According to ICI, three out of five owners have incomes between $25,000 and $99,999.

According to the latest data in from ICI (as of 2006), the mutual fund business is comprised of 8,719 mutual funds, 653 closed-end investment companies, 211 exchange traded funds and 5 sponsors of unit investment trusts. ICI reports that its members manage 98 percent of all mutual fund assets.

The amount of money going into mutual funds is staggering when one considers the numerous scandals surrounding the mutual fund business. In the first three months of 2006, the ICI reports that the amount of new money going into stock mutual funds averaged $30.98 billion per month. If this trend continues, this will surpass annual new inflows of money of $302 billion in 2000 and $325 billion in new money in 2004. These amounts do not include additional cash flows into taxable and non-taxable bond funds, money markets and so on.

The tax-deferred cousin to mutual funds known as *variable annuities* passed the $1 trillion mark in 2003 and it has grown to about $1.5 trillion in 2006. Unfortunately, investors tend to follow the herd into the slaughter. In the late 1990s, about sixty to eighty cents of every mutual fund dollar was going into a technology fund. As we would later find out, roughly $7 trillion of wealth was erased in the high tech dot.com meltdown.

New Pension Reform Act: Automatic Enrollment, a Permanent Bonanza for Mutual Fund Companies

Mutual funds now control a major portion of all liquid savings within America. In August, 2006, the "Pension Reform Act of 2006" was instigated in large part due to the impending implosion of the airlines' related massive underfunding of their defined benefit pensions. The act contains provisions, which will benefit the mutual fund business immensely for years to come.

This bill, which was lobbied for by the Investment Company Institute and fund companies such as Fidelity, now lets employers set up *automatic payroll deductions* on retirement plans for new employees. This bill virtually guarantees the mutual fund business additional trillions of dollars in assets and billions in revenues. The act also opened the door for mutual fund

---

[49] All information obtained from Investment Company Institute, online, www.ici.org.

80

companies to offer investment advice directly to 401(k) plan participants. It allows money managers to charge additional and varying fees for investment advice and squeeze out independent advice providers such as Financial Engines and Morningstar.[50]

The pension act will also benefit the mutual fund industry, as tax incentives from 529 college savings plans, another sweet spot in profits for the mutual fund industry, are made permanent with the passage of this act.

The mutual fund industry also benefited from the "2005 Bankruptcy Abuse and Consumer Protection Act" as well. Assets up to $1 million are exempt from the bankruptcy estate as long as they are in IRAs or Roth IRAs. In addition, most of those retirement assets are in mutual funds. In addition, unlimited qualified plan assets are also exempt and most defined contribution 401(k) and 403(b) plans are in mutual funds. However, this *is not* a new provision.

The Mutual Fund Business: A Perpetual Income Stream for Owners, Managers, and Institutions

The author has never met anyone who has made his or her entrepreneurial millions in mutual funds. Not one. Many people have lost a great deal of money in mutual funds. However, for the people who own, run and monitor mutual funds it is like winning the lottery.

John Bogle, founder and former CEO of Vanguard Funds, writes in his book *The Battle for the Soul of Capitalism* about the mutual fund compensation game.

"In effect, the fund industry operates under an institutionalized system of managers' capitalism, one so deeply entrenched that it will be difficult to dislodge. An institution with its own serious governance problems and riddled with conflicts of interest is hardly in a preferred position to cast stones at others.

While the shareholder wealth consumed by the managers of corporate America has been far from trivial, the shareholder wealth consumed by the managers of mutual fund America has been enormous. More than one-fifth of the robust annual gross returns generated for investors in the financial markets—stock, bond, and money market alike—during the past two decades has been siphoned off by fund managers. The awesome magic of compounding returns has been overwhelmed by the tyranny of compounding costs. Without a major reduction in the share of market returns arrogated to themselves by our mutual fund intermediaries, more than three-quarters of the future cumulative financial wealth produced by stocks over an investment lifetime will be consumed by fund managers, leaving less than 25 percent

---

[50] As the 401(k) becomes the dominant retirement vehicle in America, the vast majority of 401(k) plans are funded with mutual funds; around 400,000 corporate sponsors use the 401(k)-mutual fund combo. Doug Halonen, "Rule Hurts Advice Givers but Aids Fund Companies," *Pensions & Investment*, February 19, 2007, 1.

for the investors. Yet it is the investors themselves who put up 100 percent of the capital and assume 100 percent of the risk." (p. xxii)

Wealth created and future dependable income streams generated for mutual fund owners, managers, bankers, Wall Street brokers, accountants, lawyers, and suppliers (*The Pirates of Manhattan*) can be astronomical and reach into the stratosphere. Extracted from the latest 2006 *Forbes* magazine *400 Richest Americans* report[51] and from previous research, the following is what the author discovered about the wealthy involved in the mutual fund business.

Fidelity Investments, Edward "Ned" Johnson, III, and his daughter Abigail Johnson own the largest mutual fund company in America. Between them, they have an aggregate net worth of around $20.5 billion. Edward is estimated at $7.5 billion, while his daughter exceeds him at $13 billion. Edward Johnson started the family business in 1946 when he acquired Fidelity Management & Research or FMR.

Fidelity manages roughly $1.384 trillion for twenty million investors. In March 2006, the *Boston Globe* reported that the company's profits rose 20 percent at Fidelity to $1.3 billion in 2005 while gross revenues grew by 10 percent to $11.1 billion. In 2006, revenues grew to $12.9 billion, a 16 percent increase. At the top of the bull market in 2000, Fidelity earned about a $2 billion dollar profit. Because the mutual fund giant had also doubled its marketing budget, the *Boston Globe* reported that its sales of new and existing funds went up about 62 percent in 2006. Overall, according to an annual report of the company, new inflows into the mutual fund arm of the company increased to $60.4 billion despite a lackluster year in mutual fund performance.

Franklin Resources is another family business started by Charles Johnson's father in 1947. Along with half brother Rupert Johnson, Charles took over the company in 1969 and acquired Templeton mutual funds in 1992. Franklin Resources now manages about $500 billion in assets, with Charles Johnson estimated to be worth $4.5 billion and Rupert Johnson $3.7 billion. Franklin was fined $50 million for the market timing of its mutual funds, and $21 million for its revenue sharing/kickback arrangements. Elizabeth Wiskemann, who is worth about $1.1 billion, inherited 6 percent of the Franklin Resources money management firm from her husband R. Martin Wiskemann.

John Calamos founded Calamos Asset Management in 1977 and took the company public in 2004 where the family net worth took off. Today the Calamos family is worth about $2 billion and has about $44 billion under management.

---

[51] The author was well aware of some of the fortunes created in the mutual fund business, but *Forbes* clarified much. "The 400 Richest People in America," *Forbes*, October 9, 2006.

William "Bill" Gross is probably the highest paid bond trader in the world, worth about $1.2 billion. Gross learned the bond business when he was an analyst for Pacific Life Insurance Company. PIMCO (Pacific Investment Management Company), the bond company spin-off, was sold to giant German insurer Alliance for $4.7 billion. Gross' share was $400 million. PIMCO has since been fined in the range of $50 million in market timing and $11.6 million for undisclosed revenue sharing/kickback arrangements.

Thomas Bailey made his money with Janus Funds of Colorado, a company that was heavily involved in the market timing of mutual funds, which gave preferential treatment to traders. Janus was later fined about $100 million. Bailey is worth about $1.2 billion according to *Forbes*.

Jonathan Lovelace, Jr. and his family inherited a money management firm founded in the 1930s by his father called Capital Research and Management (American Funds). Most of the company was sold off; however, the Lovelace family still owns only about 10 percent, which is worth $1.1 billion.

Joseph Mansueto does not own a mutual fund business but has made a fortune trying to bring transparency to the industry. Mansueto owns mutual fund monitoring company, Morningstar, worth about $1.2 billion.

Mario Gabelli of Gabelli Asset Management is worth around $900 million. In 2003, Mario took home $41 million in 2003 and $55 million in compensation in 2004 and 2005. From when he took his company public in 1999 to 2004, Mario's total compensation package has been around $325 million—an amount that came close to surpassing what his combined companies earned. Since Mario owns a complex labyrinth of companies involved in electronics components, cable TV, a broker–dealer and more, it is hard to figure out his total compensation. His mutual fund performance has been lukewarm. In July 2006, according to *Forbes*, Mario paid a $130 million settlement in which he illicitly obtained cell phone licenses from the FCC.

Adding to the list is Richard Strong, the former CEO and founder of Strong Mutual Funds. At one time, Strong's net worth was $800 million. In 2004, he personally had to pay a $60 million dollar fine for improper trading of mutual funds against the interests of his own shareholders. Between Strong and the company, the total fines for mutual fund malfeasance added up to a hefty $140 million.

The mutual fund business can be an extremely lucrative business even when you are hired help. Larry J. Lasser was once the chief executive of Putnam Investments in Boston. While Putnam's inside managers were caught making a million on the inside market timing of mutual funds, Larry did very well for himself.[52] Putnam ended up paying $55 million for market timing violations and $40 million for undisclosed revenue sharing/kickback

---

[52] Gretchen Morgenson, "At Putnam The Buck Stays Put In the Pocket," *New York Times,* November 11, 2003.

arrangements. Between 1998 and 2003, Larry took home about $5 million in salary, $100 million in bonuses and $22 million more in restricted stock options.

In 1997, Larry also received a special employment contract worth $15 million for a special retirement package to honor a non-compete agreement and for post-retirement consulting. Lasser's contract was amended again in 2001 to include another special payment that was disbursed in December 2005. If Larry was not busy enough, he also received an additional $200 thousand for his work as trustee on various mutual funds. Before Lasser left Putnam, he received total cash compensation of about $100 million, with about $163 million in total compensation.

According to an article by Ross Kerber of the *Boston Globe* in November 2006, compensation for mutual fund managers in 2006 was the highest it has been in years. A senior manager earns around $225 thousand a year and can earn annual bonuses up to four times that amount. Columbia Funds, which is owned by Bank of America, pays their managers between $150 and $300 thousand, and they can earn an annual bonus up to six times their base salaries.

The average mutual fund manager makes $436 thousand for managing other people's money, with the top 10 percent of fund managers making around $1.7 million per year[53]. High-end fund managers can make much, much more as evidenced by the likes of Bill Gross and Mario Gabelli. The directors of mutual funds, who often just rubber stamp investment policies and attend a few meetings, have annual compensation ranging from $170 to $230 thousand. Then you also have extremely lucrative directors who are called trustees. Robert M. Gates is chairman of Fidelity trustees. He was paid $373 thousand for monitoring 328 funds[54]. Mr. Gates' real job, however, was president of Texas A&M University—a position he recently departed to become the new Secretary of Defense of the United States. What does a guy who used to work in the CIA know about mutual funds? Where is the connection?

Regardless, it is very difficult to figure out exactly what the mutual fund managers really make. This author tried numerous times to get information that was more empirical, but came up short-handed. Gretchen Morgenson, in an article in the *New York Times* on April 16, 2006, called "Fund Managers May Have Some Pay Secrets, Too," talks about the difficulties of getting mutual fund manager compensation.

"Amid all the talk about executive compensation and pay for performance, one group of managers has been pretty much untouched: those who run mutual funds.

---

[53] Kurt Linn, *The Trouble with Mutual Funds* (Seattle: Elton-Wolff Publishing, 2002).
[54] Gretchen Morgenson, "How To Find A Fund's True Colors," *New York Times,* September 10, 2006.

Pay disclosure for them is scant, because many fund management companies are private and do not need to file pay figures with regulators. Others are subsidiaries of large organizations, and the fund executives are not necessarily among their company's five highest paid people, whose compensation must be detailed...

For most funds, however, the only hint of how much managers receive is the total figure paid by the funds to the management companies that have been contracted to run them. There is no way for shareholders to see the compensation paid to a specific fund manager or even to the five most highly paid executives of the management company.

As such, investors have no way to compare what their fund managers made with how well they performed. That could be eye opening...

Some will argue that money managers operate in a free market and that their pay reflects the demand for their services, plain and simple. But with so many fund customers locked into their funds through retirement plans that are run by their employers, the free market in mutual fund managers is by no means as free as some make it out to be."

Total fees collected by the mutual fund industry were somewhere in the neighborhood of $70 billion in 2003. If we assume that the fund industry gets roughly a minimum of one percent net on running mutual funds, then the total income for the industry should be around $93 billion in 2006. Total fees of running a mutual fund can run as high as 4 percent.

Also disturbing is that a good portion of the fees goes into marketing and advertising, which make every attempt to make mutual fund managers and companies appear they can do no wrong—attracting new investors and new deposits. As we have seen with Fidelity, this increased advertising activity definitely brings in more assets into mutual funds.

The Lure and Bait of Celebrities

Fund companies like to hire high profile celebrities to cushion their credibility. Fidelity has hired Paul McCartney of the Beatles fame who has a net worth around $1.6 billion and income approaching $100 million. American Century Funds has been successful in hiring the powerhouse, Lance Armstrong, who is reimbursed $200 thousand just to speak at an executive conference. This author likes Lance Armstrong as much as anybody does, but you have to wonder why he is paid so much to represent something about which he knows little.

Why the Mutual Fund Business Has Grown

The mutual fund business has grown significantly because of one significant and major trend, which is going on throughout the retirement planning system in America—defined benefit pension plans for average

85

citizens in the private sector, which guarantee an income for life for the retiree and his or her spouse, have been declining for years. The 401(k) was really meant to be a supplement to retirement plans, but now because so many defined benefit plans are being terminated, the 401(k) is being served up as the main course in retirement planning.

There are exceptions to this rule, particularly in the case of government workers such as military, teachers, firefighters, police personnel, legislators, senators, members of congress, federal workers, and most state and municipal workers. Their pensions are actually growing, yet with cradle-to-grave health insurance programs, all government entitlement programs in the years ahead have the potential to become municipal Enrons. If you need proof, just look at the city of San Diego. By the year 2009, that city's unfunded pension liability is estimated to be in the realm of $2 billion. Its liability for retiree healthcare will be another $1.1 billion. In November 2006, the beautiful City by the Sea was also given a cease-and-desist order by the SEC for securities fraud for not disclosing these liabilities to the public when offering new municipal bond sales in 2002 and 2003.

However, for the average worker in corporate America, the shift in retirement planning to the defined contribution model essentially means the employee now sets aside a portion of his or her salary in a tax-deferred account with an employer match of some sort. Big companies such as Verizon, IBM, Fidelity, and MetLife are freezing defined benefit pension plans for existing employees and locking out new hires with defined contribution retirement plans such as the 401(k). In addition, corporations are doing so to relieve them of their long-term liabilities of maintaining a corporate pension and to get the price of their stock up.

In this sleight of hand, investment risk has been removed from the employer and shifted onto the employee. Unfortunately, the costs to manage the money in the defined contribution mutual fund model are exponentially higher than defined benefit pension plans, which usually use low-cost independent money managers. Higher costs to run money were confirmed in a study done by a Professor Stewart Brown of Florida State University and a Professor John P. Freeman of the University of South Carolina. In an article done for the *Journal of Corporation Law* in 2001, Brown and Freeman found that mutual fund shareholders pay nearly twice as much in money management fees as institutional investors.

In an additional report prepared January 27, 2004 for the US Senate Subcommittee on Financial Management, the Budget, and International Security, Professor Freeman testified on the mutual fund fee mess:

"For our efforts, in calling attention to the waste, my co-author and I have been called "irresponsible" by ICI President Matthew Fink. Our sin is that we had the brass to suggest that advisory fees are excessively high.

According to the ICI's Fink, fund advisory fees are highly competitive, and the fund industry epitomizes disclosure transparency. He's wrong on both counts. Fund advisory fee gouging is a national disgrace.

*Consider these facts. Recently, Alliance Capital was charging 93 basis points (.93 percent) for managing the $17.5 billion Alliance Premier Growth Fund. This is a fee paid by shareholders of $162.7 million per year. At the same time as it was charging 93 basis points to its **own shareholders**, Alliance was managing the Vanguard U.S. Growth Fund for 11 basis points (.11 percent)—less than 1/8 of what it was charging Alliance shareholders. Alliance was also managing a $672 million portfolio for Kentucky Retirement System for 24 basis points, a $1.7 billion portfolio for the Minnesota State Board of Investment for 20 basis points, a $730 million equities portfolio for the Missouri Retirement System for 18.5 basis points, and a $975 million equity portfolio for the Wyoming Retirement System for 10 basis points.*

These price discrepancies cannot be justified on the basis of differences in service. According to the prospectus for the Alliance Stock Fund, the management company's institutional accounts shared "substantially the same investment objectives and policies" and were managed with "essentially the same investment strategies and techniques" as the Alliance Premier Growth Fund. Moreover, the different clients "shared a nearly identical composition of investment holdings and related percentage weightings."

Defined contribution retirement plans are commonly known as 401(k) plans for regular businesses and 403(b) plans for non-profits such as hospitals, museums, and universities. What investors get in the end for the defined contribution model is anybody's guess. In the absence of guarantees, the total final sum is an Alice in Wonderland projection. Furthermore, what is clearly omitted in these "projected sums" by mutual fund companies are the final costs an individual would incur such as high management fees to run the fund, market risk, taxes, inflation, and lost opportunity costs.

Administration and Communication Play a Dominant Role in Plan Selection

While one would think that the most important thing would be to select the most appropriate investments for a 401(k) plan (e.g. index funds, exchange traded funds, or separate accounts), more often than not the administrative process plays the dominant role in plan selection. What this means is that most often a plan is chosen by employers based on record keeping, reporting, and communication services. What happens is that many plans end up stuffed with high cost actively managed mutual funds and newer generation lifestyle funds, which have even greater costs due to an extra layer of fees. Most plan executives who oversee these 401(k) plans make little effort to monitor overall financial costs. Fewer still know how to measure these costs as the mutual fund company does not disclose all of them as line items.

401(k) Plans Are Now the Dominant Retirement Plan

According to a 2006 study conducted by the Investment Company Institute (ICI) and the Employee Benefits Research Institute (EBRI), 401(k)s are now the most popular retirement plan in America, with about 47 million workers participating and $2.4 trillion in assets.[55]

The median account balance was about $54,591 in a 401(k) account, but because some people have large accounts, the average balance was around $102,014. The EBRI/ICI study prided itself on having available a very large database, which gives the study immense credibility, as it included 17.6 million plan participants, 42,256 employer plans, and over $1 trillion in assets. In addition, according to a recent study done by AXA Equitable in 2007, the average American worker saved about $696 monthly into their retirement plan.

An overwhelming *two-thirds* of account balances are allocated to equity securities, which are the most profitable line of business for mutual fund companies and Wall Street, yet the most volatile for investors. Yet in the United States of Amnesia, this 401(k) program stuffed with stocks may end up being a depressing travesty. Authors William Wolman and Anne Colamosca warn us all in the book, *The Great 401(k) Hoax.* Wolman has a Ph.D. in economics from Stanford, and he was an editor and Chief Economist for *Business Week,* an economics commentator for *CNBC* for more than ten years, and named one of the leading business journalists of the century. Colamosca, a former staff writer and reporter for *Business Week,* and has written for the *Columbia Journalism Review, Christian Science Monitor,* the *New Republic,* and the *New York Times.*

"By mid-February 2002, American investors had lost $5 trillion or 30 percent of their stock wealth since the spring of 2000. Yet Wall Street's propaganda in favor of the family market continued to be backed by gobs of advertising dollars and millions in campaign contributions and lobbying, along with brokers and analysts hired to promote stocks day after day, no matter how bad things got. Andrew Smithers, the brilliant British financial analyst, once told the authors that he could make a lot more money by being a bull and being wrong than being a bear and being right.

---

[55] Sarah Holden, the Investment Company Institute, and Jack Van Derhei, the Employee Benefit Research Institute, "401(k) Plan Asset Allocation, Account Balances and Loan Activity in 2005," Investment Company Institute, www.ic.org, August 2006.

The same cannot be said of those who depend upon their 401(k) programs. The American public has been hoodwinked by political and corporate forces into relying on the 401(k) as the primary long-term investment mechanism. In doing so, the stock market has been put at center stage in providing for a comfortable retirement for the average American. The 401(k) represents an implicit promise to middle-class Americans that they can live off the income that they receive from stock ownership, just like the rich do. It is a promise impossible to fulfill; it is the great 401(k) hoax." (p. 12).

Sticky Money in a Lock Box

The EBRI/ICI study is very, very good news for those in the mutual fund business and their Wall Street suppliers. Defined contribution 401(k)s and 403(b) plans are captive funds or sticky money for financial institutions to manage and make fees off. Assets locked up in a retirement plan become a perpetual motion income machine for mutual fund companies. Unlike taxable investments which can be readily cashed in to buy a car, put a down payment on a home, or start a small business, defined contribution money in 401(k)s, 403(b)s, and IRAs are funds restrained in straight jackets. Getting funds out of these plans is quite painful from a tax standpoint. Funds withdrawn before normal retirement and before 59½ are subject to full income taxation at marginal tax rates as well as an additional 10 percent excise tax.

To access funds within a defined contribution plan, many plans, but not all, offer loans up to 50 percent of one's vested interest to a maximum of $50,000. However, repaying the loan is a nightmare for both the participant and the employer if there is a break in employment. It should come as no surprise that fund companies and plan sponsors go out of their way to discourage loans. Fund companies do not like loans because they have less money on which to collect fees. For employers, loans are an administrative maze and take on the characteristic of a high maintenance unintended employer-sponsored Christmas Club.

Nevertheless, hordes of people are hitting up and cashing in their 401(k)s anyway. A report in 2006 done by the National Association of Securities Dealers (NASD) titled, "Think Twice before Cashing out Your 401(k)" says that 45 percent of Americans cash out their 401(k) plans when they leave their jobs. In addition, according to IRS figures, about 4.9 million people paid out $3.5 billion in penalties for cashing out their retirement plans too soon in 2003.

Problems with Over-Diversification in Mutual Funds: A Loss of Power and a Mount Everest of Paperwork

The average investor is told to diversify with mutual funds, jump into asset allocation models, or whatever is the hottest and latest fad such as a *life cycle fund*. Fees associated with these funds are usually substantial. The mantra is diversify, diversify, and diversify some more. This generates a Mount Everest of paperwork. The investor becomes even more confused. Efforts to move ahead financially are scattered. It becomes extremely difficult to analyze mutual funds impartially. This confusion makes the individual overtly dependent upon the mutual fund companies for guidance. That is something they like.

This author, who has literally reviewed hundreds of portfolios, has seen some individuals own as many as sixty or so different mutual funds. One recently had forty-one different funds.

Funds Do not Perform nor Are They Safe and Secure

"History does not repeat itself, but it rhymes."

Mark Twain

Regardless of all the problems with over-diversification in mutual funds, another problem with the mutual fund business is that they just do not perform. According to Lipper Analytical Services, the vast majority of funds, around 94 percent have underperformed the market. Other research confirms this as well. Gary Weiss in *Wall Street Versus America* comments on overall mutual fund performance.

"Academic researchers have been studying mutual fund performance for a long time and they have plenty to say—most of it none-too-flattering. Studies have proven consistently since the 1970s that mutual funds do not beat the market...One came out in the same month in which the media was engaged in its quarterly mutual fund kissing competition. A scholarly publication called The Financial Review published a paper by a professor of finance at Princeton University named Burton G. Malkiel, describing in meticulous detail how poorly mutual funds have stacked up against the indexes over the years.

Malkiel's figures made the S&P numbers seem understated by comparison. He found that in 2003, 73 percent of actively managed funds failed to beat the S&P 500. The failure rate was just as bad over the long term—72 percent over three years, 63 percent over five years, 86 percent over ten years, and (this is the one source of that number cited earlier) 90 percent over twenty years. The very oldest and most long-lasting funds were generally losers.

These numbers seem all the more distressing when you realize that Malkiel is not some crank, but is one of the most esteemed financial authorities alive." (pp. 73-74).

David Swensen, author of *Unconventional Success* and the manager for the $14 billion Yale Endowment, puts it this way in his book:

> *"As I gathered information for my new book, the data clearly pointed to the failure of active management by profit-seeking mutual-fund managers to produce satisfactory results for individual investors…*
>
> *The colossal failure of the mutual-fund industry carries serious implications for society, particularly regarding retirement security for American workers. I share with most economists the bias that free markets generally produce superior outcomes, believing that government intervention often creates more problems than it solves. However, the market failure resulting from the mutual-fund industry's systematic exploitation of individual investors requires government action. Without an appropriate policy response, I worry about the level of resources available to support future generations of American retirees."*

Actively managed mutual funds are not guaranteed; they have no downside protection and usually do not perform over the long haul. They are not safe or secure. Even index mutual funds have no downside protection. Yet misinformation in regards to mutual funds comes from the highest of places. Here is what George W. Bush said at a speech at Auburn University in Montgomery, Alabama, in 2005.

> *"When I was young, I didn't know anything about 401(k)s because I don't think they existed. Defined-benefit plans were the main source of retirement. Now they have got what they called defined-contribution plans. Workers are taking aside some of their own money and watching it grow through safe and secure investments."*

George forgot to tell us about the tax problems with 401(k)s.

Taxes on Retirement Plans: The Subject about which Mutual Fund Companies Would Prefer You Know Little

> *"The only difference between the taxman and the taxidermist is that the taxidermist leaves the skin."*   Mark Twain

> *"After paying taxes due today, no doubt many prospering citizens are comforted by the amazing growth in their 401(k) or IRA or other retirement vehicles. But to understand that swelling figure on your screen, do a little calculation: Take $650,000 and subtract the value of your home and other assets. The remainder is how much your IRA you really own; sooner or later the government will confiscate the rest.*
>
> *We exaggerate, but only slightly. You can of course spend all of your IRA money, in which case the federal government will not take more than 40 percent, or including state levies, close to 50 percent in a tax hell like New York or California. But if you hope to leave some of your money to your kids, they will have to pay not*

only the tax bite, but on top of it any inheritance tax that currently applies to estates more than $650,000—a level reached by your ordinary successful American citizen. The combination of the income and estate tax boost the tax to something like 80 percent"

Editorial, Review & Outlook
The Wall Street Journal, April 15, 1999

"Pensions are widely thought to be attractive shelters which encourage savings for retirement. They allow people to save before-tax dollars and to compound investment returns without current taxation. However, the taxation of pension assets as they are distributed at retirement or as they pass through an estate may turn the shelter into a trap, at least for large pension accumulations. Pension distributions can face marginal tax rates as high as 61.5 percent; pension assets passing through an estate can face virtually confiscatory marginal tax rates between 92 and 99 percent. The analysis of this paper shows the circumstance under which these extraordinary high marginal tax rates will be encountered. They are not limited to the rich. In fact, people of modest incomes who participate in a pension plan over a long career may face such rates."

John B. Shoven, School of Humanities, Stanford
David A. Wise, School of Government, Harvard
Abstract- The Taxation of Pensions: A Shelter Can Be a Tax Trap, October 1996

"Having been so busy chasing investment returns all their working lives, they've probably neglected the distribution part of the equation, and thus risk losing a whopping amount of what they've saved to the taxman.
As this greatest transfer of wealth in human history reaches its apex in the coming years, there will be an explosion of excessive taxation that will reach epidemic proportions (especially given the population affected), an explosion that will give millions of ill-prepared and under protected American savers like yourself the financial shock of their lives."

Ed Slott,
The Retirement Savings Time
Bomb and How to Diffuse It

Until the early eighties, a retirement plan balance was exempt from the taxable estate. This meant retirement accounts were not subject to any estate taxes, yet retirement accounts have always been subject to income taxes. Finally, the federal government, in an effort to raise taxes, limited the exemption amount in retirement plans to $100 thousand from the taxable estate. Any amount over $100 thousand was then includable in the taxable estate for estate tax purposes. Today, unless a retirement plan balance is left to a charity, it is at minimum subject to income taxes (even with a "stretch IRA") and often to estate taxes, too.

Although easily forgotten in the United States of Amnesia, until about 1997, there was an additional 15 percent excise tax or "success tax" on all retirement accounts with balances of $750 thousand or more. It was a "success" tax because the government thought you had too much money in your retirement plan.

There is on the books a rarely implemented additional tax of 50 percent if you do not start taking money out from your IRA or 401(k) when you are supposed to at seventy and one-half years.

The SEC and the NASD are Asleep at the Wheel

"Martha Stewart got hurt very badly for something that happens every single day on Wall Street. It's falseness and a hollowness to the capitalist system when you are pretending that things are pristine and they are not. Either the SEC should get very, very serious and prosecute a lot of people or forget about it."

Herbert A. Denton,
President, Providence Capital
New York Times, Aug. 27, 2006,
Commenting on rampant insider
trading in the stock market.

"Questions have also been raised as to why securities industry regulators, such as the Securities and Exchange Commission (SEC) and the National Association of Securities Dealers (NASD) did not detect the undisclosed market timing arrangements and late trading abuses. Instead, the New York State Office of the New York Attorney General (NYSOAG) uncovered the abuses in the summer of 2003 after following up on a tip provided by a hedge fund insider. SEC, which has direct supervisory oversight responsibility for mutual fund companies, did not detect the undisclosed arrangements through its routine examination program...By November 2003, SEC estimated that 50 percent of the 80 largest mutual fund companies had entered into undisclosed arrangements permitting certain shareholders to engage in market timing practices that appeared inconsistent with the funds' policies, prospectus disclosures, or fiduciary obligations."

United States Government Accountability Office
Mutual Fund Trading Abuses: Lessons Can Be
Learned from SEC Not Having Detected
Violations at an Earlier Stage, April 2005

"It's not unreasonable to expect that it would take the SEC awhile to absorb the study—say a couple of months, or a couple of years. The more time the better, right? So the SEC took the study and began reading it very carefully, for...oh, about thirty-seven years. That is how long it took for the SEC to turn its attention to fund kickbacks to brokerages after the were detailed in Public Policy Implications of Investment Company Growth, which the SEC sent over to the House Committee on Interstate and Foreign Commerce on December 2, 1996."

Gary Weiss, Wall Street Versus America
Commenting on how revenue sharing/kickback
arrangements were problems with the mutual fund

"Examining the history of the mutual-fund industry leads to the
disheartening conclusion that legislation and regulation prove no match for the
greed-inspired creativity of mutual-fund companies. Sometimes, as in the case of 12b-
1 fees and soft dollars, the regulators create the problem by providing explicit
authorization for investor-unfriendly practices. In other cases, authorities fail to act
in the face of widespread understanding and acknowledgement of fund company
abuses. Finally, in those instances where the regulators get it right, the fund
management industry finds new mechanisms to pursue old abuses. Mutual-fund
managers win. Mutual-fund investors lose. (p. 271).
David Swenson, Unconventional Success

Scandals in investments and Wall Street are nothing new in America.
Thomas Jefferson hated the speculative mania that accompanied wartimes and
post-war booms. John Adams abhorred the whole banking system. Charles
Dickens was appalled by Americans' lust for money. Herman Melville
thought that America's love of speculation was a sign of spiritual malignancy.
Mark Twain warned about the dangers of speculation in *The Gilded Age,* and
he knew very well of the consequences, as Twain found himself in bankruptcy
after speculating his own funds in the stock market. Speculators such as
Vanderbilt, Drew, Fisk, and Gould helped loot the public treasury when the
Erie Canal was being built. Speculators such as J.P. Morgan made immense
fortunes speculating during wartime.

Mutual funds are offspring of investment trusts, which originated in
England and Scotland. They were put together so that small investors and
those with small sums could participate in the stock market. Around 1921,
there were a few investment trusts in America. According to John Kenneth
Galbraith in his book *The Great Crash of 1929,* by 1927, 160 trusts, and by
1928, an additional 265 investment trusts were added. In 1927, investment
trusts, which morphed into closed end mutual funds, sold $400 million of
securities and by 1929, these trusts increased their assets eleven fold and
exceeded $8 billion.

Sponsorship of these investment trusts came from people like Joseph
P. Kennedy, the House of Morgan, and Goldman Sachs. Sponsorship was not
without its financial rewards. They collected fees based on a percentage of
assets or earnings, could receive commissions on the purchase of securities,
and when sponsored by investment bankers, could manufacture more
securities to give them additional income streams.

Yet the investment trust business has not had a clean history. The
United and Allegheny Corporations, sponsored in part by the House of
Morgan in raising $25 million later collapsed. Goldman Sachs, a late entrant
to the investment trust game, brought Goldman Sachs Trading Corporation
public for $100 a share, raising $100 million while selling it for $104 a share

to an eager public; a few years later, it would be worth less than $2 a share. Before the passage of the Investment Company Act of 1940, which is the governing body of rules for mutual funds today, the mutual fund business had a history of operating in the interests of the owners and not the investors.

In the 1960s, the American public lost immense sums of money in the mutual fund business with funds such as the Overseas Corporation and the Mates and Enterprise Funds. You also had very shady mutual fund operators like Bernie Cornfield, who became better known for his scantily clad women and exploitation of his customers than for his mutual fund performance. In addition, in Japan, equity mutual funds declined by as much as 95 percent from their peak in the 1990s.

In the old days, insiders often used the mutual fund/investment company as a source of capital for their own ventures. They used the cash within the funds to dump unsalable securities. Outright embezzlement and larceny were common. Management investment advisory contracts were sometimes non-cancelable. Mutual fund sales loads could be as high as 20 percent on the mutual fund purchase (contractual plans). Likewise, investment advisory contracts could be extremely lucrative to fund company owners.

The business of buying mutual fund shares at stale prices, which is known as *market timing,* has been with us since the 1920s. Purchasing on stale prices, or market timing, is being able to purchase mutual fund shares at a prior date at a discounted price. For instance, it you could purchase shares on Tuesday with the lower prices of Monday that would be market timing. The exploitation of market timing of mutual funds was found money and guaranteed profits for insiders and other favored customers. Like today, market timing came at the expense of normal shareholders, as they would have to incur a sales load.

The practice of *late trading* is somewhat similar, but allows an individual to purchase mutual fund shares after the markets close. The practice of late trading is akin to being able to place a bet on a winning horse after it has already past the gate. Major Wall Street firms, like Bear Stearns, were involved in the late trading practice, and in 2006, that company paid a $250 million fine for its activity in that area.

Gary Weiss, in *Wall Street Versus America,* documents that the practices of market timing and late trading were going on as recently as 2001 and the SEC knew about it. However, the SEC did not do anything to enforce it other than have SEC lawyer Douglas Scheidt write a letter to the lawyer Craig S. Tyle who represented the mutual fund trade group, Investment Company Institute (ICI). He writes:

"According to studies at Stanford University, trading on stale prices (market timing) had resulted in losses to long-term investors of $4 billion a year, while trading at night and back stamping of orders (late trading) had resulted in losses of

$400 million. Those $4 billion/$400 million annual losses were achieved by, as the Scheidt letter indicated, "diluting" the value of fund shares."

Since time immemorial, Wall Street, banking, and the mutual fund industry have fought regulation tooth and nail. Wall Street believed any over sight or regulation would drive investors away. In 1933, The Glass–Steagall Act was put in place and the SEC was created to protect the consumer from Wall Street. In 1999, the Glass–Steagall Act was torn down.

The more things change, the more they remain the same. Even today, the American Stock Exchange (AMEX), a 164-year old institution, still actively does business with fly-by-night public companies with flaky balance sheets. Around 2000 and today, the Justice Department went after the AMEX, along with other exchanges, in regards to a conspiracy to fix equity options spreads.

So much of the securities business is based upon *self-regulation,* which is allowing the fox to protect the hen house. Consider the New York Stock Exchange (NYSE), a company that bills itself as "a private company with a public purpose." Every security traded on the NYSE is assigned to a specialist. A specialist sees every order to maintain a "fair and orderly market." The SEC bans floor brokers from trading for their own accounts, but like many things in the securities businesses, specialists are given exception because they are supposedly providing a public purpose in maintaining the market. Specialist firms were some of the people responsible for Richard Grasso's $180 million payday. Some specialists make hundreds of millions in dollars trading for their own accounts.[56]

Instead of sticking up a store, financiers loot America. The system is amuck in corruption. Late trading, market timing, insider trading, front running (using one's knowledge to trade for one's own account ahead of the client), and marking the tape (trading late in the day to inflate the stock price) are commonplace, yet few in the banking, securities, or mutual fund industries go to jail. They may pay some fines when their hands are caught in the till, but they rarely go to jail.

Concerning having the SEC and government prosecution of securities crimes, there are a myriad of problems. You would think that the SEC, with an annual budget of about $888 million, would do a better job, but the agency is always under political pressure and lacks transparency and follow through. In addition, with banking deregulation, there are even more obstacles than ever. Some of the problems today are in regards to prosecuting securities crimes are as follows:

One: The SEC and the NASD are asleep at the wheel. The whole securities scandal went largely undetected by the federal government regulator called the SEC, and the self-regulatory, self-policing agency known

---

[56] John Bogle, "Specialist Man," *Wall Street Journal,* September 19, 2003.

as the National Association of Securities Dealers (NASD). William Galvin of Massachusetts and Eliot Spitzer of New York brought more light and exposure to the mutual fund business in six months than the SEC brought in sixty years. Not only has the SEC been asleep at the wheel in regards to the mutual fund scandals, it has shown a poor track record in regards to pinpointing the problems with hedge funds (unregulated entities with around $1.3 trillion in assets), problems with boiler room stock frauds and overlooking the stock exchanges, such as the NYSE.

Edward Siedle, a former SEC attorney and now the President of Benchmark Financial Services, commented that the SEC needs a shake up in a November 27, 2006, issue of *Forbes*. Among other things, Siedle commented that the SEC is too vulnerable to political pressure, relies too much on self-regulation by the securities industry, lacks transparency as it allows the financial industry to control the content and timeliness of information to the public, and lacks follow through. In 2005, the SEC found that conflicts of interest were rampant and disclosure was abysmal in the pension consulting industry. Did the SEC allow pension plan sponsors access to the information? Nope, the SEC just issued a vague warning to pension plan sponsors to be careful in hiring investment consultants.

Securities scandals came to light because of state laws and efforts from state regulators, not because of federal laws or that federal regulators were on the top of their game. Eliot Spitzer of the state of New York used a state law known as the Martin Act to bring the first prosecution against Merrill Lynch where a doctor from Queens lost $500 thousand in highly recommended Internet company stocks. Under the Martin Act, Spitzer and his office were able to subpoena many documents to put together investigations for securities cases.

In their analysis, Spitzer's office found that the very same Merrill analysts who scorned the securities in private had been recommending them to the public. Companies like Infospace were considered "a powder keg and had a bad smell." Aether System had "horrible fundamentals." Excite was "a piece of crap." Goto.com— "nothing interesting about the company except investment banking fees."

Lawyers at Spitzer's office also learned that some of these companies, which were touted by analysts in public, were also investment banking clients of Merrill Lynch, which was a definite conflict of interest. When negotiations were being stalled, Spitzer went to a judge, and under the Martin Act, forced Merrill Lynch to expose its conflict of interest. He soon went public speaking about Merrill's betrayal of trust.[57]

---

[57] Charles Gasparino, *Blood on the Street: The Sensational Story of How Wall Street Analysts Duped a Generation of Investors* (New York: Free Press, 2005). Gasparino gives one of the best overviews of the conflicts of interest in commercial and investment banking and how deregulation made crimes once illegal now legal.

Federal regulators at the SEC were upstaged and declined to help Spitzer. Merrill Lynch dug in its heels in essentially telling the overeager attorney that he had overstepped his boundaries and did not understand high finance. Eliot Spitzer displayed a tremendous act of courage, as he was very alone in his fight.

However, following the announcement about Merrill's conflicts of interests in its analysts' reports, the market hammered the value of the company's stock. Merrill wanted to settle and make the bad news go away. Spitzer managed his first victory—Merrill Lynch paid a $100 million dollar fine and agreed to change its practices.

Later, it would be Spitzer, with the assistance and courage of one Noreen Harrington who roped in one of the first major violations in regards to late trading in mutual fund scandals. Spitzer fined hedge fund manager Edward Stern of Canary Capital Partners $40 million for late trading in mutual funds. The SEC and the NASD were nowhere to be found. It has also been Spitzer, not the federal regulators, who has been involved in a running feud with billionaire Kenneth Langone, the former director of the New York Stock Exchange, over the exchanges former chairman, Richard Grasso who received a $180 million dollar retirement package from the NYSE.

Other states, such as the Commonwealth of Massachusetts along with Attorney General William Galvin, also exposed the market-timing problem in mutual funds, not the SEC. In fact, the SEC was the first to learn of the original market timing problems at Putnam Mutual Funds from William Scannell, but the SEC did not find any violations and did not act on the documented information Scannell had.

The state of New Hampshire, where this author lives, found that ING, the giant Dutch financial services conglomerate, which handles the state's 457(b) accounts was involved in undisclosed revenue sharing arrangements with Oppenheimer and American Mutual and had allowed market-timing arrangements of mutual funds with certain brokers. ING is to pay state workers $2.75 million for its malfeasance.

Two: Securities laws are very complex. Prosecutors must prove criminal intent. It is not a crime to be wrong about a stock or mutual fund.

Three: The overall tone in Congress was to give the securities and banking industries more deregulation, which they received, after intense lobbying that cost millions. Congress has been totally reluctant to act on "carried interest" which is where hedge fund managers, private equity, and venture capital financiers pay capital gains taxes of about 15% instead of ordinary income taxes of 35%+.

Securities arbitration with *Shearson/American Express vs. McMahon*, a landmark case in 1987, clearly made arbitration a stacked deck in favor of the securities industry and not the consumer.[58]

With deregulation, actions, which were once illegal such as tying, are now legal practices under the Gramm-Leach-Bliley Act of 1999. Deregulation gave the Federal Reserve, a private corporation, the right to veto the US Treasury in regards to new financial powers. Further legislation such as the 2005 Bankruptcy Abuse and Protection Act and the Pension Reform Act of 2006 also favored banking and mutual fund industries as well.

The hedge fund business is unregulated and in 2006, the SEC lost its battle to have hedge funds registered as investment advisors. There is no federal requirement for a hedge fund to be registered; it only depends on the state in which it is doing business. Many hedge funds are actually registered offshore. Hedge funds do collapse. Long Term Capital Management had to be rescued with the assistance of Alan Greenspan, the Federal Reserve, and major money center banks.

Losing huge sums of money in the market does not appear to have too many repercussions for hedge fund managers either. John Meriwether, the founder of Long-Term Capital Management, left Salomon Brothers in 1991 over a Treasury bond auction scandal. After Long-Term Management imploded, Meriwether was able to raise another couple of billion dollars for his latest firm. Even so, with little or no oversight, public pension plans are depositing more and more money into hedge funds.

Four: There is usually a lack of urgency in prosecuting securities crimes. Laws are broken because laws are not enforced. Laws are broken because the media does not care. With lack of urgency, attention spans wane. Securities fraud enters into the United States of Amnesia.

Five: There is high turnover in the legal area. Good people leave. There is no long-term consistency concerning SEC legalities. Congress may pass laws to penalize security crimes but enforcing the law is another thing entirely. The SEC is clearly outmatched and outgunned by the huge legal forces the securities and banking industries have. While private sector legal staffs mushroomed, staffs at the SEC remained flat. When major scandals like accounting fraud take place with companies such as WorldCom, staff resources are used up. No one is available to monitor the mutual fund business.

The relationship between the mutual fund business and the SEC is quite incestuous at times. Law Professor John P. Freeman of the University of South Carolina said this in his testimony before the Senate Governmental

---

[58] Gary Weiss, *Wall Street Versus America, The Rampant Greed and Dishonesty that Imperils Your Investments* (New York: Penguin Group, 2006). Gina Holland, "Court Deals Blow to Investor Lawsuits," *National Telegraph-Associated Press,* March 23, 2006.

Affairs Subcommittee on January 27, 2004 regarding the troubled relationship between the fund business and the Securities and Exchange Commission:

The SEC is MIA

"I referred to conflicts of interest infecting the way the industry is regulated. The SEC's Division of Management ("DIM") presents a classic case of "regulatory capture." It is conflicted as well. Bluntly stated, over time, DIM has become far too differential to the industry. The SEC's Division of Investment Management represents a Chihuahua watchdog, not the Doberman shareholders need.

And there are the DIM alums. What we almost always find when SEC staffers move on are SEC-honed skills being put to work protecting the wealth of fund managers, not fund shareholders. My analysis of SEC personnel movements, using data I obtained from the SEC under FOIA, shows that most of the SEC's senior personnel who leave the DIM go to work form mutual funds as officers or directors, for the ICI, or for service suppliers (law firms or accounting firms) who advise fund sponsors. These professionals are dedicated to protecting the industry's managers, and the industry's managers have an agenda that does not place the fund shareholders first.

When I was working with the SEC in DIM years ago, I was told by a fellow staff lawyer: 'Let's face it, in five years we'll all be working for these guys.' Then and now, that staff lawyer's observation holds true. I tell you bluntly the SEC has failed the mutual investors."

Six: Disclosure of wrongdoing in the securities business is absolution of the crime. In the case of the revenue sharing/kickback arrangements between mutual fund companies and broker–dealers who distributed their products, once the kickbacks were disclosed, everything was magically okay.

Seven: Settlements are all the rage even when malfeasance has been proven, whether it be insider trading, bad analysts reports, late trading, market timing or what have you, the violator often pays only a fine and calls it a day. You then see the settlement in the newspaper, in the familiar legalese, *neither admits nor denies any wrongdoing.*

There are exceptions but you have to hunt for them. James P. Connolly was formerly Vice Chairman of Fred Alger Management. He was involved in market timing mutual fund scandals at that company. Connolly had to pay a $400 thousand fine but also received a *criminal* sentence of one to three years for tampering with evidence. He was one of only a few people to do time for a mutual fund-related crime.

The preferential treatment of firms and individuals involved in mutual fund wrongdoing is eye opening. Yet the predatory nature of securities crimes can get down right disgusting. Take the example of Israel Englander and Millennium Partners. According to the *Forbes'* 2006 issue of the 400 richest people in America, Englander is now worth about $1.2 billion. He collects

100

some pretty stiff fees for running money, generating a 4 percent base management fee and an additional 20 percent of profits on the hedge funds he operates. *Institutional Investor Alpha* magazine reports that Mr. Englander made around $230 million in 2005.

Englander was a protégé of the financier Ivan Boesky, one of the few who did do minimal time for securities fraud. Israel "Izzy" Englander later started a securities firm with a John Mulheren. However, Mulheren was later convicted on insider trading charges. According to *Forbes*, Izzy, having an insatiable temper, would fire traders for losing money.

On December 1, 2005, the SEC announced a *"settled administrative procedure"* against Millennium Partners LP, Millennium Management, LLC, Millennium International Management, L.L.C., Israel Englander, Terence Feeney, Fred Stone, and Kovan Pillai in a fraudulent scheme to market time mutual funds. The respondents will pay $180 million in total fines and disgorgement, but that is a drop in the bucket when you are worth over a billion.

According to the SEC, these were some of the activities that Millennium Partners was involved in between 1999 to 2003 in regards to taking advantage of mutual fund investors:

1. Created approximately one hundred new legal entities with unrelated names to execute market-timing trades
2. The entities opened up over one thousand accounts at various brokerage firms in order to conceal market-timing trades further
3. Also engaged in market timing, through variable annuities, Millennium misled that annuities were for long-term retirement needs when they were in fact used solely for market timing
4. The company used brokers with multiple registered representatives' numbers to avoid and evade certain mutual fund market timing restrictions
5. They also used other tactics to avoid detection such as breaking up larger trades into a series of smaller ones, leaving small positions in funds to avoid suspicion, and using clearing brokers to conceal the identities of the individual

In the all too familiar legalese *"without admitting or denying the Commissioners findings,"* it appears that these billionaire hedge fund operators, who made their astronomical incomes at the expense of smaller investors, will be back in business by simply adding a compliance officer. Others who paid fines but did not do any time were:

Jack Grubman of Citigroup/Smith Barney was fined for undue influence on investment banking clients, omission of facts, violations of ant-fraud, etc. He paid a $15 million fine and he was banned from the securities business for life. Grubman was the foremost analyst for Citigroup/Smith

Barney and played a major role in hyping stocks such as WorldCom. Grubman's severance package when he left Citigroup exceeded thirty million dollars.

Henry Blodget of Merrill Lynch paid a $4 million fine. The stocks Blodget touted in public were scorned in private.

Eliot Spitzer caught *Edward Stern* of Canary Capital Partners' hedge fund in late trading Bank of America (Nations) mutual funds. Stern paid a $40 million fine without further prosecution. Stern is the heir to the Hartz Mountain Industries pet supply dynasty and a son of Leonard Stern, a real estate magnate. Other firms, such as PIMCO, were also involved with Stern.

Speaking of Edward Stern…*Stephen J. Treadway,* the CEO of PIMCO equity funds, was found liable by a Manhattan court jury in July 2006 for allowing "round trip trades" with Canary Capital Partners for more than $4 billion. Treadway faces civil penalties and other sanctions.

Kenneth W. Corba was the former CEO of another PIMCO subsidiary, PEA Capital. In July of 2006, he agreed to permanent injunctions and a $200 thousand civil penalty.

Richard Strong, CEO and founder of Strong Mutual Funds paid a personal fine of $60 million, and his firm, Strong Capital Management, paid an additional fine of $80 million for improper trading of mutual funds against the interests of their own customers.

Harold Baxter and partner, *Gary Pilgrim,* of Pilgrim Baxter & Associates, both paid $80 million for undisclosed market timing of mutual funds. Their firm also paid an additional $90 million fine for undisclosed market timing. The firm was sold at the top of the market in 2000 for $400 million but apparently, that was not enough. Gary Pilgrim set up a hedge fund with his wife and several others and was caught rapidly trading in and out of his own mutual funds at the expense of the investors.

John D. Carifa made tens of millions as the former chief of Alliance Capital, which has about $453 billion in assets, making it one of the largest mutual fund companies in the United States. Alliance ended up paying a $250 million dollar fine, but Carifa walked away.

Mark Whitson of Janus Capital Management and the Janus mutual fund giant received a $13.7 million in cash and mutual funds when he resigned from Janus in April of 2004 amid the mutual fund scandal at his firm. Janus later paid $100 million in fines for its role in the mutual fund scandals.

The white shoe investment bank *Bear Stearns* who cleared trades for A.R. Baron in the 1990s, settled with the SEC for a $250 million dollar settlement in March of 2006. Certain customers at Bear Stearns were treated to late trades by falsifying order tickets, giving access to some clients to let them trade mutual funds until 5:45 and some clients were even allowed to *cancel unprofitable transactions the next day.* Bear Stearns employees even received gifts from customers who participated in these illegal activities, yet no one from Bear Stearns went to jail.

The SEC did not fine *Mario Gabelli*, but the FCC did fine him for illicit phone deals for about $130 million.

Jefferies & Company and Excessive Gifts to Fidelity Traders

In December 2006, the NASD fined Jefferies & Company of New York $5.5 million for providing lavish gifts and excessive entertainment to equity traders employed by FMR Co., Inc., an investment advisor to the Fidelity family of mutual funds. If you do not think there is money in receiving stock trading business from a mutual fund company, think again.

Jefferies & Company hired Kevin Quinn as an institutional sales trader to drum up business with mutual fund giant Fidelity. Jefferies paid Quinn a base salary of $4 million in 2002 and 2003, and $4.75 million in 2004. Jefferies also gave Quinn an annual travel and entertainment budget of $1.5 million for entertaining Fidelity traders so that new business would flow into Jefferies. NASD rules set the limit at $100 per individual gift per year. However, here is a record of just some of the money Jefferies spent to get a piece of Fidelity's stock trading mutual fund business.

     *   One Fidelity trader received a round trip chartered jet from Bedford, Massachusetts to Bermuda at a cost exceeding $17 thousand in 2002, and in 2003, more chartered jet flights from Boston to Los Angeles and Florida with a cost exceeding $70 and $31 thousand respectively. In 2004, the same trader received another private chartered flight from Bedford, Massachusetts to Puerto Rico with a cost exceeding $23 thousand.

     *   Another Fidelity trader was given tickets to the Wimbledon tennis tournament for a cost exceeding $19 thousand, a second set of tickets to women's and men's Wimbledon tennis for $31 thousand, tickets to the Justin Timberlake/Christina Aguilera concert for $1,200, tickets to the U. S. Open tennis tournament for $7,000, twelve bottles of 1993 Chateau Petrus wine for $7,500, an additional eight bottles of miscellaneous wine exceeding $5,900, and a third set of tickets to Wimbledon with hotel accommodations for $38,000 and $12,000 respectively.

     *   A third Fidelity trader received in a portable DVD player valued at $1,000 in 2002, six bottles of Opus One wine exceeding $2,600 in 2003, and a private chartered jet from Bedford, Massachusetts to Turks and Caicos Islands for a cost exceeding $47,000 in 2004.

If that were not enough, Kevin Quinn, through his employer Jefferies, entertained Fidelity traders.

*   In 2002, Quinn treated several traders to a four-day golf classic in Las Vegas and Cabo San Lucas, Mexico. Quinn provided lavish hotels and private air travel for a total cost of $225 thousand. In 2003, the destinations were Las Vegas and Scottsdale, Arizona with a price tag of $140 thousand.

*   The following year Quinn and his family accompanied a Fidelity trader and his family to Florida where they stayed at the Breakers in Palm Beach and enjoyed round-trip private chartered air travel. The total cost exceeded $157 thousand.

*   In 2003, Quinn, being the good sport, paid more than $75 thousand for limousine and round trip private air travel between Boston and Miami for several Fidelity traders and other guests to attend a bachelor party.

*   In 2004, Quinn invited several Fidelity traders to join him and another Jefferies trader in Houston for Super Bowl weekend. Quinn paid out more than $125 thousand for weekend-related expenses, which included Maxim and Playboy pre-game parties, a car service, private round trip chartered flights, Super Bowl tickets, and lodging. It must have been a good time.

Jefferies, Kevin Quinn, and Quinn's boss, Scott Jones, settled the actions with the NASD with the all too familiar, *without admitting or denying the allegations*. Jefferies paid a $5.5 million dollar fine, Quinn was permanently barred from associating with any NASD registered broker–dealer, and Jones paid a $50,000 fine and he was suspended for three months from associating with any NASD broker–dealer.

The SEC fined Kevin Quinn, in the all too familiar, *without admitting or denying the Commission's findings or allegations,* a $1 fine for disgorgement and $468 thousand for the benefit of the fund advisors' clients. Jefferies, who was hit up for $5.5 million by the NASD, had to pay a $4.2 million dollar fine for disgorgement to the SEC.

Of course, like just about all securities crimes, no one did any time…

But What about Martha Stewart and Frank Quattrone?

Those who are prosecuted for securities crimes are not always indicted for those specific crimes. Martha Stewart did not go to jail for securities fraud, but for a hubris crime—obstruction of justice. On August 7, 2006, the SEC settled with Martha. For someone like her, this was just a minor bump in the road. According to an SEC press release, Martha only paid a total of $58,062 for her insider trading and a civil penalty of $137,019.

Frank Quattrone, the investment banker who became well known for ladling out lucrative initial public offerings to VIP clients and who personally made tens of millions brokering deals on companies that never posted a profit, was also roped in on the obstruction of justice call. For procedural reasons, the obstruction of justice charge against Mr. Quattrone was later thrown out of court.

Fines are more like a domestic housecat than a wild tiger. They lack bite. By various estimates, the various fines levied against banks, investment firms and mutual fund companies have only amounted to five percent of total gross profits. In comparison to what they have taken from the public, this is a paltry sum.

Adding insult to injury is that these fines are many times tax deductible, which means that the taxpayer subsidizes these crimes. Fines simply come out of shareholder returns, so the executives who were at the helm manage to dodge the penalties all together.

Hats off to the Heroes

With all the scandals and negative publicity, you have to wonder why people continue to trust in Wall Street and the mutual fund industry. In researching this book and after being in the financial business for more than two and one-half decades, it is easy to feel depressed and discouraged. Never have people done so little, yet gained so much economically.

In the murky waters, this author did find heroes—folks who stood up, told the truth, and fought for what they believed in regardless of the consequences. One, for example, was Edwin Grey, the bank commissioner who stood alone trying to bring justice to the Savings and Loan crisis. By power of example, these individuals help motivate us to do the next right thing.

Eliot Spitzer, of course, is a shoe-in. You have to admire someone who took a stand against the mighty behemoth, Merrill Lynch. Spitzer also brought light to the corruption in the mutual fund business, but Spitzer did not act alone. He was tipped off by Noreen Harrington of the hedge fund Canary Capital Partners after she learned that the fund was engaged in rapid late trading.[59] She left the firm and realized that contacting the SEC was the right thing to do, knowing that the commission would probably never follow through with the complaint. In the end, she had the courage to tell Eliot Spitzer, the Attorney General of New York, which opened up a Pandora's Box of problems.

You also have to admire the courage shown by William Scannell,[60] who once worked for Putnam Funds in Boston. Scannell documented the

---

[59] Henry Sandler and Gregory Zuckerman, "Behind the Mutual Fund Probe: Three Informants Open Up," *Wall Street Journal,* December 9, 2003.
[60] Jayne O'Donnell, "The Guy Who Blew The Whistle," *USA Today*, November 23, 2003. Not only did it take a great deal of courage for William Scannell to approach the SEC in Boston, and later William Galvin of Massachusetts, but Scannell was also physically threatened by people who did not want his discoveries of the mutual fund malfeasance to come to light.

problems of market timing on spreadsheets, where various fund customers were involved in widespread abusive market timing practices. Scannell had the guts to go to the SEC office in Boston, where they thanked him for his efforts and told him they would get back to him.

According to the GAO report, the Boston SEC office reviewed the insider Scannell's allegations, and deemed that the violations were not a violation of any federal securities laws, and, based upon the information provided by the Putnam prospectuses, did not merit further investigation. Scannell, who had threats for his own safety because of the information he possessed, proceeded further and persisted with his findings and brought them to the attention of Massachusetts Attorney General William Galvin, who leveled charges against the giant Putnam mutual fund company.

In closing, we all need to thank the efforts of people like Noreen Harrington and William Scannell, as these two people were the catalysts in the mutual fund scandal exposure.

Should I Own Individual Stocks?

Mutual funds are starter kits for investors. Big money on Wall Street is still made in individual stocks. In researching this book, reviewing hundreds of proxy statements and from experience working with clients, individuals do make millions owning individual stocks. When the stars align just right for the insiders, stocks and stock options are a way for individuals to loot a company legally. Moreover, with the backdating of stock options, the looting has become much easier. In the final analysis, the words are CAVEAT EMPTOR. All investments, whether it be stocks or mutual funds have inherent risks and most of these risks are shifted onto the consumer, not the fund manager or Wall Street insiders.

The author has personally witnessed fortunes wiped out from people who had large single stock holdings in Enron and WorldCom—thousands of employees who had their 401(k) plans locked in with these volatile companies.

Dan Reingold

Dan Reingold was once one of the top institutional stock analysts on Wall Street. Reingold first worked for MCI, then in research for Morgan Stanley and Merrill Lynch, ending his career at Credit Suisse First Boston. Along with Jack Grubman of the Citigroup/WorldCom disaster, Reingold was known as one of the top telecommunications analysts in the securities business. In fact, the *New York Times* said that Jack Grubman and Dan Reingold were the Siskel and Ebert of telecom investing.

Reingold, in his book, *Confessions of a Wall Street Analyst: A True Story of Inside Information and Corruption in the Stock Market* warns us about investing in individual stocks. He writes:

"Individuals should not be investing in individual stocks. I know this is a radical statement, especially from a guy who researched individual stocks for a living. But there are simply too many insiders with too many unfair advantages. Biased research or not, the markets are, and will remain, rampant with uneven information flow. Some privileged or talented professionals will always receive or ferret out information earlier than everyone else. To be an investor in this environment is like being a drug-free athlete whose competitors are all juiced up on steroids....

Stronger enforcement of insider-trading rules can help to reduce some but not all of this unevenness. Nevertheless, individual investors should assume that the information and advice they receive regarding individual stocks are stale and, to a large degree, already incorporated into stock prices. Even the majority of professional investors find the deck is stacked against them, since it is only a minority of well-connected, high-commission-paying, deal-absorbing institutions that receive the favored information flow...

But if individual investors do buy individual stocks and bonds, the rule should be caveat emptor: investors need to be reminded that the various strands of advice they are receiving come from people who have their own, potentially conflicted, agendas. That could be anyone from television commentators to journalists, analysts, bankers, or other groups...

Of all the lessons I've learned in my time on the Street, the most difficult one to swallow is that I no longer believe in the transparency of the American financial system. When I came to the Street, I saw it as a place where there were plenty of sharks, but also as a place where American capitalism reigned supreme, a place where everyone had a chance to do well if they were smart, hardworking, and a little bit lucky. It was a game I enjoyed playing—at least until I realized how corrupted the game had become.

But I also came to realize that for people who don't have access to this inner sanctum, Wall Street is not a game at all. It's deadly serious, and it's rigged against most of the participants—everyone but the few with a seat at Wall Street's special tables. If you take anything from this book, I hope it is this unfortunate truth." (pp. 313-315).

Securities and Exchange Commission—Various Enforcement Actions Against Investment Advisors, Broker–dealers and Mutual Fund Companies—From 2002 to 2007
Conflicts of Interest, Mutual Fund Abuses, Confirmed Fines and Disgorgements, *Does Not* Include Pending Cases, State Fines, Class Action Lawsuits, Etc.

Investment Advisor, SEC #	Date	Reason for Penalty/Fine	Amount of Fine & Penalty
Credit Suisse First Boston #2002-14	January 2002	Abusive allocation of initial public offerings (IPOs)	$100,000,000
Merrill Lynch #2003-32	March 2003	Aiding & abetting Enron's securities Fraud	$80,000,000
Joint Release SEC/NASD/NYSE State of New York	April 2003	Conflicts of interest between research & investment banking	
Bear Stearns			$80,000,000
Credit Suisse First Boston			$200,000,000
Goldman Sachs			$110,000,000
JP Morgan			$80,000,000
Lehman Brothers			$80,000,000
Merrill Lynch			$200,000,000
Morgan Stanley			$125,000,000
Piper Jaffray			$32,500,000
Salomon Smith Barney (Citigroup)			$400,000,000
UBS (United Bank of Switzerland)			$80,000,000
JPMorgan Chase #2003-87	July 2003	Settle allegations that it helped Enron commit fraud	$135,000,000
Citigroup #2003-87	July 2003	Settle SEC charges that it helped Enron and Dynergy commit fraud	$120,000,000
Goldman Sachs, MFS, Peter Davis #2003-107	September 2003	Trading based upon non-public information on 30-year Treasury bills	$10,300,000
JPMorgan #2003-129	October 2003	Unlawful IPO allocations	$25,000,000
Morgan Stanley #2003-159	November 2003	Inadequate disclosure-mutual funds	$50,000,000
Alliance Capital #2003-176	December 2003	Illegal market timing-mutual funds	$250,000,000
Mass Financial Services #2004-14	February 2004	Widespread market timing-mutual funds	$225,000,000
Joint Release SEC/NASD	February 2004	Penalties for breakpoint violations on mutual fund sales	
Wachovia Securities			$4,844,465
UBS Financial			$4,621,768
American Express			$3,706,693
Raymond James Financial			$2,595,129
Legg Mason Wood Walker			$2,315,467
Linsco/Private Ledger			$2,232,805
H.D. Investment Services			$725,216
Bank of America Securities #2004-29	March 2004	Repeated failures to produce documents	$10,000,000
Bank of America #2004-33	March 2004	Permitted market timing-mutual funds	$375,000,000
Fleet Boston-Bank of America #2004-34	March 2004	Undisclosed market timing-mutual funds	$140,000,000
Mass Financial Services #2004-44	March 2004	Failure to disclose brokerage commissions for mutual fund "shelf space"	$50,000,000
Putnam Investments #2004-19	April 2004	Improper market timing/late trading mutual funds	$55,000,000
Strong Capital Management, Richard Strong, #2004-69	May 2004	Undisclosed frequent trading of mutual funds "round trip trades"	$140,000,000

Pilgrim & Baxter Ass. #2004-84	June 2004	Undisclosed market timing, mutual funds	$90,000,000
Banc One Investment Advisors Corporation #2004-90 Mark Beeson, former CEO	June 2004	Excessive short term trading mutual funds Civil penalty	$50,000,000 $100,000
Franklin Advisors, Inc. #2004-103	August 2004	Rapid in and out trading of mutual funds	$50,000,000
Fidelity Brokerage Services#2004-103	August 2004	Destruction of books and records	$2,000,000
Conseco Equity Sales, Inc. #2004-109	August 2004	Market timing of variable annuities	$20,000,000
Janus Capital #2004-111	August 2004	Undisclosed market timing-mutual funds	$100,000,000
Deutsche Bank Securities#2004-120 Thomas Weisel Partners	August 2004 " "	Conflicts of interest between research and investment banking " " "	$87,500,000 $12,500,000
Van Wagoner Capital Mgmt#2004-122	August 2004	Misstatement of securities-mutual funds	$800,000
Invesco Mutual Funds former employees #2004-123 Timothy J. Miller, CIO Thomas A. Kolbe, Nat' Sales Mgr Michael Legoski	August 2004	Widespread market timing-mutual funds	$150,000 $150,000 $40,000
PIMCO Equity Mutual Funds, PA Fund Mgmt, PEA Capital, PA Distributors #2004-127	September 2004	Undisclosed market timing-mutual funds	$50,000,000
Charles Schwab & Co. #2004-128	September 2004	Late trading, mutual funds	$350,000
PIMCO Funds Multi-Manager Series Funds #2004-130	September 2004	Failure to disclose use of directed brokerage for mutual fund shelf space	$11,600,000
Bridgeway Capital #2004-131	September 2004	Illegal performance fees, mutual funds	$5,000,000
RS Investment Management #2004-142	September 2004	Frequent short timing, mutual funds	$25,000,000
Invesco Funds Group, Inc. #2004-143 Aim Advisors, Inc. Aim Distributors, Inc. Raymond C. Cunningham, former CEO, Invesco	October 2004	Widespread market timing, mutual funds	$315,000,000 $30,000,000 $30,000,000 $1,500,000
Fremont Invest. Advisors#2004-153	November 2004	Market timing, mutual funds	$4,000,000
Harold Baxter Gary Pilgrim #2004-157	November 2004	Undisclosed market timing-mutual funds	$80,000,000 $80,000,000
Franklin Advisors #2004-168 Franklin Templeton	December 2004	Settle charges, brokerage commissions for mutual fund "shelf space"	$21,000,000
Edward D. Jones #2004-177	December 2004	Failure to disclose revenue sharing agreements for select mutual funds	$75,000,000
Southwest Securities#2005-2	January 2005	Market timing/late trading-mutual funds	$10,000,000
Morgan Stanley #2005-10 Goldman Sachs	January 2005	Unlawful allocations, IPO shares	$40,000,000 $40,000,000
Citigroup#2005-39	March 2005	Failure to provide shareholders information about mutual fund purchases	$20,000,000
Putnam Investments #2005-40	March 2005	Mutual fund brokerage commissions for for "shelf space"	$40,000,000
Citigroup, Inc., Citigroup Global Smith Barney Fund Mgmt#2005-80	May 2005	Misrepresentation and omission of material facts, placing profits ahead of mutual funds it served	$208,000,000
Federated Investment Mgmt#2005-164	November 2005	Undisclosed market timing and late trading of mutual funds	$72,000,000
American Express, Ameriprise	December 2005	Failure to disclose revenue sharing, mutual	

Financial, Inc. #2005-168		funds to customers	$30,000,000
American Express #2005-169	December 2005	Market timing of mutual funds	$15,000,000
Millennium Partners, LP Israel Englander #2005-170	December 2005	Fraudulent scheming in market timing in mutual funds	$180,000,000
Daniel Calugar, Security Brokerage, Inc. #2006-5	January 2006	Improper late trading and market timing of mutual funds	$150,000,000
Bear Stearns & Co. Inc. #2006-38	March 2006	Securities fraud, unlawful late trading and market timing in mutual funds	$250,000,000
Prudential Equity Group, LLC #2006-145	August 2006	Defrauded mutual funds by concealing identities, market timing mutual funds, etc.	$600,000,000
BISYS Fund Services #2006-163	September 2006	Aided and abetted two dozen mutual fund companies in defrauding investors, entered into undisclosed side agreements with advisors	$21,000,000
Hartford Financial Services #2006-188	November 2006	Failure to disclose revenue sharing/kickback arrangements with mutual funds and annuities for shelf space with 61 broker–dealers, Hartford directed $51 million of shareholder assets to certain broker–dealers	$55,000,000
Jefferies & Company, Inc. #2006-198	December 2006	Lavish gifts, private jets, entertainment to Fidelity mutual fund traders	$5,500,000
Kevin Quinn			$1,468,000
Fred Alger Management #2007-6	January 2007	Allowed market timing and late trading of mutual funds with various hedge funds	$40,000,000
Banc of America Securities #2007-42	March 2007	Failure to safeguard non-public information, issuing fraudulent research	$26,000,000

NASD (National Association of Securities Dealers)-Various Press Releases Disciplinary Actions-Confirmed Fines & Disgorgements Only-Does Not Include Pending Cases

Advisor/Organization	Date	Reason for Action	Total Fine
Banc One Corporation	April 5, 2001	Insufficient customer reserves, inadequate net capital, inaccurate books & records	$1,800,000
Knight Securities	January 7, 2002	Market making & trading violations	$800,000 to clients
Hornblower & Weeks, Inc.	May 7, 2002	Baseless projections, misleading & exaggerated omission of facts, violation of anti-fraud & advertising rules	$100,000
John Rooney, Principal			$85,000
Josephthal & Co.	July 8, 2002	Refusal to comply with NASD arbitration	$10,000
Credit Suisse First Boston George W. Coleman, J. Anthony Ehinger	August 15, 2002	Excessive commissions in exchange for allocations of "hot" initial public offerings	$200,000
Salomon Smith Barney-Citigroup	September 23, 2002	Materially misleading research reports in regards to Winstar Communications, Inc.	$5,000,000
Deutsche Bank Securities	December 3, 2002	Failure to preserve electronic records	$1,650,000
Goldman Sachs			$1,650,000
Morgan Stanley			$1,650,000
Salomon Smith Barney			$1,650,000
U.S. Bancorp-Piper Jaffray			$1,650,000
American Express	December 4, 2002	Sales practice & supervisory violations	$350,000
JPMorgan	February 3, 2003	Unlawful profit sharing activities w/Hambrecht & Quist, received millions of dollars in inflated commissions for "hot" initial public offerings	$6,000,000
Jack Grubman-Smith Barney	April 28, 2003	Undue influence of investment banking interests on investment analysts at brokerage firms, aided & abetted Salomon Smith Barney violations of antifraud, omission of facts, etc.	$15,000,000
Henry Blodget-Merrill Lynch	April 28, 2003	Issuing fraudulent research under Merrill Lynch name, expressing views which were inconsistent with private views	$4,000,000
Morgan Stanley	September 16, 2003	Conducting prohibited sales contests to promote Morgan Stanley mutual funds	$2,000,000
Bruce Alonso			$250,000
Prudential Equity Group, Inc.	January 29, 2004	Failure to comply with variable annuity replacement Procedures	$2,000,000
Customer Restitution			$9,500,000
Credit Suisse First Boston	February 2, 2004	Failure to provide "best price"	$150,000
Restitution		MP3.COM	$600,000
State Street Research	February 19, 2004	Market timing, mutual funds	$1,000,000
AXA Advisors	February 26, 2004	Failure to obtain sale charge waivers	$250,000
Ameritrade	March 11, 2004	Improperly extending credit	$10,000,000
Christine Gochuico-Smith Barney	April 5, 2004	Misleading research, telecommunications	$100,000
Robertson Stephens, Inc. Richard Davies-Fleet Boston	April 7, 2004	Threats to discontinue research unless awarding investment banking business	$275,000 $75,000
David Lerner Associates	April 12, 2004	Promoting proprietary mutual funds	$100,000

111

Bear Stearns	May 18, 2004	Engaging in improper IPO allocations	$4,950,000
Deutsche Bank		receiving unusually high commissions	$5,290,000
Morgan Stanley			$5,390,000
Nationwide Investments	May 20, 2004	Inadequate procedures & systems	$175,000
American Express			$300,000
Phua Young-Merrill Lynch	May 25, 2004	Violation in regards to research activities, Tyco, Honeywell, disclosure non-public information	$225,000
D.A. Davidson & Co	June 24, 2004	Failure to implement adequate	$150,000
TD Waterhouse Investor Services		supervisory systems to prevent and detect	$150,000
Stifel Nicolaus & Company		"late trading" of mutual funds	$125,000
National Planning			$100,000
SII Investments			$100,000
Citigroup	July 19, 2004	Failure to comply with discovery	$250,000
Merrill Lynch		obligations, arbitration cases	$250,000
Morgan Stanley			$250,000
Goldman Sachs	July 28, 2004	Excessive markups or markdowns,	$5,000,000
Deutsche Bank		inadequate record keeping, supervisory	$5,000,000
Miller Tabak		violations	$5,000,000
Citigroup Global			$5,000,000
Morgan Stanley	July 29, 2004	Late reporting, supervisory failures	$2,500,000
National Securities Corporation	August 19, 2004	Facilitating deceptive market timing & late trading of mutual funds	$300,000
Sentinel Financial Services, Inc.	October 7, 2004	Failure to prevent market timing mutual	$700,000
Restitution		funds	$659,000
Citigroup Global Markets, Inc.	October 25, 2004	Disseminating inappropriate information in regards to hedge funds, unsubstantiated claims	$250,000
29 Securities firms	November 30, 2004	8,000 late disclosures in regards to reporting information about their brokers	$9,200,000
CitigroupGlobal Markets, Inc.	December 7, 2004	Unsuitable recommendations, failed record keeping inadequate risk disclosures, commodities	$250,000
H&R Block, Inc.	December 21, 2004	Enabling hedge fund customers to engage in market timing of mutual funds	$500,000
Reimbursement			$325,000
Banc One Securities	January 12, 2005	Failure to implement adequate supervisory systems to prevent & detect "late trading"	$400,000
Jefferson Pilot Corporation	March 16, 2005	Failure to have adequate supervisory systems to prevent excessive trading in VUL	$325,000
Restitution		accounts	$235, 697
Failure to retain emails			$125,000
Raymond James	April 27, 2005	Failure to maintain supervisory systems	$750,000
Restitution		on asset based accounts	$138,000
Waddell & Reed, Inc.	April 29, 2005	"Churning" thousands of variable	$5,000,000
Restitution		annuity policies	$11,000,000
Royal Alliance	June 8, 2005	Directed brokerage for preferential	$6,600,000
H.D. Vest Investments		treatment with mutual fund companies	$4,015,000
Alliance Bernstein			$3,984,087
Linsco/Private Ledger			$3,602,398
Wells Fargo Investments			$2,970,000
SunAmerica			$2,500,000
FSC Securities			$2,400,000
Securities America			$2,400,000
RBC Dain Rauscher			$1,700,000
McDonald Investments			$1,500,000
AXA Advisors			$900,000
Sentra Securities/Spelman & Company			$780,000
Advantage Capital			$450,000
Advest			$286,415

Morgan Stanley	August 2, 2005	Failure to supervise fee based business	$1,400,000
Restitution			$4,600,000
Edward D. Jones	September 29, 2005	Failure to disclose yields on 86,000 municipal bond transactions	$300,000
First Allied Securities	October 3, 2005	Facilitating deceptive efforts in market timing of mutual funds with hedge funds	$400,000
Restitution			$136,700
ING Funds	October 3, 2005	Improper market timing mutual funds	$1,500,000
Restitution			$1,400,000
Janney Montgomery Scott, LLC	October 3, 2005	Improper market timing & other violations with mutual funds	$1,200,000
Restitution			$1,000,000
IFC Holdings	October 10, 2005	Receipt or payment of directed brokerage for preferential treatment with mutual fund companies	$1,520,000
Commonwealth Financial			$1,400,000
National Planning			$1,308,000
Mutual Service Corporation			$1,300,000
Lincoln Financial			$950,000
SII Investments			$658,000
Investment Centers			$363,000
Lord Abbott Distributors			$255,000
Ameriprise Financial	October 26, 2005	Failure to supervise sales of 529 college savings plans	$500,000
Restitution			$750,000
SC Americas Securities	October 31, 2005	Excessive markups or mark downs in bond trades, other violations	$3,750,000
Restitution			$728,000
RBC Capital			$2,000,000
Restitution			$108,000
RBC Dain Rauscher			$1,000,000
Restitution			$158,000
Debt Traders			$120,000
Expelled from industry			
State Street Global	November 22, 2005	Failure to report thousands of bond trades	$1,400,000
Ameriprise Financial	December 1, 2005	Directed brokerage in return for preferential treatment with mutual fund companies	$12,300,000
Chase Investments	December 13, 2005	Failure to have adequate supervisory controls in place to prevent deceptive market timing of mutual funds with hedge funds	$150,000
Restitution			$140,000
Merrill Lynch	December 19, 2005	Improper sales of "B" & "C" shares of mutual funds	$14,000,000
Wells Fargo			$3,000,000
Linsco-Private Ledger			$2,400,000
Stanford Bernstein & Company	February 8, 2006	Trading contrary to analysts recommendations, conflicts of interests	$350,000
Charles Hintz			$200,000
Diversified Investors	February 14, 2006	Facilitating impermissible market timing of mutual funds	$1,300,000
Restitution			$950,000
Merrill Lynch	March 15, 2006	Supervisory failures, registration violations, impermissible sales contests, other violations	$5,000,000
Boston Captial	March 21, 2006	Violations in regards to public offerings of tax-advantaged limited partnerships	$1,200,000
American General/AIG	April 5, 2006	Directed brokerage for preferential treatment with mutual fund companies	$1,100,000

Steven W. Norin–Citigroup Global	April 26, 2006	Improper short sales, personal accounts	$400,000
Lasalle Street Securities	May 31, 2006	Failure to supervise Frank Devine	$200,000
Frank Devine		Wire fraud, tax fraud, restitution, etc.	$3,000,000
Trillium Trading, LLC Schonfeld & Company, LLC	June 29, 2006	Misuse of NASDAQ trading system	$225,000 $175,000
Citigroup Credit Suisse Morgan Stanley	July 17, 2006	Ignored warnings from NASD to cease violating analyst's disclosure reports	$350,000 $225,000 $200,000
BRUT, LLC	August 3, 2006	Publishing erroneous executions	$2,200,000
ING-Financial Network Investment ING-Financial Partners ING-Multi-Financial Services Corp. ING-Prime Vest Financial Services, Inc.	August 9, 2006	Directed brokerage in exchange for preferential treatment with mutual funds	$3,400,000 $1,300,000 $1,200,000 $1,000,000
Citigroup Global Markets Restitution	August 10, 2006	Brokers improperly obtained mutual fund sales load waivers by falsely claiming customers were disabled, even hedge funds	 $400,000 $715,000
American Funds–Capital Research	August 30, 2006	Directed brokerage to securities firms that were top sellers of mutual funds	 $5,000,000
Morgan Stanley	September 5, 2006	Extensive violations, reporting obligations, best execution short sales, and other violations	 $2,900,000
Securities America Restitution	September 14, 2006	Investment scheme aimed at Exxon retirees, failure to adequately supervise	 $2,500,000 $13,800,000
MetLife Securities, Inc.	September 19, 2006	Providing inaccurate and misleading information to NASD, permitting late trading of mutual funds, failure to produce emails, etc.	 $5,000,000
Oppenheimer & Company	October 4, 2006	Failure to respond to regulatory requests	$800,000
Citizens Bank-CCO Investments Corp	October 16, 2006	Failed to implement procedures in regards to selling variable annuities to seniors, etc.	 $850,000
James River Capital Corporation Paul Saunders	October 25, 2006	Deceptive market timing in variable annuities	 $2,250,000
EKN Financial Services Anthony Ottimo, Thomas Giugliano William Baker, Michael Benvenuto	November 2, 2006	Engaged in short selling of unregistered securities	 $200,000
Chase Investment Services Restitution MetLife Securities Restitution	November 6, 2006	Supervisory violations in 529 College savings plans	$500,000 $288,500 $500,000 $376,000
Jefferies & Company	December 4, 2006	Improper gifts & excessive entertainment for Fidelity Traders	 $5,500,000
Edward Jones Restitution RBC Dain Rauscher Restitution Royal Alliance Associates Restitution Morgan Stanley DW Restitution	December 13, 2006	Supervisory failures mutual fund charges	$250,000 $25,000,000+ $250,000 $6,800,000+ $250,000 $1,600,000 $100,000 $10,400,000
USAllianz Securities	December 18, 2006	Record keeping violations	$5,000,000

Friedman, Billings & Ramsey Co. Inc.	December 20, 2006	Improper short selling	$7,700,000
Emanuel Friedman, Chairman			$500,000
SEC civil penalty			$750,000
Nicholas J. Nichols, Chief Compliance Officer			$50,000
SEC civil penalty			$60,000
Four Fidelity-Affiliated-Broker–dealers	February 5, 2007	Registration, supervision and email retention violations	$3,750,000
Scudder Distributors, Inc.	February 12, 2007	Firms improperly entertained brokers, reimbursed guest expenses	$425,000
Putnam Retail Management			$175,000
Alliance Bernstein Investments			$100,000

LIFE INSURANCE AND THE HUMAN LIFE VALUE CONCEPT

"The capitalized worth of the earning power of life, when properly appraised, is an economic asset just as truly as appraised property. If we choose to apply indemnity contracts to our property possessions, it follows even more logical that we should be equally sensible with the monetary worth of our lives...The human life value is the creator of all utility in tangible property. The life value is the "cause" and the property value is the "effect." Were it not for human life values there would be no property values at all. Human life values, as reflected by current earning power, constitute an economic asset quite as much does tangible property. The capitalized value of the nation exceeds by ten the aggregate total its national wealth."

Solomon S. Huebner
The Economics of Life Insurance

"If I had my way I would write the word insurance over the door of every house because I am convinced that for the sacrifices which are inconceivably small families can be secured against catastrophes which could otherwise smash them up forever."

Winston Churchill

"Life insurance has to do with the most sacred things that stir the human affections...its management involves a higher duty and more constant devotion than we associate with a mere business enterprise."

Grover Cleveland, U. S. President, 1905

"Life insurance increases the stability of the business world, raises its moral tone, and puts a premium upon those habits of thrift and saving which are so essential to the welfare of the people as a body."

Theodore Roosevelt

"To carry adequate life insurance is a moral obligation incumbent upon the great majority of citizens."

Franklin D. Roosevelt
When he died in 1945, $562,142 of life insurance was owned by the Georgia Warm Springs Foundation. Roosevelt's net estate was $1.3 million.

"I have always found them (life insurance policies) to be comforting possessions, and if I had my life to live over, I would seek to take more rather than less."

Warren Harding

"It is established that the protection of one's family, or those near to him, is the one thing most to be desired, and there is no medium of protection that is better than life insurance."

Calvin Coolidge

"A materialization of the doctrine of duty...an instrument of the ethical code, practiced by civilized man...the most reliable system of economic security which has been yet devised."

> Carlyle R. Buley, Equitable Life,
> 1960s historian on value of life insurance

"People are your most valuable asset. Only people can be made to appreciate in value."

> Stephen Covey

"A man who does not believe in life insurance deserves to die once without it."

> Will Rogers.
> When Rogers died in a plane crash with
> Willie Post, life insurance was one
> of the largest financial assets in his estate.

"What you're really asking me is: Are all lives equal, why isn't everyone getting the same amount of money? A very fair question, ladies and gentlemen. The answer is: Congress told me that is not the way to compute these awards. Congress told me you must take into account the economic loss suffered by the victim's death."

> Kenneth Feinberg,
> the presiding Master for the
> 9/11 Victims Compensation Fund in which the
> United States government paid close to $7 billion
> in life insurance and injury claims

The actual first known examples of the use of life insurance are associated with the Greeks around 1750 BC, when a sum of money was set aside for member of a household that was murdered during a robbery. It was during the times of the Roman Empire when the first mutual benefit associations, which provided their members with stated benefits and required regular contributions, were formed.

During the Middle Ages, guilds developed more sophisticated forms of insurance, by covering a host of covered perils for relief—death, illness, capture by pirates, shipwrecks, the burning of one's home and the loss of one's tools associated with one's trade. In England, the first mutual groups of insurance were formed in connection with particular crafts or religions. They were called "Friendly Societies."

In Muslim nations, where the Koran prohibits the payment of interest and gambling, Islamic insurers set up a *tarafu*, which is a form of life insurance. This is a collective pooling arrangement to protect heirs against unforeseen events that could financially hurt them.

Today the life insurance industry in the United States provides life and health insurance benefits to millions of consumers and businesses. Life insurance companies are an integral component of the overall American economy. They provide consumers with numerous financial benefits such as stable savings, tax benefits, disability, health, and death benefits.

According to the American Council of Life Insurers (www.acli.com), Americans purchased about $3 trillion in new life insurance in 2005. Total life insurance coverage in the United States is about $18.4 trillion. Fifty-four percent of life insurance owned in the US is individually owned life insurance, with the vast majority of that being sold by individual life insurance agents. Other life insurance is issued through group life plans, credit insurance, and so on.

As financial intermediaries, life insurance companies provide consumers and businesses exemplary financial strength and indispensable insulation from the everyday vicissitudes of a volatile world economy. Life insurance companies, while still very strong, do not maintain the prominent position that they once did within the economy. Banks, mutual fund companies and securities firms have displaced the life companies in the competition for the consumers' discretionary savings dollar. This movement of savings into more speculative instruments, which is known as disintermediation, has been clearly accelerated by the deregulation and de-supervision of the financial service industry.

When viewed from a historical context, from about 1933 to about 1980, it was the life insurance companies who were the dominant architects, engineers, builders, and custodians of the nation's savings and pension systems, from small employers to large publicly traded companies.

Although life companies have never been, and will never be, known for shoot-out-the-lights stock market performance, as custodians of money, the life companies have consistently demonstrated unmatched expertise for preserving capital. Banks, securities firms, and mutual fund companies have never been able to duplicate the track record that life insurance has in preserving capital.

The financial planning profession, as we know it in America, has definite roots within the life insurance industry as life insurance professionals have been pioneers in the progression of financial planning. High-end entrepreneurial life insurance agents still actively nurture the profession today. Some of the most influential and dominant players in the financial industry come out of the life insurance business.

The employee benefits industry, particularly small and medium-sized employers and, to some extent, large publicly traded companies are well served by life insurance professionals. Leading producers in the employee benefits business with specialty disciplines in qualified retirement plans, group benefit programs, or in selective executive retirement plans more than likely got their careers initially started in, or were in some way heavily influenced by, the life insurance business.

Stock and Mutual Life Insurance Companies

Life insurance companies generally take two corporate forms. One form is that of shareholders or stockholders of a corporation owning the company. In this arrangement, the primary emphasis is to reward the stockholders with overall growth and profits of the life insurance company. This is known as a *stock life insurance company.*

The second type of life insurance company is the *mutual life insurance company.* In this arrangement, the policyholders are the owners of the company. Overall growth and profits are for the policyholders, not stockholders.

Both stock and mutual life insurance companies, to keep their products competitive, can reward, and have historically rewarded, policyholders with dividends or interest earnings from the general account of the life insurance company. However, from a practical point of view, a policyholder will most likely be rewarded with more financial benefits from a mutual life insurance policy because of company ownership.

This dividend or interest from the life insurance company is technically a *return of the premium* under the Internal Revenue Code. This is a major benefit to the owner of the policy, as the return of the premium is *non-taxable.*

Together, stock and mutual life insurance companies provide about 94 percent of life insurance and annuities underwritten in the United States. Fraternal organizations and the U.S. Department of Veteran Affairs underwrite the remainder of life insurance benefits.

Origins of the Economic or Human Life Value Concept

The philosophical concept regarding the economic value of a human life or human life value has evolved over the ages. [61] The economist, William Petty (1623-1687), was one of the first to conceive the idea that human life had value, known as the *economic value of a man.* Richard Cantillon (1680-1734) was the one to form the concept of *human capital.*

Other economists who have addressed the economic value of a man include Adam Smith (1732-1790), Johan Heinrich von Thunen (1783-1850), and John Stuart Mill (1806-1873). Recently, economist Gary Becker won the Nobel Prize in Economics in part for his related work with the human life

---

[61] Kenneth Black and Harold D. Skipper, Jr., *Life & Health Insurance* (New Jersey: Prentice Hall, 2000).

value concept and the way in which education improves the economic potential of a human being.

It was William Farr, an economist and statistician, who generated the first set of equations used to define human life value around 1853. Farr's work laid the initial foundation for the concept of human life value, as we know it today.

Contemporary economists who have also written about life insurance in light of the economic value of a human life include Laurence J. Kotlikoff of Boston University, B. Douglas Bernheim of Stanford University, Jagadeesh Gokhale of the Federal Reserve Bank of Cleveland, and Solange Berstein of Boston University and the Central Bank of Chile.

One of the most important economists of the past century, John Maynard Keynes, believed in the value of permanent life insurance as an economic instrument. For a time, Keynes was at the helm of one of the largest life insurance companies in Great Britain. However, he was later dismissed from the company when his attempts to improve policy yields with speculative securities became highly unsuccessful.[62]

The Austrian School of Economics

The Austrian school of economics supports the value of permanent life insurance. F.A. Hayek, who went on to win the Nobel Prize in Economics in 1974, maintained that voluntary disciplined savings through permanent cash value life insurance and the purchase of a home were two of the most important economic investments anyone could own.[63]

Richard von Strigl, another Austrian economist, makes explicit reference to the extraordinary importance of permanent cash value life insurance as an economic tool in the formation of private capital.[64]

Jesus Huerta de Soto, an internationally renowned Spanish economist, has written extensively in regard to the importance of permanent life insurance as an economic tool. In his major work, *Money, Bank Credit and Economic Cycles*, de Soto explicitly reviews the multiple economic uses of life insurance throughout one's entire economic life. He also reaffirms the superior stability of the life insurance companies over banks and other financial intermediaries for the past two hundred years. In his book, de Soto writes:

---

[62] Jesus Huerta de Soto, *Money, Bank Credit and Economic Cycles*, trans. Melinda A. Stroup,(Auburn, AL: Ludwig von Mises Institute, 2006).
[63] Ibid.
[64] Ibid.

"The institution of life insurance has gradually and spontaneously taken shape in the market over the last two hundred years. It is based on a series of technical, actuarial, financial and juridical principles of business behavior which have enabled it to perform its mission perfectly and survive economic crises and recessions which other institutions, especially banking, have been unable to overcome. Therefore, the high "financial death rate" of banks, which systematically suspend payments and fail without the support of the central bank, has historically contrasted with the health and technical solvency of life insurance companies. (In the last two hundred years, a negligible number of life insurance companies have disappeared due to financial difficulties.) ...

"Thus life insurance companies tend to underestimate their assets, overestimate their liabilities, and reach a high level of static and dynamic solvency which makes them immune to the deepest stages of the recessions that recur with economic cycles. In fact when the value of financial assets and capital goods plunges in the most serious stages of recession in every cycle, life insurance companies are not usually affected, given the reduced book value they record for their investments. With respect to the amount of their liabilities, insurers calculate their mathematical reserves at interest rates much lower than those actually charged in the market." (pp. 590-591).

Solomon S. Huebner and the Human Life Value Concept

Most credit in regards to refining the intellectual argument for the human life value concept in regards to the purchase of life insurance for consumers today must go to Solomon S. Huebner. Huebner, the author of *The Economics of Life Insurance*, was a distinguished professor at the Wharton School at the University of Pennsylvania. Huebner, although few people in this country realize it, was also one of the key catalysts and pioneers of today's modern financial planning profession.

In his classic work, Huebner laid down the following major tenets in regards to the value of the human life and the purchase of life insurance.[65] They were:

One. Human life should be *carefully appraised* and *capitalized*.
Two. The human life value should be *recognized* as the *creator* of all property values.
Three. The family is an *economic unit* organized around the *human value* of its members.
Four. The human life value and *its protection* should be regarded as the *principle economic link* between the *present* and *future* generations.
Five. In view of the significance of human life values, the *scientific principles* of business management utilized in connection with

---

[65] Solomon S. Huebner, *The Economics of Life Insurance*, (Executive Asset Mgmt. 3rd ed. 1996) (1927). This work is Huebner's classic work and the foundation for much of financial planning within America today.

property values *should be applied* to life values.

The Courtroom

In wrongful death cases, the courtroom has consistently ruled in favor of the *economic replacement value of a human life.* Rulings in the courtroom over monetary compensation for a beneficiary's pain and suffering in relation to wrongful death cases have deep roots in economic replacement or the human life value concept. Virtually all favorable courtroom financial awards are based upon the economic value of a human life.

This economic concept was reaffirmed unequivocally in the courtroom in the summer of 2005. In a landmark case brought against pharmaceutical giant Merck for a Vioxx wrongful death, the jury awarded Carol Ernst, the victim's spouse, $24 million for her pain and suffering, and an additional $229 million in punitive damages.

Although this case is an extreme example, it reaffirms the important role that economics plays in the death of a human.

The Titanic: The Coexistence of Property and Human Life Values

The concept of insuring the value of a human life is nothing new in America and can peacefully coexist when insuring one's property value. When the Titanic sunk in April of 1912, the ship was insured for $5.5 million, the equivalent of about $154 million today. Back then, when there were no income tax or estate taxes per se, two very wealthy individuals, John Jacob Astor and Benjamin Guggenheim, intuitively knew the inherent economic benefits of life insurance and the importance of human life value as the main contributor in the creation of property values.

When Astor and Guggenheim died, they were insured for $1.7 million, which equates to about $54 million today. Henry Blank, a former Prudential life insurance agent on board the Titanic, who was then a wholesale jeweler, was one of the most heavily insured at $800 thousand.

Americans and the Human Life Value Concept

America has become a nation that spends more on car insurance than it does in insuring the economic value of its lives. This has been confirmed by the author's own work over the past twenty-five years, independent economists, and by numerous empirical studies performed by life insurance companies.

Large portions of Americans are doing their financial planning in risk management in *reverse.* Most risk management and asset protection strategies

focus on protecting the golden eggs (autos, homes, possessions, etc.) rather than protecting the golden goose (the human life).

As a country, Americans are in the dark when it comes to purchasing life insurance as a means of thrift and protection. In the 1990s, Swiss Re, a major international life reinsurance company, performed a study that confirmed America's malaise in this area. The United States ranked last among large industrial countries in terms of per capita spending on life insurance. Japan was first at $3,236, Switzerland ranked second at $3,106, France was third at $1,559, the United Kingdom came in at $1,433, and America was last at $1,079.

The author's own research revealed a frightening trend—even though the population of the country has increased, actual new purchases as a percentage of the population have gone down dramatically on individual policies. The following is consolidated information from the United States Census Bureau, the National Association of Insurance Commissioners, and LIMRA International:

Year	Total US Population in Millions	New Life Insurance Individual Purchases in Millions	Purchases as Percentage of Population
1940	150,622,754	17,872,000	11.865%
1950	154,233,234	20,203,000	13.00%
1960	183,285,009	21,021,000	11.469%
1970	203,235,298	18,550,000	9.127%
1980	226,500,000	17,116,000	7.5%
1990	248,709,873	14,199,000	5.7%
2000	281,421,906	13,345,000	4.7%
2004	293,655,000	12,581,000	4.28%

From the above figures, we can see that as a percentage of the population, Americans are purchasing less and less life insurance as a means of thrift and protecting their loved ones. You would think that particularly with more education, the war on terror, and the higher costs of living, life insurance purchases, and patient capital formation would be going up. Statistics prove otherwise. Regretfully, most savings, if Americans are saving

123

at all, are going into the untested waters of mutual funds and the Wall Street Casino.

Conversely, you will see in the next chapter, "Bank-Owned Life Insurance," that banks, unlike the American consumer, are depositing as much as 25 percent of their reserves in permanent life insurance—sometimes depositing as much as 40 percent!

Research done by the Life and Health Insurance Foundation for Education (LIFE) in 2004 confirms Americans' dysfunctional approach to life insurance and the human life value concept. According to LIFE, the average male in America today has an average economic worth of about $1 million, yet on average had only about $288 thousand of life insurance or about 29 percent of his economic value. Women, whose economic value was somewhat less with on average of about $661 thousand, had life insurance amounts on average of about $165 thousand or about 25 percent of their human life value.

In 2004, MetLife, the largest life insurance company in the United States, performed a survey, "Financial Impact of a Premature Death: The Value of Adequate Life Insurance Coverage When Tragedy Strikes." The study found that 39 percent of all families had no life insurance whatsoever, and that the average amount of life insurance in place was only about 2.1 times annual income.

In 2005, MetLife did an additional study, "MetLife Study of Employee Benefit Trends." The study found that 60 percent of the population was extremely concerned about premature death, yet 34 percent of the group thought that life insurance less than three times annual income was adequate.

This author wrote an article for a national magazine back in 1999. In researching that article, statistics from the national research firm of Roper Starch revealed that most people were more concerned about having a retirement account versus having adequate life insurance. The tragedy is that few Americans realize that permanent life insurance can be a protection plan, a savings plan, and a viable methodology to provide additional retirement income. Retirement plans such as a 401(k) and IRAs have never been able to perform multiple economic jobs simultaneously as life insurance can.

A survey done by J. Walter Thompson in May of 2005 essentially confirms the MetLife study done in 2004. Their study found that over 80 percent of Americans have become more anxious about life and death matters. However, around 35 percent of the population had no life insurance whatsoever.

Application of the Human Life Value Life Concept Concerning Life Insurance

"What is a human life worth? You may not want to put a price tag on it. But if we really had to, most of us would agree that the value of a human life would be in the millions. "
Peter Singer, Professor of Bioethics, Center for Human Values
Princeton University, On Giving, New York Times, December 17, 2006

We most often purchase property insurance to replace the economic value *of* material goods such as automobiles, homes, and fine jewelry. We do not purchase insurance to replace our needs and goals. If we purchased a brand new Mercedes and the car was stolen or totaled in an accident, we would want the economic value of the Mercedes replaced. We would not be happy if we were given a Yugo automobile to replace our mode of transportation.

If we purchased a million dollar home and it burned down while we were away for a weekend, we would want the economic value of the home restored. We would not be satisfied with a $250,000 home or be content with permanent housing in the local trailer park. Similarly, if we owned a business, had an inventory of finished goods worth $3 million, and insured the inventory for that amount, we would want the economic value of that inventory replaced if it were lost in a fire or other natural disaster.

Ideally and for most practical purposes, we purchase insurance to replace intrinsic or economic value, not to meet our needs and goals. Why is it then we get so far off track when it comes to insuring the economic value of our lives, the greatest asset of them all? The truth is there are many reasons, such as:

- No one wants to talk about the greatest risk of them all: premature death. Yet it is the greatest risk we all face. Every person on the face of the planet is guaranteed at least one death.

- The media and the entire speculation mania promoted by banks, securities firms, and mutual fund companies distort reality, because it is in their best economic interests to promote speculation and misinform the public every day.

- Many self-appointed financial gurus who influence public opinion by promoting speculative strategies such as "buy term life insurance and invest the difference" in mutual funds, skew the realities of the economic value of life. These gurus

125

never differentiate between savings and investing nor do they make the public aware of the lost opportunity costs involved with term life insurance. The "buy term and invest" strategy never worked over an extended period for the consumer, but life companies still make money on term life sales so they are happy. Instead of promoting thrift, wisdom, and an overall understanding of how financial products work within an economy, condescending fear is used by various gurus to promote their agendas and term life insurance sales.

- Few people understand the greatness of life insurance as a multifaceted financial product, which is not just a death benefit, but also a wonderful financial tool being actively used by the country's banks, corporations, and wealthy individuals. This book will attempt to show scientifically, that permanent life insurance is being consistently used throughout the strongest sections of our national economy.

- The majority of people do not reject the human life value concept or the wonderful economics of permanent life insurance once they understand it. The problem comes down to cost. It behooves the reader to work with a high-end life insurance or other financial planner for viable strategies, which enable them to structure the correct cash flow techniques to purchase it. Most often, it is just a question of repositioning cash flow and assets to maximize the efficiency for the consumer.

9/11 Victims Compensation Fund Reaffirms, Like no Other, the Human Life Value Concept Concerning Life Insurance

The payment of close to $6 billion in benefits to deceased victims of the 9/11 Victims Compensation Fund reaffirmed the importance of the economic value of a life. On *CSPAN* September 11, 2005, Kenneth Feinberg, said that he had complete and unfettered discretion to distribute the Victims Compensation Fund. Payments were based upon the economic value of a human life.

In the final analysis, no matter which way you slice it, even though the benefits did not come from a life insurance company, 9/11 Victim Compensation awards were life insurance because the benefits were received totally income tax-free. The awards also reaffirmed the human life value concept as compensation was based upon the economic value of a life.

The federal government is already in the life insurance business and it has been for years. Although one does not think of it because the life insurance payments do not come from a traditional life insurance company. In 1939, amendments were made to the Social Security Act, which created *survivor benefits* for widows and their dependents. This is life insurance.

Robert J. Shiller, an internationally acclaimed Yale economist known for his book, *Irrational Exuberance,* says this in his book, *The New Financial Order,* concerning survivor benefits as life insurance:

> *"The ultimate change for life insurance in the United States came when the federal government began to provide it for all its working citizens, and gave it a different name. In 1939, in amendments to the U. S. Social Security Act created survivors insurance, a form of life insurance whose beneficiaries are the children and spouse of a worker.*
> *Survivors insurance is important. For most people in the United States, the value of these survivors' insurance policies is greater than the value of their life insurance policies.*
> *By labeling it survivors insurance rather than life insurance, the U.S. government achieved a major change in framing without which it might have been politically impossible for the government to start providing life insurance, since it would collide head on in competition with the already large life insurance industry. By calling the program "survivor insurance" and by not advertising it, the U.S. government guaranteed that few families fully understand that they have government provided life insurance, even to this day." (pp. 243-244).*

In July, 2002, two other noted economists, Laurence J. Kotlikoff of Boston University and Jagadeesh Gokhale of the Federal Reserve Bank of Cleveland, in their published paper, "The Adequacy of Life Insurance" reaffirmed that Social Security benefits are a form of life insurance. However, due to the deep financial trouble Social Security was in, it is was unwise to rely further on the government for additional life insurance benefits.

Public Opinion Reaffirms the Human Life Value Concept

Kenneth Feinberg, the appointed Special Master for the 9/11 Victim Compensation Fund, said that the overwhelming correspondence he received reiterated that he had done the right thing by awarding 9/11 compensation based upon economic or human life values. Feinberg went on to write, *What Is A Life Worth?* In it, he said:

> *"The controversy that initially characterized gradually yielded to a studied calm as the program took shape, then to grudging acceptance, and finally to admiration. I was helped by my efforts by overwhelming public support. The*

American people not only endorsed the program but embraced it. The few critics who spoke out against the fund were overwhelmed by public enthusiasm. The editorial pages of the New York Times, Washington Post, Chicago Tribune, and other major newspapers offered support for my difficult task, then urged me success by highlighting the generosity and compassion of the American people. I got plenty of encouragement from the ordinary American citizens too."

Feinberg did have a tremendous amount of discretion to promote the idea of the human life or economic value of a human being. He did back out existing life insurance and other employee benefits, which is in many ways tragic, as it penalized those who had the discipline and foresight to take care of their families. Ironically, many of those who died in the 9/11 tragedy, those who had multi-million dollar incomes, those you would think would know better, had minimal personal life insurance.

Feinberg had complete discretion in making financial awards, using an open checkbook from the United States Treasury. Feinberg, while on *CSPAN,* told the story of a firefighter who died in the 9/11 tragedy. This firefighter was "Mr. Mom" according to his surviving spouse. He gave a monetary award to his spouse and remaining two children. Feinberg mentioned that on the side, "Mr. Mom" had a girlfriend. Subsequently, Feinberg said he paid both parties.

He also admitted that he had a young mother in her early twenties who had two young children, ages four and five. Upon hearing that this young mother was terminally ill, Feinberg doubled the award.

In reaffirming the economic or human life value concept, Feinberg paid out many claims for single people who are thought to have no human life value in the traditional life insurance sense of today. The idea that senior citizens had no economic or human life value over age seventy was turned over as well. The 9/11 fund paid out over nineteen claims to people age seventy or more, with the average award being $632 thousand.

Sadly, the 9/11 Victim Compensation Fund represents another sign of bailout for two privileged industries, the airlines and New York finance. The financing for the Victims Compensation Fund did not originate in the kindness of Americans' heart. Taxpayer funds came out of a bill, which was passed two weeks after the tragedy to protect the airline industry from future litigation.

Congress created the Air Transportation Safety and Stabilization Act, which, in addition to the billions in economic awards granted to the beneficiaries of the 9/11 tragedy, awarded billions of dollars in loans, grants and limited liability to the airline industry. Even Federal Express was paid $110 million under the act (but now the U. S. Transportation System is asking FedEx to pay back $29 million).

The awards reaffirmed the power of New York and airline industry and banking industries in this country. If you were a bond trader or stockbroker on the 103rd Floor of the World Trade Center, your beneficiaries could receive $6 million in tax-free life insurance compensation. The average claim was around $2 million. The highest claim was $7.1 million.

Conversely, if you are in the armed services today, and you take a bullet for Uncle Sam in the war on terror, the death benefit for soldiers is $100 thousand. A few years ago, it was only $12 thousand. Servicemen's Group Life Insurance is still today limited to $400 thousand.

Human Life Value Guidelines for Individuals and Their Families as It Pertains to Life Insurance

The human life value concept is nothing cast in stone, but as an economic formula, it is generally about 20-25 times annual income until age forty or so. As we get older, and our life expectancy declines, our human life value or life insurance value also drops. There are always exceptions. One should always seek *qualified professional advice.*

This book is only meant to motivate your thinking, and to use the information as a benchmark when working with a qualified life insurance agent or financial planner. The key is to *change your way of thinking from needs and goals to the concept of economic replacement value.*

Since the tragic events of September 11, 2001, MetLife now considers amounts up to thirty times annual income when it evaluates the economic value of life. The point is that when one purchases life insurance, whatever one finally decides, the human life value should be given consideration first. This is not an argument over what type of life insurance to buy. Whole life insurance is the product of choice, but huge chunks of term life insurance may also be needed as well. This author is not against term life insurance for the short-term.

The 9/11 Victim Compensation Fund was the largest life insurance claim ever at $6 billion. Whether one dies in a tragedy such as 9/11, cancer at a young age, a heart attack, or in some other unforeseen event, the economic devastation remains the same for the families left behind.

A Summary of the 9/11 Victim Compensation Fund

In addition to direct economic payouts, the fund also gave a non-economic award of $250 thousand for each victim of the fund. An additional $100 thousand was given for each dependent qualifying under the fund (e.g. children). Here is a summary of claims paid by the Victim Compensation Fund.

129

Claims for Death*

Income Level	Number of Claims	Average Claim	Highest Claim
No Income	17	$ 788,022.03	$2,219,390
$24,999 or less	163	$1,102,135.44	$3,048,255
$25,000 to $99,000	1,591	$1,520,155.41	$4,361,482
$100,000 to $199,000	633	$2,302,234.80	$5,512,520
$200,000 to $499,000	310	$3,394,624.91	$7,100,000
$500,000 to $999,999	89	$4,749,654.40	$7,100,000
$1 million to $1,999,999	52	$5,671,815.64	$7,100,000
$2 million to $3,999,999	17	$6,253,705.42	$7,100,000
$4 million or more	8	$6,379,287.70	$7,100,000

Source: September 11th Victim Compensation Fund of 2001

Claim Summaries

In addition, Special Fund Master Feinberg also explained the methodology for actual claims paid. Below are real-life examples, and more are posted at (www.usdoj.gov/archive/victimcompensation/payments). For clarification, collateral offsets include items such as existing life insurance, employer pension benefits, Social Security Survivor benefits, and so on.

- A married military officer, age twenty-six with no dependents and a base compensation of $44 thousand, received a net award of more than $1.8 million after offsets of $168 thousand.

- A married broker, age thirty-four, with one dependent and a base compensation of $82 thousand, received an award of just over $2 million, after $466 thousand in collateral offsets.

- A single trader, age thirty-four, with no dependents and a base salary of $100 thousand, received an award of just under $1.4 million after collateral offsets of $150 thousand.

- A married business official, age thirty-eight, with one dependent and a base compensation of $65 thousand,

130

received an award just under $990 thousand, after collateral offsets of just under $600 thousand.

- A single business official, age forty-two with no dependents and a base compensation of $120 thousand, received a net award of $954 thousand after collateral offsets of $300 thousand.

- A single professional, age forty-three, with no dependents and a base salary of $94 thousand, received an award close to $1.2 million after collateral offsets of $50 thousand.

- A married laborer, age forty-seven, with three dependents and a base compensation of $58 thousand, received an award of just over $1 million after collateral offsets of $299 thousand.

- A married civilian working at the Pentagon, age fifty-four, with no dependents and a base compensation of $116 thousand, received an award of $686 thousand after collateral offsets of $509 thousand.

- A single civilian employee working on building maintenance and recycling, age twenty-four and a base compensation of $32 thousand, received a net award of $1.2 million (including value of caring for a seriously ill parent) after collateral offsets.

- A married project manager, age thirty-six, with one dependent and a base salary of $231 thousand, received a net award of almost $3.5 million after $940 thousand in collateral offsets.

Explanation of Economic Loss Calculation for Military Victims

Growth Rates (Table 3), Decedent's Personal Expenditures or Consumption as Percent of Income (Table 4), and Assumed Before-tax and After-tax Discount Rates (Table 5).

ILLUSTRATION

September 11th Victim Compensation Fund of 2001
Illustration of Presumed Economic and Non-Economic Loss Calculation -- Military Claimant

Assumptions

Victim Name:		Representative Military
Date of Death:		09/11/01
Age:		33
Marital Status:		M
Children's Ages at 09/11/01:	Child #1	Age 9
	Child #2	Newborn
Employer:		U.S. Military E-7
Total Annual Compensation Including BAH, BAS and Tax Advantage at 9/11/2001:		$54,210
Military Basic Pay as of 9/11/2001:		$31,057
Years in Military Service as of 9/11/2001:		15

Total Economic Losses Before Collateral Offsets

Loss of Earnings & Benefits Including Loss of Lifetime Military Pension Benefits From Continued Military Service After 09/11/01 — **$1,787,580**

Total Non-Economic Losses — **$550,000**

Total Economic and Non-Economic Losses Before Known Collateral Offsets — **$2,337,580**

Less:

Known Offsets:

Past and Present Value Future Children's Social Security Benefits	$214,175
Past Spouse's DIC Benefits	$13,024
Past and Present Value Future Children's DIC Benefits	$62,394
Death Gratuity	$6,000
Service Members Group Life Insurance	$250,000
Total Known Offsets	**$545,593**

Amount of Award — **$1,791,987**

132

Explanation of Economic Loss Calculations for FDNY or NYPD Victims

ILLUSTRATION

September 11th Victim Compensation Fund of 2001
Illustration of Presumed Economic and Non-Economic Loss Calculation -- FDNY Claimant

Assumptions

Victim Name:		FDNY Claimant
Date of Death:		09/11/01
Age:		30.0
Marital Status:		M
Number Children Under Age 18:		2
Children's Ages at 09/11/01:	Child #1	Age 9
	Child #2	Newborn
Primary Employer:		FDNY
Total Annual Earnings From All Employers:		$80,000
FDNY Annual Earnings:		$75,000
Years in FDNY as of 09/11/01:		6.0
Assumed Start Date of FDNY Pension:		10/01/20

Total Economic Losses Before Collateral Offsets:

Loss of Earnings & Benefits Including Loss of Lifetime FDNY Pension Benefits From Continued FDNY Service After 09/11/01*	$2,712,391
Total Non-Economic Losses	$550,000

Total Economic and Non-Economic Losses Before Known Collateral Offsets	$3,262,391

* Includes the excess of the victim's "vested pension" over the value of the survivor pension, if any, assuming FDNY survivor annuity is elected instead of lump sum.

Less:

Known Offsets:

Present Value of FDNY Survivor Annuity Pension Benefit Reduced by Present Value of Victim's FDNY Vested Pension as of 09/11/01:

FDNY Survivor Benefits	$1,354,813	
Less: Victim's Vested Benefit	($89,395)	$1,265,418
Present Value of Estimated Children's Social Security Benefits		$359,350
FDNY Group Life Insurance		$8,500
Mayor's Office Benefit (one year's pay)		$75,000
Contractual Benefit		$25,000
Total Known Offsets		$1,733,268

Amount of Award	$1,529,123

133

Explanation of Economic Loss Calculations for Port Authority Fire and Police Victims

ILLUSTRATION

September 11th Victim Compensation Fund of 2001
Illustration of Presumed Losses for Port Authority Fire or Police

Assumptions

Victim Name:	Port Authority Fire or Police
Date of Death:	9/11/01
Age:	30
Marital Status:	M
Number Children Under Age 18:	2
Children's Ages at 09/11/2001: Child #1	9
Child #2	newborn
Occupation:	Police
Employer:	Port Authority
Total Annual Earnings From All Employers:	$70,000
Fire or Police Annual Earnings:	$70,000
Hire Date at Last Employer:	9/11/95
Years of Creditable Fire or Police Service at 09/11/2001	6.0
Assumed Start of New York State or Local Fire or Police Pension:	10/1/20

Total Economic Losses Before Collateral Offsets

Loss of Earnings & Benefits Including Loss of Lifetime Port Authority Pension Benefits From Continued Port Authority Service After 09/11/2001*	$2,454,281
Total Non-Economic Losses	**$550,000**

Total Losses Before Collateral Offsets	**$3,004,281**

* Includes amount of pension projected at ultimate retirement less amount of vested benefit prepaid in the form of survivor benefits.

Less:
Known Offsets:

Present Value of Survivor Lump Sum Pension Benefit Reduced by Present Value of Victim's Vested Pension as of 09/11/2001:		
Past Survivor Benefits	$68,036	
Present Value Future Survivor Benefits	$1,263,387	
Less: Victim's Vested Benefit	($40,718)	$1,290,705
Social Security One-time Lump Sum Death Benefit		$255
Past Social Security Survivor Benefits	Spouse	$0
	Children	$52,356
Present Value of Children's Future Social Security Survivor Benefits		$317,386
Basic Life Insurance (3 times pay)		$210,000
Total Known Offsets		**$1,870,702**

Amount of Total Award	**$1,133,579**

134

BANK-OWNED LIFE INSURANCE

Permanent life insurance is perhaps the most underutilized and least understood financial product in America today. Unfortunately, knowledge of this product is minimal. Even many employees in the home offices where the life insurance is manufactured do not fully comprehend the strengths and economic benefits of permanent life insurance.

However, one segment of the nation's economy completely understands the economic value of high cash value permanent life insurance as a golden asset. This section of the economy is arguably the strongest and most potent force in the entire economy. This section controls everything— how much you pay for your car, how much you pay for a mortgage, how much you pay in usury credit cards—it is the nation's banks, particularly large money center commercial banks.

Banks buy permanent life insurance by the tractor-trailer loads. Banks own so much that the cash values on their balance sheets actually make them look like life insurance companies unto themselves. Most people, perhaps the vast majority of the population, are unaware that the banks with whom they do business, own such great amounts of permanent life insurance. Many life insurance professionals are unaware of this, too, and banks are reluctant to talk about their mammoth purchases. It is a relatively new phenomenon in the banking industry, which developed over the past twenty years or so.

Five of the six largest banks in the world—Citigroup, JPMorgan Chase, HSBC Holdings, Bank of America, and the Royal Bank of Scotland (through its Citizens Banks)—own significant amounts of high cash value permanent life insurance. Other large U. S. banks with high ownership rates include Wells Fargo, TD BankNorth, Sovereign, Bank of New York, Washington Mutual, Wachovia, Key Bank, LaSalle, US Bank, PNC Bank, AmSouth, Branch Banking & Trust, Mellon, Fifth Third Bank, Harris National, Bank of the West, SunTrust, Charter One, and Marshall & Ilsley among thousands more.

Banks buy high cash value life insurance for a variety of reasons, including funding bank executive and director supplemental pensions, healthcare costs and other employee benefits; to improve the income statement; to enjoy tax benefits, and to strengthen the financial stability of the bank. Due to their level of purchases, it is now known as bank-owned life insurance or BOLI. There are several other scenarios where life insurance is purchased in massive quantities, including corporate-owned life insurance (COLI) and trust-owned life insurance (TOLI), which are discussed in other chapters of this book.

Banks purchase regular payment high cash value life insurance, but more often purchase very high cash value policies, known as single-premium life insurance, which can be paid with a single premium. Management of the cash within the policy is generally handled by investment professionals with insurance companies or alternatively can be done by outside investment managers. This is known as *variable, separate account,* or *private placement* life insurance.

Bankers have wholeheartedly embraced high cash value life insurance as a safe economic power tool and have found the product to be healthy for the bottom line. Generally, banks today purchase permanent life insurance on the top 35 percent of their employees ranked by compensation.[66] From all indications, purchases of permanent high cash value life insurance polices are very much on the upswing in the banking industry. In confirmation of this trend, one advisor with whom the author spoke discussed having a game of golf one day with the CEO of a Midwestern bank. The CEO confessed to the advisor that the bank-owned life insurance was the bank's best performing asset. The CEO went on to tell the advisor that he liked BOLI so much, he ordered his people to purchase the maximum amount that the laws and regulators would allow.

The life insurance companies who manufacture the life insurance products for banks and other corporate institutions do not openly promote or publicize their offerings. Some life insurance companies that are active in the BOLI marketplace include New York Life, Mass Mutual, MetLife, Nationwide, John Hancock/Manulife, Mutual of New York (MONY), The Hartford, AIG, Pacific Life, Security Life of Denver, CIGNA, and Northwestern Mutual. In a press release, Northwestern, an otherwise quiet company, reported a record year in 2004 for the amount of single premium bank-owned life insurance premiums that it sold in that year.

Midland National Life claims to be one of the first life companies to write bank-owned life insurance policies in 1982. Today Midland, on its Web site, claims to have more than 1,000 commercial BOLI customers.

Sun Life of Canada and Munich America Reassurance Company, two large life insurance reinsurance companies who insure and share the risk with the life companies, are very active in reinsuring BOLI and COLI business as the underwriting of this type of life insurance requires high reserves.

Why do Banks Purchase so much Permanent Life Insurance?

Let's face it; banks are in the *money* business. Banks have immense resources. They have legions of economists, analysts, attorneys, and

---

[66] Tom Wamberg, CLU, *Separate Account Bank-Owned Life Insurance* (The American College Press, 2006). Today banks limit their purchases of life insurance to the top 35 percent of the workforce based on compensation. In the past, banks and other corporations would sometimes purchase life insurance on their entire workforce.

136

accountants to help each bank *maximize the efficiency and economic output* on its money. These professionals must make sure that the money within a bank is working *as hard as it can* with the *maximum amount of safety*. Banks would not purchase billions of life insurance lightly. It would be foolish to think otherwise. Banks buy a great deal of life insurance because it provides immeasurable economic benefits, financial stability, and safety—which is superior to the banks themselves.

The Numbers Do the Talking

According to the Federal Deposit Insurance Corporation and research this author performed in 2005, 2006, and 2007, at least 4,082 of the nation's commercial and savings banks owned bank-owned life insurance (BOLI) in 2006, whereas only 3,474 banks owned BOLI in 2004. As of December 31, 2006, the aggregate cash surrender value in these policies was an astounding $106.825 billion whereas at the end of 2004, aggregate cash surrender value was only $65.8 billion.

In twenty-four months, banks have increased their cash value life insurance holdings by $41.02 billion, or a 62 percent increase over 2004. Moreover, according to a report published by the General Accounting Office (GAO) of the United States in 2004, approximately 88 percent of the cash surrender value BOLI was owned and concentrated in about 259 banks and thrifts, which had one billion or more in assets. The remaining 12 percent of cash surrender value was spread among the remaining 3,100 banks.

As mentioned previously, a primary reason why banks, as well as other corporations, buy high cash value permanent life insurance is to fund executive and director supplemental executive retirement plans commonly known as SERPs or deferred compensation plans. In funding executive pensions, high cash value permanent life insurance is a smart purchase and the ideal funding mechanism as it gives banks and other corporations a method of *cost recovery*. What is meant by cost recovery is that at the death of a retired executive, the residual death benefit comes into the bank income tax-free and the bank recaptures much of the money it set aside to pay for the executive pension.

Another major reason why banks purchase permanent life insurance is to fund future health and welfare benefits such as retiree health plans. One of the nation's largest banks, Wachovia of Charlotte, North Carolina, requested consent from all of its officer level employees in January of 2005[67] to increase its corporate life insurance funding to help fund employee benefit cost. According to figures from the FDIC, Wachovia's aggregate cash surrender

---

[67] Rick Rothbacker, "Wachovia Looks to Life Insurance on Workers to Defray Costs," *The Charlotte News Observer*, January 27, 2005.

value increased $512 million between December 31, 2005 and March 31, 2006. Between March 31, 2006, and December 31, 2006, Wachovia's cash value on its life insurance increased an astounding $2.274 billion, which means in one year, Wachovia added $2.786 billion in permanent life insurance cash surrender values! Citibank increased its permanent life insurance benefits as well from March 31, 2006, to December 31, 2006. Citibank and its Banamex subsidiary added more than $1 billion in values in nine months. During the same period, Washington Mutual increased its permanent life insurance holdings over $929 million and Sovereign Bank increased its holdings over $694 million.

Bank-owned life insurance also has the ability to boost a bank's income statement in a low interest rate environment. BOLI improves the overall profits of the bank and can even improve the share price of stock.

Tier One Capital: The Core Capital of a Bank

A very important point to understand is how the cash surrender value of BOLI is classified on the bank's balance sheet. Unlike traditional retirement plan benefits, which are segregated in separate trust accounts (e.g. pensions and 401(k) plans), the cash surrender values of BOLI are classified as a general asset of the bank and an integral component of *Tier One capital*, the *most important* component of any bank.

Tier One capital is at the very core capital of all banks. It is a bank's bedrock, its foundation and structural steel. The following is an explanation of Tier One capital: If the original stockholders of a bank contributed $100 to buy their stock, and each year for ten years, a bank made $10 in profits, paid out nothing in dividends, and incurred no losses, then the Tier One capital of the bank would be $200—which is equal to common stock and retained earnings.

The larger the Tier One capital, the stronger the bank. A primary purpose of this capital is to cushion the bank in times of adversity and to support other balance sheet assets. A strong Tier One is what all banks strive for, since this asset determines how much money they can lend to the public. This is a bank's lifeblood.

As one would imagine, Tier One is comprised of very safe assets[68] such as cash, gold bullion, loans guaranteed by the federal government, and

---

[68] Tier One Capital is given various risk weightings by bank regulators by asset class, with "0" risk weight being the strongest and safest: 0 percent risk weight—cash, gold bullion, loans guaranteed by the federal government; 20 percent risk weight—demand deposits, banker's acceptances and letters of credit, short term notes, bank-owned life insurance; 50 percent risk weight—residential mortgages, mortgage backed securities, municipal revenue bonds; and 100 percent risk weight—cross-border loans, commercial loans, derivative mortgage backed securities, industrial revenue bonds, intangibles and goodwill.

balances due from Federal Reserve Banks. (Equity stocks are not allowed in Tier One capital, as they can be quite volatile.). Separate account BOLI, according to the Office of Thrift Supervision in a letter dated December 14, 2004, titled, "Interagency Statement on the Purchase and Risk Management of Life Insurance," has given a 20 percent weighting in regard to a bank's *risk-based capital*. This means that BOLI is considered a strong financial asset on par with banker's acceptances and letters of credit, demand deposits, checks in the process of being collected, and short-term claims maturing in one year or less.

Much of the BOLI banks purchase for their Tier One accounts is single premium life contracts, which are often written on a guaranteed issue basis. These BOLI policies are usually modified endowments, but because these contracts will be held until the death of the insured, benefits will be income tax-free. The cash within these policies is generally backed by the general account of the life insurance company or alternatively invested in stable separate accounts backed by mortgage-backed securities or other conservative investments.

The Officer of the Comptroller of the Currency (OCC) does detail allowable uses for BOLI, such as key person insurance, insurance on borrowers, compensation, and benefits and for security on loans. More recently, the OCC has issued Bulletin #2000-23, which explains guidelines for the use of BOLI. Letter #848 specifically addresses BOLI as a funding medium for deferred compensation. FDIC statistics will verify how much banks hold in life insurance.

Bank Owned Life Insurance: Twenty-Five Percent or More of Tier One Capital

As we have just learned, Tier One capital is a critical and fundamental component of a bank and perhaps its most important asset. In 2004, the General Accounting Office (GAO) found that, on average,[69] for the banks that owned BOLI, the cash surrender value of life insurance generally accounted for up to 25 percent of the total Tier One capital.

The GAO also found that in over 58 institutions, the cash surrender value accounted for more than 40 percent of their Tier One capital. Over 467 institutions reported more than 25 percent of Tier One invested in BOLI![70]

---

[69] United States Government, "Business-Owned Life Insurance. More Data Can Be Useful in Making Tax Policy Decisions," GAO, released May 2004.
[70] Ibid.

To give you an idea how important permanent life insurance is to the Tier One capital of the bank, here are the statistics of some banks' overall Tier One core capital, the dollar amount of BOLI (bank-owned life insurance) located in their Tier One accounts, and the percentage of Tier One that is BOLI. Figures are as of December 31, 2006.

Institution	Total Tier One Capital Assets/$Billions	Total BOLI Assets/$Billions	BOLI as a Percentage of Tier One of the bank
Bank of America	$95.348	$14.402	15%
Wachovia	$32.919	$12.874	39%
JPMorgan Chase	$68.726	$7.874	10%
Washington Mutual	$21.081	$4.285	20%
Wells Fargo	$29.191	$3.693	12%
Citibank	$59.860	$3.281	5.4%
U.S. Bank, NA	$12.359	$3.241	26%
Keybank, NA	$6.809	$2.602	38%
Branch Banking	$8.075	$2.381	29%
Bank of New York	$5.474	$1.721	31%
Sovereign Bank	$5.023	$1.717	34%
PNC Bank	$6.159	$1.617	26%
National City	$8.382	$1.565	18%
Regions Bank	$11.095	$1.253	11%
Harris National	$3.297	$1.155	35%
Huntington Nat'l	$1.989	$1.115	56%
M & T Bank	$3.355	$1.074	32%
Bank of the West	$4.551	$1.046	23%
LaSalle-Chicago	$6.542	$.985	15%
LaSalle-Troy, MI	$3.803	$.660	17%
Fifth Third-Cincin.	$5.300	$.906	17%
Fifth Third-GR	$5.341	$1.402	19%
TD BankNorth	$2.433	$.791	32%
Comerica	$5.649	$.854	15%
Mellon	$2.103	$.772	36%
Marshall& Ilsley	$3.192	$.730	23%
First Tennessee, NA	$2.489	$.576	23%
SunTrust	$12.856	$.564	4%
RBC Centura Bank	$1.889	$.547	28%

NY Comm. Bank	$1.735	$.525	30%
Compass Bank	$2.350	$.474	20%
Colonial Bank	$1.536	$.473	31%
North Fork Bank	$3.886	$.434	11%
Associated Bank-WI	$1.457	$.411	28%
Astoria-NY	$1.415	$.385	27%

What Are We to Learn from This?

The nation's banks as a group are arguably the strongest and most influential economic power in the United States, as they ultimately control the entire nation's money supply. They have chosen, with precision and scientific analysis, to invest a very large percentage of the bank's assets and critical reserves prudently into permanent life insurance, treasury bills, cash, and other high-quality liquid assets such as gold bullion. Banks are not investing in mutual funds, speculative stocks, or high-flying real estate deals.

Here are some of the main reasons why some of America's largest banks and corporations are investing in permanent high cash value life insurance:

Reason One. Banks, at the end of the day, are highly transactional in nature and do poorly in managing conservative investments for the long haul. If you have any doubts, remember the Savings and Loan crisis, the bailout of Continental Illinois, or the rescue of the Mexican peso. If you are still not convinced about banks' expertise in managing money conservatively and safely, remember the Crash of 1929 or the current sub prime mortgage meltdown.

Whether it is general account backed or conservatively managed separate account life insurance, the rates of return for a life insurance company will generally be two to three hundred basis points (2 to 3 percent) above the yield of a ten-year US treasury bill. For banks, life insurance acts like an extremely safe municipal bond with a tax-free death benefit thrown in. Banks, in the final analysis, only provide financing with money they create, and are generally not involved in the day-to-day operations of the people to whom it lends money. Much of the loans banks originate today are packaged, securitized, and sold off to investors. Life insurance companies, on the other hand, are generally more active participants in the substantial investments and loans they make. They have much longer time horizons of five, ten, and fifteen years out. As fiduciaries, life insurance companies are contractually bound to look out for policyholder interests for a long period.

Furthermore, due to state regulations and regulators (one could argue that state regulators are superior to federal regulators in light of the mutual

141

fund scandals and so on), life insurance companies are required to keep very structured, conservative and regulated investment portfolios. A typical life insurance company portfolio may have bonds with durations of six-and-a-half years. The credit rating of the bonds may be A+. Investment grade bonds may compromise about 80 percent of the portfolio. Another 12 percent may be in mortgage loans, 3 to 4 percent in non-investment grade bonds, 3 to 4 percent in policy loans, and less than 1 percent in equities. These portfolios are known as the *general account* of a life insurance company.

The track record of life insurance companies in conservative investment management over the long haul is exemplary[71]. To reduce investment risk, investments within the general account portfolio are diversified by industry, geography, and duration. As a result of life insurance companies' expertise in conservative long-term investing, consumers can often get a better long-term savings rate with an annuity offered by a life insurance company than they can with a bank savings account.

Reason Two. Tax benefits are crucial in all of our financial decisions, whether it is personal or business. Bankers are very smart people. There is no annual taxation of capital gains or cash value increases in life insurance, whereas most company- or bank-owned taxable investments are subject to interest, dividends, and capital gains tax. Although corporate dividends are now taxable at a lower rate, they are still taxable. Since dividends are technically part of the return of premium from life insurance companies, they are *not taxable* under the Internal Revenue Code.

Reason Three. Life insurance provides a minimum guaranteed death benefit to the bank or corporation whereas taxable investments do not. The death benefit provides funding for a bank to finance supplemental survivor benefits.

Reason Four. Life insurance benefits come into the bank or corporation income tax-free. Inevitably, there is a net gain to the bank at death on an insured employee or executive. This is not subject to income taxes. In reviewing the financial statements of various banks, there were several documented instances whereby the bank reported significantly improved quarterly earnings when it received the proceeds of key person bank-owned life insurance. For example, in March 2004, Cornerstone Bank of Stamford, Connecticut, reported non-taxable proceeds from a key man executive life insurance policy of $342 thousand—greatly improving its income in the first quarter of that year.

Reason Five. Unrealized gains or losses cannot be recorded on taxable investments, but *banks can recognize the increase in cash surrender value as a credit to earnings*. In this way, banks and other corporations can

---

[71] During the Great Depression, cash savings within legal reserve life insurance companies remained 99.9 percent safe. Conversely, during this period, over ten thousand banks failed.

improve their income statement between 1 to 2.5 percent. For instance, in 2002, The Bank of America, reported $570 million in additional revenue and $170 million in net profits to the bank by using bank-owned life insurance.

A 1 or 2 percent increase in earnings may not sound like much, but it is extremely significant in the eyes of Wall Street. Wachovia, for instance, says BOLI contributes about 3 percent to earnings whereas Branch Banking and Trust Company in Winston-Salem, North Carolina says BOLI contributes 1 percent to earnings.

Reason Six. In periods of low interest rates, *banks have cheap access to money* through their central bank, the Federal Reserve System. They can borrow at bargain basement rates with the Fed, invest it in life insurance, and not only gain all of the above benefits, but also make money on the spread.

Reason Seven. Investing in permanent life insurance, particularly when banks make mammoth purchases, *offers banks professional money management options.* Purchasing life insurance based upon the investment return of the general account of a life insurance company is the safest and most prudent course of action for consumers. However, through their purchasing clout and financial sophistication, banks can negotiate more pass-through income to their bottom line.

Reason Eight. Life insurance companies lend money out to third parties in a similar manner to banks. However, unlike banks that inflate their money supply to the public through fractional reserve banking; life insurance companies do not have this ability. This makes the life insurance company inherently stronger than a bank, as it has less exposure than an overleveraged bank.

Uncovering the Amount of Life Insurance that Banks Own

Finding out how much each bank holds in bank-owned life insurance was not an easy task initially. Newspaper accounts conflicted with data compiled by the Federal Deposit Insurance Corporation. Proxy statements filed with the SEC were difficult to decipher. Sources within the life insurance industry did not want to discuss the topic with the author. It was a couple of years of trial and error. The author felt like the Detective Colombo out of the 1970s television series. An analyst from the FDIC did divulge that although banks may own BOLI, they do not always account for it properly. The author agrees wholeheartedly.

Not until August 2006, did the author obtain information in regards to BOLI owned by JPMorgan Chase, Citibank, Wells Fargo, Bank of New York, Sun Trust, and FIA Card Services (the old MBNA credit card company now owned by Bank of America). Therefore, even though a bank may own cash value life insurance, it does not necessarily show up on the official report of the Federal Deposit Insurance Corporation.

Most often life insurance surrender cash surrender values are classified as "other assets" on a banks balance sheet. Getting banks to pinpoint the types of policies they own, the death benefits they will ultimately receive is difficult, as they call it "immaterial." Specifics of actual policies do not have to be reported or disclosed. The term "immaterial" means that the content of the information is essentially not meaningful or material enough to affect an investor's decision as to whether or not they should invest in the bank's stock. However, according to this author's research, it is safe to say that around 90 to 95 percent of large money center banks have made a significant financial investment in BOLI.

While banks may make it difficult to find the exact nature of the policies purchased and the resultant death benefits to be paid, cash surrender values, which are as liquid as any financial instrument can be, are often accounted for properly by the FDIC. (Generally, death benefit is four to five times surrender cash values for single-premium life and twenty-five times for regular payment life.)

The following numbers should be an eye opener and erase all doubts about the beauty of high cash value life insurance as a quality asset. Banks do not do anything, which is not in their best economic interest. The irony is, and we shall see later in the chapter "Life Insurance is Something Good for the Consumer," cash value permanent life insurance will do more for the consumer than it will for the banks or corporations.

This author also noticed something, which the FDIC did not notice. As banks consolidate in this Wild West era of deregulation, their consolidated aggregate cash values grow exponentially. For instance, Citizens Bank (which is owned by the Royal Bank of Scotland) with the acquisition of Charter One, will have aggregate BOLI cash values of $1.759 billion. National City, when you add all of their divisions, adds up to $1.346 billion in aggregate BOLI cash surrender value. When you add Fifth Third Bank of Grand Rapids and Cincinnati together, their aggregate values are $1.865 billion. Lastly, LaSalle Banks (Troy, Michigan and Chicago, Illinois that are now owned by ABN Ambro) together command a healthy $1.571 billion in cash surrender value. All values are approximate as of March 31, 2006.

Many Banks Own More in the Cash Surrender Value of Their Life Insurance than They Do in Their Entire Defined Benefit Pension Plan

Once in awhile you get assistance from other powers. In researching this book, this author reached out to various experts to verify information, as data relating to BOLI is scarce. In researching the actual rates of return, which corporations and financial institutions make on their defined benefit pension plans, the author ran into William Strauss, the president of FutureMetrics of Bethel, Maine (www.futuremetrics.com) Bill is an economist. His firm does advanced economic modeling, forecasting, and simulation. Among other things, Bill's firm each year pulls together a survey such as its *2006 Annual Pension Plan Best and Worst Investment Performance Report.*

FutureMetrics collects data on pension plans by reviewing annual reports and various financial statements of public corporations on file with the SEC, the Department of Labor, the Pension Benefit Guaranty Corporation, and other government agencies. From this information, FutureMetrics extracts the total pension obligations, market value of entire defined benefit portfolio, asset-to-liability ratios, one- and five-year composite rates of return, and so on. FutureMetrics' numbers must be considered *estimates*, as pension plans are somewhat of a moving target, given that plans have different fiscal years and different funding levels and a wave of retirees could theoretically drain a significant amount of assets from the pension plan.

Regardless of whether or not FutureMetrics numbers are estimates, they are probably more reliable than anything the government has. In analyzing some of the raw data put together by FutureMetrics, something struck the author as very odd. Many large banks owned and had more equity in their bank-owned life insurance programs than they had in their entire defined benefit pension plans covering all of their employees! Although not all the banks were in this situation, some of the following very large banks were.

Institution	US Market Value Of Defined Benefit Assets/ $Millions 12/31/2005 *(Separate Trust Accounts)*	Bank Owned Life Insurance Assets/$Millions 03/31/2006 *(Balance Sheet/Tier One)*
Amsouth Bancorporation	$855.629	$1,166.00
Bank of New York	$1,333.000	$1,679.00
Branch Banking & Trust Company	$1,029.000	$2,147.00
Fifth Third Bancorp	$238.000	$1,886.24
Huntington Bancshares	$440.787	$1,085.00

KeyCorp	$1,096.000	$2,534.00
US Bancorp	$2,419.000	$2,950.00
Wachovia	$5,378.000	$10,600.00
Bank of America (including MBNA)	$13,097.000	$14,123.00
Associated Banc Corp	$100.660	$399.783
BancWest Corp	$438.662	$1,008.00
Bank of Hawaii	$59.924	$151.859
Compass Bancshares	$178.903	$459.833
FirstMerit Corp	$133.050	$274.539
M&T Bank Corp	$452.271	$1,044.00
Zions Bancorporaton	$124.888	$193.300
Washington Mutual	$1,621.00	$3,356.00
Sovereign Bank	$82.000	$1,023.00
TD BankNorth	$304.00	$767.04

Another downside—FutureMetrics only tracks pensions for about one hundred large financial institutions. Bank pensions have become increasingly difficult to track because of all the mergers and acquisitions in the past decade. Many other banks owned significant amounts of BOLI; however, the plans did not exceed the total assets of the banks' defined benefit pension plans.

Deregulation of Banks in Financial Planning and Life Insurance

Although banks purchase huge amounts of life insurance for their own accounts, you have to question their sincerity to sell it properly and do a good job in financial planning for their clients in this newly deregulated environment. As you can see in the chapter, "Never Met a Man Who Made His Millions in Mutual Funds," banks and their broker–dealer subsidiaries were waist deep in the mutual fund scandals.

Through deregulation, banks are actively engaged in the financial planning business. They have incredible advantage over other financial intermediaries, as they have carte blanche access to a client's savings and checking accounts and so on: and this advantage can be easily abused. This abuse became apparent when Fleet Bank and Nation's mutual funds solicited the author's elderly mother, who is now deceased, several times. This family of funds, which is now owned by Bank of America, subsequently became involved in one of the largest market timing, late trading mutual fund scandals.

In another situation, the author filed a formal complaint against another major bank in regards to the bank's *twisting of life insurance* on a client. Twisting is essentially selling a consumer a new life insurance product, which is not in the consumer's best interest but generates a new commission for the person selling it. In this case, it was a bank. One regulator called the author back and essentially agreed that the bank financial planning department was taking advantage of an unsophisticated client. Some regulators were actually worried about this type of unprofessional behavior in the newly deregulated banking environment.

However, the client could not do anything because he had not filed a complaint against the bank. In addition, the regulator, who also happened to be an attorney, did not even have a full-time assistant to oversee bank financial planning sales. He was in many ways, the entire police force for the entire state.

The author was overwhelmed by the aggressive solicitation in the financial planning area in one bank where he maintained several checking accounts. In opening an additional checking account, the author was told he would have to go to the financial planning desk. This author told the financial planner at the bank that all he wanted was an additional checking account for another entity.

The bank's planner, when she found out the author was a business owner, started to probe the author aggressively about the need for other financial products. The author told the planner that he was not interested in any financial products and had been working in employee benefits, financial planning, advisement, and consulting for more than twenty years. However,

147

the planner at the bank ignored the author's comments and, with decided persistence, solicited the author for term life insurance, investments, a SEP retirement plan, and long-term care insurance.

The checking account ended up a disaster. The planner set the author up on a $50 a month minimum fee checking account, which he had explained was only going to be used for writing two or three checks a month. The author had to go back later to get the fee reduced. The bank manager, whom the author had known for more than fifteen years from another bank and another business venture, apologized profusely and was upset and embarrassed that the financial planning division of the bank could make such a mistake—the wonders of bank deregulation.

In March of 2006, a Portland, Maine, superior court found Bank of America—the Higher Standards Bank—guilty of professional negligence and mismanaging an entrepreneur's $27 million dollar nest egg. A unanimous verdict of nine jurors awarded Darrell Mayeux $7.4 million for the bank's failure to provide financial advice and the protection it had promised.[72] This same bank has paid over $610 million in fines for market timing and late trading of mutual funds with various hedge funds.

In the case of Citizens Bank, they simply give the consumer erroneous advice. In a brochure distributed by Citizens Bank Investment Services (#003-012805Mktg-CIS R-0162 02/05) in 2005, it stated customers should consider life insurance to pay estate taxes if they are single with estates approaching $700 thousand; if they are single with $1.4 million or more; or if they are married. This is false and misleading information given. The "Economic Growth and Tax Relief Reconciliation Act of 2005" exemption amount for single people was $1.5 million in 2005, and for married couples it was $3 million. In 2006 through 2008, the exemption amount for singles is $2 million and for married couples, $4 million.

Citizens Bank has also been in trouble for selling unsuitable financial products to senior citizens. In July of 2005, William F. Galvin, Secretary of the Commonwealth of Massachusetts, fined Citizens Bank $3 million for unethical and dishonest conduct in pushing the sale of variable annuities to elderly bank customers and failing to maintain internal emails. The complaint against Citizens arose when unlicensed tellers at the bank earned compensation by referring depositors, particularly those with maturing certificate of deposits, to stockbrokers. Galvin, in a press release, said, "The company pressured elderly bank customers into buying variable annuities without regard for the appropriateness of such an investment."

Citizens Bank affiliate CCO was also fined $850,000 by the NASD in October 2006, for failing to establish, maintain, and enforce a reasonably

---

[72] Gregory D. Kesich, "Jury Awards $7.4 Million to Bank Client," *Portland Press Herald,* March 21, 2006.

designed supervisory system and written procedures including customer suitability reviews, telemarketing compliance, review of written correspondence, registration of offices, and review and approval of 529 plan business.

What is far more troubling is the mixed message that Citigroup gives to consumers in regards to the purchase of life insurance. You would think that Citigroup, with the way it misled an entire public with Enron and the WorldCom stock disasters, would be consistent with consumers in its communications concerning the financial products it sells to the public, *but it is not*. If one visits the Primerica Web site, www.primerica.com, which is a wholly owned Citigroup company, it states on its information page under "Two Kinds of Insurance" the following:

> *"At Primerica, we sell 100 percent term insurance, 100 percent of the time because we believe it's the best choice for most families. Contact a representative near you for more information on our life insurance products and our "Buy Term and Invest the Difference" philosophy. Check your local yellow pages for listing."*

On the Smith Barney Web site, www.smithbarney.com, another Citigroup subsidiary, it says this about the purchase of life insurance:

> **Life insurance-** *The appropriate life insurance policy can help preserve the assets that you spend years accumulating. Life insurance can be used in many different ways for different purposes. It not only is for your beneficiaries, but can also be used as an investment vehicle during your lifetime. It can be structured to provide tax-deferred growth and a tax-free death benefit.*

It is obvious that Smith Barney, which serves a more affluent clientele than Primerica, understands that *buy term and invest the difference philosophy does not work.* Citigroup, which is the largest bank and financial institution in the world, obviously knows the value and strength of permanent life insurance particularly as it relates to its balance sheet. As of December 31, 2006, Citibank reported $3.281 billion in cash surrender value for its BOLI Tier One account.

Lastly, there is the case of Chase Insurance Direct, which is part of JPMorgan Chase, one of the new super banks brought to you through deregulation. JPMorgan Chase acts a lot like Citigroup. Chase Direct, in its solicitation offer to this author, says this.

"Dear Barry J. Dyke

If you were to buy additional life insurance to protect your family, your current insurance company would want you to buy it from them. So they certainly wouldn't want you to know how easy it is to get more coverage at a lower price from someone else."

Later in the letter, Chase says:

*"Chase Insurance Direct offers a choice of 10, 15, 20 or 30-year plans ranging from $100,000 to $5,000,000. We can help you choose the **term** that best suits your situation. Only pay the amount you need. No matter which policy you choose, your rates are locked in for the initial term of your policy. Discover how you may get more coverage for less money."*

In the solicitation, it looks as if the only way to go is to purchase Chase term life insurance. However, upon visiting the company's web site, the author quickly found out that it also recommends whole life. So what is the deal?

One of the JPMorgan Chase subsidiary companies offers non-qualified retirement, split-dollar life, bonus, and supplemental employee retirement plans. All of these plans are funded with cash value permanent life insurance. Then there is the final litmus test. JPMorgan Chase Bank, like Citibank, does not buy term life insurance for its own account. Instead, as of December 31, 2006, JPMorgan Chase had $7.181 billion in cash surrender value BOLI for its own Tier One account. This amount of BOLI makes JPMorgan Chase one of the largest owners of permanent life insurance in the world. Once again, what banks recommend to the public and what they do for themselves are two different things—ah, the wonders of bank deregulation.

Regardless, in the four pages that follow, you will see how much permanent life insurance banks own under the column BOLI starting with Bank of America at $13.883 billion. With the BOA acquisition of MBNA-FIA Card Services (which owns about $519 million in cash value BOLI), Bank of America total cash surrender value in life insurance approaches $14.4 billion. Bank of America, according to the most recent reports and experts, is now the world's most profitable bank.

Ultimate death benefits to the banks are probably in the range of anywhere from four to five times the cash surrender value.

Cert	Name	City	State	Zip	BOLI
3510	Bank of America, National Association	Charlotte	NC	28255	13,883,173
33869	Wachovia Bank, National Association	Charlotte	NC	28288	12,874,000
628	JPMorgan Chase Bank, National Association	Columbus	OH	43240	7,181,000
32633	Washington Mutual Bank	Henderson	NV	89014	4,285,247
3511	Wells Fargo Bank, National Association	Sioux Falls	SD	57104	3,693,000
7213	Citibank, National Association	Las Vegas	NV	89109	3,281,000
6548	U.S. Bank National Association	Cincinnati	OH	45202	3,241,119
17534	Keybank National Association	Cleveland	OH	44114	2,602,193
9846	Branch Banking and Trust Company	Winston Salem	NC	27104	2,381,077
639	The Bank of New York	New York City	NY	10286	1,721,000
29950	Sovereign Bank	Wyomissing	PA	19610	1,717,999
6384	PNC Bank, National Association	Pittsburgh	PA	15222	1,617,688
6557	National City Bank	Cleveland	OH	44114	1,565,441
12368	Regions Bank	Birmingham	AL	35203	1,253,146
16571	Harris National Association	Chicago	IL	60603	1,155,926
6560	The Huntington National Bank	Columbus	OH	43216	1,115,130
588	Manufacturers and Traders Trust Company	Buffalo	NY	14203	1,074,533
3514	Bank of the West	San Francisco	CA	94104	1,046,847
993	Fifth Third Bank	Grand Rapids	MI	49503	1,042,235
15407	LaSalle Bank National Association	Chicago	IL	60603	985,278
6672	Fifth Third Bank	Cincinnati	OH	45263	906,289
983	Comerica Bank	Detroit	MI	48226	854,311
18409	TD BankNorth, National Association	Portland	ME	04112	791,489
7946	Mellon Bank, National Association	Pittsburgh	PA	15219	772,273
1020	M&I Marshall and Ilsley Bank	Milwaukee	WI	53201	730,332
22488	LaSalle Bank Midwest National Association	Troy	MI	48084	660,463
4977	First Tennessee Bank, National Association	Memphis	TN	38101	576,248
867	SunTrust Bank	Atlanta	GA	30308	564,617
33184	RBC Centura Bank	Raleigh	NC	27604	547,685
16022	New York Community Bank	Westbury	NY	11590	525,390
33318	FIA Card Services, National Association	Wilmington	DE	19801	519,221
19048	Compass Bank	Birmingham	AL	35233	474,664
9609	Colonial Bank, National Association	Montgomery	AL	36101	473,002
15985	North Fork Bank	Mattituck	NY	11952	434,418
5296	Associated Bank, National Association	Green Bay	WI	54305	411,422
29805	Astoria Federal Savings and Loan Association	New York City	NY	11103	385,952
13718	Wells Fargo Bank Northwest, National Association	Ogden	UT	84401	363,000
18562	Citizens Bank of Massachusetts	Boston	MA	02110	295,248
57282	Citizens Bank of Pennsylvania	Philadelphia	PA	19103	288,722
13675	Firstmerit Bank, National Association	Akron	OH	44308	282,656
18221	Webster Bank, National Association	Waterbury	CT	06702	259,318
17985	First Hawaiian Bank	Honolulu	HI	96813	238,905
27334	People's Bank	Bridgeport	CT	06604	222,212
34967	Banco Popular North America	New York	NY	10019	206,331
57890	HSBC Bank USA, National Association	Wilmington	DE	19801	202,674
2270	Zions First National Bank	Salt Lake City	UT	84111	202,034
3709	First Midwest Bank	Itasca	IL	60143	201,391
20852	California Bank & Trust	San Diego	CA	92130	194,513
24107	Amegy Bank National Association	Houston	TX	77027	191,815
27068	Greater Bay Bank, National Association	Palo Alto	CA	94301	190,909
9396	Valley National Bank	Passaic	NJ	07055	189,157
16954	Citizens Bank of Rhode Island	Providence	RI	02903	181,045
26665	First Republic Bank	Las Vegas	NV	89117	178,985
22826	Union Bank of California, National Association	San Francisco	CA	94104	177,074
19629	International Bank of Commerce	Laredo	TX	78040	176,574
26849	Carolina First Bank	Greenville	SC	29601	170,986

151

11813 BancorpSouth Bank	Tupelo	MS	38801	168,005
15951 Provident Bank of Maryland	Baltimore	MD	21202	160,822
18053 Bank of Hawaii	Honolulu	HI	96813	156,115
19977 Israel Discount Bank of New York	New York	NY	10017	153,853
5982 Sky Bank	Salineville	OH	43945	150,136
28671 Mid America Bank, FSB	Clarendon Hills	IL	60514	149,496
4214 Bank of Oklahoma, National Association	Tulsa	OK	74172	147,345
7468 First Commonwealth Bank	Indiana	PA	15701	142,006
30012 Third Federal Savings and Loan Association of Cle	Cleveland	OH	44105	140,826
32158 Sterling Savings Bank	Spokane	WA	99201	139,206
3832 Old National Bank	Evansville	IN	47708	133,889
7888 First National Bank of Pennsylvania	Greenville	PA	16125	133,333
20001 Republic Bank	Lansing	MI	48912	119,462
32247 BankUnited, FSB	Coral Gables	FL	33134	119,154
873 Columbus Bank and Trust Company	Columbus	GA	31902	118,880
12010 The Provident Bank	Jersey City	NJ	07303	116,271
18261 NewAlliance Bank	New Haven	CT	06502	116,194
3628 MB Financial Bank, National Association	Chicago	IL	60607	114,134
12229 First Bank	Creve Coeur	MO	63141	112,409
5510 The Frost National Bank	San Antonio	TX	78205	111,742
28178 Northwest Savings Bank	Warren	PA	16365	110,864
6214 Citizens Bank New Hampshire	Manchester	NH	03105	110,579
4063 MidFirst Bank	Oklahoma City	OK	73118	108,987
7579 Susquehanna Bank PA	Lititz	PA	17543	105,878
17281 City National Bank	Beverly Hills	CA	90213	105,552
3735 Amcore Bank, National Association	Rockford	IL	61110	105,425
16004 First Niagara Bank	Lockport	NY	14094	104,965
17308 Central Pacific Bank	Honolulu	HI	96813	102,394
20347 Mercantile-Safe Deposit and Trust Company	Baltimore	MD	21203	100,833
28932 Charter One Bank, National Association	Cleveland	OH	44114	100,077
21716 Citizens Business Bank	Ontario	CA	91764	99,861
7414 National Penn Bank	Boyertown	PA	19512	98,666
27515 Mercantile Bank	Orlando	FL	32801	96,494
4886 First Charter Bank	Charlotte	NC	28262	95,891
27471 American Express Centurion Bank	Salt Lake City	UT	84184	95,787
32526 American Savings Bank, FSB	Honolulu	HI	96813	95,741
19842 Bank Leumi USA	New York	NY	10170	95,626
31628 East West Bank	Pasadena	CA	91101	90,598
986 Citizens Bank	Flint	MI	48502	90,322
9694 Susquehanna Bank	Hagerstown	MD	21740	87,773
28892 Investors Savings Bank	Short Hills	NJ	07078	86,186
16026 Ridgewood Savings Bank	New York City	NY	11385	86,139
18169 Pacific Capital Bank, National Association	Santa Barbara	CA	93102	85,586
26870 Franklin Bank, S.S.B.	Houston	TX	77042	82,791
803 Wesbanco Bank, Inc.	Wheeling	WV	26003	82,572
28166 Keystone Nazareth Bank & Trust Company	Bethlehem	PA	18017	78,361
4988 Trustmark National Bank	Jackson	MS	39205	77,767
7533 Omega Bank	Huntingdon	PA	16652	76,341
6443 Susquehanna Patriot Bank	Marlton	NJ	08053	75,203
21726 Sterling Bank	Houston	TX	77092	74,923
16045 Partners Trust Bank	Utica	NY	13501	73,879
12441 Hancock Bank	Gulfport	MS	39501	70,288
12984 CommunityBanks	Millersburg	PA	17061	68,343
28834 Columbia Bank	Fair Lawn	NJ	07410	68,287
17266 Umpqua Bank	Roseburg	OR	97470	67,738
24045 Pacific Western Bank	San Diego	CA	92101	67,512
7516 The Harleysville National Bank and Trust Compan	Harleysville	PA	19438	65,584

18117 Midwest Bank and Trust Company	Elmwood Park	IL	60707	65,220
6600 First Financial Bank, National Association	Hamilton	OH	45011	63,195
27076 World Savings Bank, FSB	Oakland	CA	94612	62,371
7230 NBT Bank, National Association	Norwich	NY	13815	62,222
17735 City National Bank of West Virginia	Charleston	WV	25304	62,007
23577 First American Bank	Birmingham	AL	35203	61,928
4865 Sandy Spring Bank	Olney	MD	20832	59,992
6784 United Bank	Parkersburg	WV	26101	59,649
32749 New York Commercial Bank	Islandia	NY	11749	59,623
679 PNC Bank, Delaware	Wilmington	DE	19899	59,389
30003 Guaranty Bank	Milwaukee	WI	53209	59,173
1105 First Interstate Bank	Billings	MT	59101	57,462
26240 Sun National Bank	Vineland	NJ	08360	57,370
3297 The Laredo National Bank	Laredo	TX	78040	57,299
22858 United Bank	Fairfax	VA	22030	57,208
4382 First Financial Bank, National Association	Terre Haute	IN	47808	57,123
17838 Wilmington Savings Fund Society, FSB	Wilmington	DE	19899	55,282
12437 Renasant Bank	Tupelo	MS	38801	54,671
30307 Placer Sierra Bank	Auburn	CA	95603	54,349
57053 Signature Bank	New York	NY	10017	54,319
33897 Bank of Nevada	Las Vegas	NV	89102	53,308
26876 Safra National Bank of New York	New York	NY	10036	52,141
34659 California National Bank	Los Angeles	CA	90012	51,877
21674 Bank of Texas. National Association	Dallas	TX	75225	50,178
6515 The Yardville National Bank	Yardville	NJ	08620	49,651
18197 Citizens Bank of Connecticut	New London	CT	06320	49,582
6544 Peoples Bank, National Association	Marietta	OH	45750	48,630
28100 Iberiabank	Lafayette	LA	70501	46,705
30125 Bank Mutual	Milwaukee	WI	53202	46,444
9712 Rockland Trust Company	Rockland	MA	02370	45,759
2111 The National Bank of South Carolina	Sumter	SC	29150	45,536
110 Bank of the Ozarks	Little Rock	AR	72211	44,229
21943 Tri Counties Bank	Chico	CA	95926	43,536
16012 The Dime Svgs. Bank of Williamsburgh	Brooklyn	NY	11211	43,456
30614 Fidelity Federal Bank & Trust	West Palm Beach	FL	33401	43,069
22574 County Bank	Merced	CA	95340	43,051
18408 Bangor Savings Bank	Bangor	ME	04401	42,616
28116 Yakima Federal Savings and Loan Association	Yakima	WA	98901	42,567
19416 Chinatrust Bank (U.S.A.)	Torrance	CA	90505	41,176
90183 Middlesex Savings Bank	Natick	MA	01760	40,906
17750 Superior Bank	Birmingham	AL	35203	40,598
16049 Flushing Savings Bank, FSB	New York City	NY	11354	40,516
15697 Beneficial Mutual Savings Bank	Philadelphia	PA	19106	40,395
33029 Hancock Bank of Louisiana	Baton Rouge	LA	70808	40,352
23623 The Washington Trust Company of Westerly	Westerly	RI	02891	39,770
12181 Monroe Bank & Trust	Monroe	MI	48161	39,631
30337 Provident Bank	Montebello	NY	10901	39,548
1331 Farmers & Merchants Bank of Central California	Lodi	CA	95240	38,444
6653 The Park National Bank	Newark	OH	43058	38,352
3603 The Old Second National Bank of Aurora	Aurora	IL	60506	38,046
28489 Banner Bank	Walla Walla	WA	99362	37,978
4392 Integra Bank National Association	Evansville	IN	47705	37,841
34336 State National Bank	Fort Worth	TX	76137	37,784
28359 OceanFirst Bank	Toms River	NJ	08754	37,145
7220 Sterling National Bank	New York	NY	10022	37,135
16701 American State Bank	Lubbock	TX	79408	36,956
33306 The PrivateBank and Trust Company	Chicago	IL	60602	36,891

16606 Standard Bank and Trust Company	Hickory Hills	IL	60457	36,883
19953 Lakeland Bank	Newfoundland	NJ	07435	36,774
33826 Columbia State Bank	Tacoma	WA	98402	36,611
15797 Broadway National Bank	San Antonio	TX	78209	36,569
33905 Heritage Bank of Commerce	San Jose	CA	95113	36,174
9087 1st Source Bank	South Bend	IN	46634	36,157
29367 Citizens Financial Bank	Munster	IN	46321	35,876
13012 First Community Bank, National Association	Bluefield	VA	24605	35,517
23220 Woodforest National Bank	Houston	TX	77015	35,406
24315 Community Bank	Pasadena	CA	91101	34,853
16298 First National Bank & Trust	Kokomo	IN	46901	34,725
18923 Citibank (Banamex USA)	Century City	CA	90067	34,555
18509 West Suburban Bank	Lombard	IL	60148	34,320
11124 S&T Bank	Indiana	PA	15701	34,251
7759 Univest National Bank and Trust Co.	Souderton	PA	18964	34,169
18213 Fairfield County Bank Corp.	Ridgefield	CT	06877	33,660
12261 First Community Bank	Taos	NM	87571	33,466
1058 Midwest BankCentre	Lemay	MO	63125	33,332
1768 The Mechanics Bank	Richmond	CA	94806	32,954
21851 Far East National Bank	Los Angeles	CA	90071	32,950
28710 Northfield Bank	Staten Island	NY	10314	32,866
6423 Amboy National Bank	Old Bridge	NJ	08857	32,323
7542 Ameriserv Financial Bank	Johnstown	PA	15901	32,256
30179 Penn Federal Savings Bank	Newark	NJ	07105	31,783
22407 Bank of the Cascades	Bend	OR	97701	31,582
34598 Mercantile Bank of Michigan	Grand Rapids	MI	49504	30,858
34383 Texas Capital Bank, National Association	Dallas	TX	75201	30,763
31286 First Mariner Bank	Baltimore	MD	21224	30,714
24811 Boston Private Bank & Trust Company	Boston	MA	02109	30,345
1536 Bank of Stockton	Stockton	CA	95201	30,330
23621 Berkshire Bank	Pittsfield	MA	01201	30,315
27688 First Place Bank	Warren	OH	44481	30,278
27235 STAR Financial Bank	Fort Wayne	IN	46802	29,839
32773 Eastern Bank	Boston	MA	02110	29,578
19695 State Bank of Long Island	New Hyde Park	NY	11040	29,542
20959 North Valley Bank	Redding	CA	96001	29,483
30895 Fidelity Bank	Wichita	KS	67202	29,275
27744 Mutual Federal Savings Bank	Muncie	IN	47305	29,121
90213 PeoplesBank	Holyoke	MA	01040	28,396
18297 Southside Bank	Tyler	TX	75701	28,322
8468 Exchange Bank	Santa Rosa	CA	95401	28,310
4879 First National Bank and Trust Company	Asheboro	NC	27203	28,303
33935 North Shore Community Bank & Trust Company	Wilmette	IL	60091	28,218
4297 Capital One, National Association	New Orleans	LA	70161	28,090
20038 Interchange Bank	Saddle Brook	NJ	07663	28,055
4857 First United Bank & Trust	Oakland	MD	21550	27,926
27708 ESB Bank	Ellwood City	PA	16117	27,525
27677 HomeTrust Bank	Clyde	NC	28721	27,389
5950 Bank of Granite	Granite Falls	NC	28630	27,254
19040 The International Bank of Miami, National Associa	Coral Gables	FL	33134	26,914
258 Stock Yards Bank & Trust Company	Louisville	KY	40232	26,824
622 Amalgamated Bank	New York	NY	10001	26,772
1039 The Bank of Edwardsville	Edwardsville	IL	62025	26,618
18204 First County Bank	Stamford	CT	06904	26,595
22597 Bank of the Sierra	Porterville	CA	93257	26,505
18190 Union Savings Bank	Danbury	CT	06810	26,481
29845 First Federal Bank of the Midwest	Defiance	OH	43512	26,149

BOARD OF GOVERNORS
OF THE
FEDERAL RESERVE SYSTEM
WASHINGTON, D. C. 20551

DIVISION OF BANKING
SUPERVISION AND
REGULATION

SR 04-19
December 7, 2004

TO THE OFFICER IN CHARGE OF SUPERVISION
AT EACH FEDERAL RESERVE BANK

SUBJECT: **Interagency Statement on the Purchase and Risk Management of Life Insurance**

The staffs of the Board of Governors of the Federal Reserve System, Federal Deposit Insurance Corporation, Office of the Comptroller of the Currency, and Office of Thrift Supervision (the agencies) have issued the attached Interagency Statement on the Purchase and Risk Management of Life Insurance. This guidance discusses the safety and soundness and risk management implications of purchases and holdings of life insurance by banks and savings associations (institutions).

Institutions may purchase life insurance on their employees or others for several appropriate business purposes. The most common purposes for which institutions purchase bank-owned life insurance (BOLI) are to recover the cost of providing pre- and post-retirement employee benefits, to recover losses associated with the death of a key person, and to obtain insurance on borrowers.

Over the past several years, purchases of BOLI by institutions have increased steadily and significantly. This has given rise to concerns among the agencies that some institutions may not have an adequate understanding of the full array of risks posed by BOLI, including liquidity, operational, reputational and compliance/legal risks. The agencies also are concerned that some institutions may have committed a significant amount of capital to BOLI holdings without properly assessing the associated risks. Over the same period, agency staffs have noticed a significant rise in the number of inquiries pertaining to BOLI posed by supervised institutions and bank examination staff.

Such developments have highlighted the need for the agencies to enhance and harmonize their supervisory guidance on BOLI. The attached guidance is for institutions and examination staff to help ensure that risk management practices for BOLI are consistent with safe and sound banking practices.

The guidance addresses the need for both a comprehensive pre- and post-purchase analysis of BOLI risks and rewards, as well as its unique characteristics. The agencies expect institutions to have comprehensive risk management processes applicable

155

to their BOLI purchases and holdings, including:

- Effective senior management and board oversight;
- Comprehensive policies and procedures, including appropriate limits regarding purchases; and
- An effective ongoing system of risk assessment, management, monitoring and internal control processes, including appropriate internal audit and compliance frameworks.

The guidance highlights the agencies' expectation that when an institution plans to acquire BOLI resulting in an aggregate cash surrender value in excess of 25 percent of the applicable concentration threshold, it should obtain prior approval from its board of directors or the appropriate board committee. The Federal Reserve's concentration guidelines applicable to state member banks define the capital base used to determine the concentration threshold as a percentage of Tier 1 capital plus the allowance for loan and lease losses.

The guidance also states that a "look-through" treatment may be applied to BOLI holdings in separate account assets for the purposes of assigning a regulatory capital risk weight, subject to a 20 percent risk weight floor. An institution using the look-through treatment should document its assessment, based upon applicable state insurance laws and other relevant factors, that the separate account assets would be protected from the insurance carrier's general creditors.

Reserve Banks are asked to distribute this SR letter and the attached interagency guidance to state member banks as well as to supervisory and examination staff. Questions pertaining to this letter should be directed to Barbara Cornyn, Senior Project Manager, Special Activities Section, at (202) 452-2434; Nancy Oakes, Counsel, Enforcement Section, at (202) 452-2743; Mark Van Der Weide, Senior Counsel, Legal Division, at (202) 452-2263; or William Tiernay, Supervisory Financial Analyst, Supervisory and Risk Policy Section, at (202) 872-7579.

Richard Spillenkothen
Director

Attachment:	Interagency Statement on the Purchase and Risk Management of Life Insurance (2,181 KB PDF)
Cross References:	SR letters 04-4, 94-23, and 93-37

SR letters | 2004

Thrift Bulletin

TB 84

Handbooks: **Thrift Activities**   **Section: 250**
Subject: **Asset Quality, Other Assets**

Interagency Statement on the Purchase and Risk Management of Life Insurance

Summary: On December 7, 2004, OTS, together with the other banking agencies, adopted the "Interagency Statement on the Purchase and Risk Management of Life Insurance." OTS is replacing its existing policy statement on life insurance in Appendix A of Section 250 of the Thrift Activities Handbook with the Interagency Statement. The preceding Appendix A is hereby rescinded. Other parts of Handbook Section 250 and attendant examination procedures will be revised at a later date.

For Further Information Contact: Your OTS Regional Office or William Magrini, Senior Project Manager, Supervision Policy, Washington, DC (202) 906-5744. You may access this bulletin at our web site: www.ots.treas.gov.

Thrift Bulletin 84

SUMMARY

The Interagency Statement addresses purchase and risk management of life insurance by banks and savings associations. OTS and the other banking agencies adopted the Interagency Statement on December 7, 2004.

The most significant change from OTS's prior policy on Bank Owned Life Insurance (BOLI) is that separate account BOLI may now be risk weighted based on the average risk weight of the underlying separate account assets, or 20 percent, whichever is higher. General account BOLI will continue to be risk weighted at 100 percent.

The Interagency Statement requires an institution's board of directors to approve any investment in cash value life insurance in excess of 25 percent of its capital. However, as indicated on footnote 2 on page 5 of the Interagency Statement, OTS retains its policy of requiring savings associations to notify their Regional Office and obtain OTS approval prior to investing more than 25 percent of their capital in BOLI.

—Scott M. Albinson
Managing Director
Examinations, Supervision, and Consumer Protection

157

Federal Deposit Insurance Corporation
550 17th Street, NW, Washington, D.C. 20429-9990

Financial Institution Letter
FIL-127-2004
December 7, 2004

BANK-OWNED LIFE INSURANCE
Interagency Statement on the Purchase and Risk Management of Life Insurance

Summary: The federal banking agencies are providing guidance on the safe and sound banking practices they expect institutions to employ for the purchase and ongoing risk management of bank-owned life insurance.

Distribution:
FDIC-Supervised Banks

Suggested Routing:
Chief Executive Officer
Chief Financial Officer
Chief Risk Officer

Related Topics:
Section 24 of the Federal Deposit Insurance Act and Part 362 of the FDIC's Regulations

Attachments:
Interagency Statement on the Purchase and Risk Management of Life Insurance, including Executive Summary

Contact:
FDIC Regional Accountant or Christine M. Bouvier, Senior Policy Analyst, Division of Supervision and Consumer Protection (202-898-7289, cbouvier@fdic.gov)

Note:
For your reference, FDIC financial institution letters (FILs) may be accessed from the FDIC's Web site at www.fdic.gov/news/news/financial/2004/index.html.

To learn how to receive FILs electronically, please visit http://www.fdic.gov/news/news/announcements/fil.html.

Paper copies of FDIC financial institution letters may be obtained through the FDIC's Public Information Center, 801 17th Street, NW, Room 100, Washington, DC 20434 (1-877-275-3342 or 202-416-6940).

Highlights:

- Institutions should have a comprehensive risk management process for purchasing and holding bank-owned life insurance (BOLI).

- The safe and sound use of BOLI depends on effective senior management and board oversight.

- Institutions should establish policies and procedures governing their BOLI holdings, including meaningful risk limits.

- A sound pre-purchase analysis helps ensure that institutions understand the risks, rewards and unique characteristics of BOLI.

- Institutions also should monitor BOLI risks on an ongoing basis subsequent to purchase.

HOME | DEPOSIT INSURANCE | CONSUMER PROTECTION | INDUSTRY ANALYSIS | REGULATION & EXAMINATIONS | ASSET SALES | NEWS & EVENTS | ABOUT FDIC

Home > News & Events > Financial Institution Letters

Financial Institution Letters

Executive Summary - Interagency Statement on the Purchase and Risk Management of Life Insurance

Institutions purchase life insurance for a variety of purposes, including recovering the cost of providing employee benefits and protecting against the loss of "key persons." Institutions should have a comprehensive risk management process for purchasing and holding bank-owned life insurance (BOLI).

The two broad types of life insurance are temporary (term) insurance and permanent insurance. Temporary (term) insurance provides protection for a specified time period, its premiums do not have a savings component, and it does not create a cash surrender value (CSV). Permanent insurance is intended to provide life insurance protection for the entire life of the insured. Its premium structure includes a savings component, thereby creating a CSV. If permanent insurance is surrendered before death, surrender charges may be assessed against the CSV.

The ability of FDIC-supervised banks to purchase life insurance is governed by state law. Some state laws permit state-chartered banks to engage in activities (including making investments) that go beyond the authority of a national bank. Section 24 of the Federal Deposit Insurance Act generally requires FDIC-supervised banks to obtain the FDIC's consent before engaging as principal in activities that are not permissible for a national bank.

The safe and sound use of BOLI depends on effective senior management and board oversight. An institution's board of directors must understand the complex risk characteristics of the institution's insurance holdings and the role this asset is intended to play in the institution's overall business strategy.

Each institution should establish internal policies and procedures governing its BOLI holdings, including guidelines that limit the aggregate CSV of policies from any one insurance company as well as the aggregate CSV of policies from all insurance companies. It is generally not prudent for an institution to hold BOLI with an aggregate CSV that exceeds 25 percent of its Tier 1 capital. Therefore, the FDIC expects an institution that plans to acquire BOLI in an amount that results in an aggregate CSV in excess of this concentration limit, or any lower internal limit, to gain prior approval from its board of directors or the appropriate board committee. In this situation, management is expected to justify that any increase in BOLI resulting in an aggregate CSV above 25 percent of Tier 1 capital does not constitute an imprudent capital concentration.

The management of an institution should conduct a thorough pre purchase analysis to help ensure that the institution understands the risks, rewards, and unique characteristics of BOLI. The nature and extent of this analysis should be commensurate with the size and complexity of the potential BOLI purchases and should also take into account existing BOLI holdings. An effective pre-purchase analysis involves the following actions by management:

(1) Identify the need for insurance and determine the economic benefits and appropriate insurance type, i.e., permanent or temporary (term) insurance.
(2) Quantify the amount of insurance appropriate for the institution's objectives.
(3) Assess vendor qualifications, including its reputation, experience, financial soundness, and commitment to the BOLI product and the adequacy of its services.
(4) Review the characteristics of the available insurance products and select those that best match the institution's objectives, needs, and risk tolerance.

159

(5) Select an insurance company after evaluating and performing credit analyses on the companies from which insurance may be purchased.
(6) Determine the reasonableness of compensation provided to the insured employee if the insurance provides additional compensation to the employee.
(7) Analyze the risks associated with the insurance and the institution's ability to monitor and respond to these risks.
(8) Evaluate alternatives to the purchase of BOLI for accomplishing the institution's objectives.
(9) Document the pre-purchase analysis and the purchase decision.

A comprehensive assessment of BOLI risks on an ongoing basis is an important element of the risk management process, especially for an institution whose aggregate BOLI holdings represent a capital concentration. Management should review the performance of the institution's insurance assets with its board of directors at least annually.

The BOLI risks that should be assessed, managed, monitored, and controlled include liquidity, transaction/operational (including the tax and insurable interest implications), reputation, credit, interest rate, compliance/legal, and price risk. All of these risks are present in permanent insurance. In particular, the CSV of permanent life insurance is one of the least liquid assets on an institution's balance sheet. In contrast, temporary insurance does not expose an institution to liquidity, interest rate, or price risk because it does not have a CSV. These risks need not be evaluated in the comprehensive assessment of the risks of temporary insurance.

Institutions should follow generally accepted accounting principles (GAAP) applicable to holdings of life insurance for reporting purposes. Under GAAP, only the amount that could be realized under an insurance contract as of the balance sheet date (that is, the CSV reported to the institution by the insurance carrier, less any applicable surrender charges not reflected by the insurance carrier in the reported CSV) is reported as an asset.

For risk-based capital purposes, an institution that owns general account permanent insurance should apply a 100 percent risk weight to its claim on the insurance company. If an institution owns a separate account policy and can demonstrate that it meets certain requirements, it may choose to apply a "look-through" approach to the underlying assets to determine the risk weight. In no case, however, may the risk weight for the separate account policy (excluding any general account and stable value protection portions, which generally receive a 100 percent risk weight) be less than 20 percent.

Last Updated 12/07/2004   communications@fdic.gov

CORPORATE-OWNED LIFE INSURANCE

"We continue to see growth in the use of COLI for informally funding both SERPS and NQDC plans. Companies understand that this is often the best funding tool available for these executive programs."

> Les Brockhurst,
> President Clark Consulting
> Executive Benefits Practice
> Press Release dated November 7, 2005

"It is vital that corporations with true key employees create an economic shock absorber to protect the corporation, its owners, and employees against the financial trauma that all too often occurs at the death of one or more key individuals. In this very common situation in American business life, the corporation should own, pay premiums on, and receive the proceeds of the coverage...

"Such insurance is not only advisable; it may be irresponsible in many cases for a corporation not to have such coverage. This is particularly true with respect to smaller publicly traded corporations, closely held businesses, and businesses with leaders who are more than usual driving forces of success for the business. So not only is there nothing wrong with corporate owned life insurance but in many cases it may be irresponsible on the part of the company's directors not to insist upon it."

> Attorney Steve Leimberg
> "Important COLI Case Settled,"
> January 10, 2004
> Regarding the Wal-Mart COLI lawsuit

According to the General Accounting Office (GAO) report released in 2004, banks purchased the majority of corporate-owned life insurance in 2001 with approximately $5.2 billion in annual premiums. The nation's public corporations spent close to that amount at $4.1 billion. More recently, however, the author's research revealed that banks in 2005 and 2006 purchased an additional $17.76 billion in permanent life insurance premiums annually, more than a three-fold increase since 2001.

Like banks, corporations purchase high cash value life insurance to fund supplemental executive retirement plans (SERPs) and to fund pre- and post-retirement employee benefit plans such as health insurance. According to information supplied by the Web site of New York Life, (www.newyorklife.com) or (www.serpplus.com) corporate-owned life insurance (COLI), based upon survey information done in 1999, about 68 percent of Fortune 1000 companies funded their SERPs with COLI. About forty-three of the top fifty banks funded their SERPs with bank-owned life insurance (BOLI).

Clarke Consulting, Inc., is a New York Stock Exchange-listed employee benefits consultant (NYSE: CLK) which serves 3,800 corporate

161

clients. It is one of the leading consultants and brokers in the country for BOLI, COLI, and TOLI (trust-owned life insurance). Clarke Consulting released the results of a survey in November 2005, titled "Executive Benefits—A Survey of Current Trends," which included data from nearly 20 percent of the Fortune 1000 companies. The following trends were cited:

1.   Of those companies, which offered a non-qualified deferred compensation plan in 2004, 61 percent of those who responded informally funded their plans with COLI, followed by mutual funds at 15 percent.

2.   Of those companies who credit a bonus rate to their nonqualified deferred compensation plans, 50 percent used COLI, 17 percent used another method other than COLI, and 33 percent of those were unfunded.

3.   When it came to discovering how corporations informally funded their SERPs, Clarke Consulting found that in 2004 over 64 percent funded these plans with COLI. In prior years such as 2001 and 2002, companies used COLI as a funding medium at levels of 69 percent and 68 percent respectively.

Like BOLI, corporate-owned life insurance, or COLI, is carried on a corporation's books as a corporate asset and not segregated into separate trust accounts such as a pension or a 401(k). The life insurance, however, may be set aside in a separate trust within the corporation to fund future executive retirement benefits. Normally, this is called a *Rabbi Trust*. However, if the corporation is ever sold, liquidated, or goes bankrupt, the life insurance is considered a corporate asset and subject to the claims of creditors.

COLI has been used as an instrument of corporate finance for decades. General Electric began using permanent cash value life insurance after World War II to fund its SERP. Today, the company still provides permanent life insurance arrangements for over 4,400 of its executives according to 2005 proxy statements filed with the SEC.

By some estimates, as many as 1,600 public companies in the United States use some type of deferred compensation plans or SERPs. A majority of these arrangements are likely to use life insurance as a funding medium, because life insurance is a proven method whereby a corporation can recover its economic costs at the death of the insured executive. This is known as *cost recovery life insurance.*

Executive Compensation

Many well-known companies use life insurance, particularly high cash value life as a tool to recruit and retain the best people. As a form of executive compensation, permanent life insurance can be structured and arranged in a number of ways.

Sometimes COLI may be structured as an *executive bonus* of premiums, whereby the executive owns the policy but the corporation pays for the premiums in a bonus arrangement. Another common method is a *split-dollar life insurance* COLI arrangement, where the premiums and economic benefits are "split" between the executive and the employer in various scenarios. Finally, COLI is used as the preferred funding medium for *supplemental executive retirement plans* where the corporation is the premium payer, the owner, and the beneficiary of life insurance proceeds.

Since the passage of the Sarbanes-Oxley Act of 2002, split-dollar has fallen out of favor as the ability to skew economic benefits to the executive has been greatly reduced. However, in and of itself, split-dollar is still a methodology to purchase life insurance, particularly for *closely held* corporations.

It is common for an executive to be covered under multiple life insurance policies for different applications within a corporation. To make this clear, it is best to give an example of the multiple uses of COLI. Kenneth D. Lewis, the CEO of Bank of America, owns split-dollar life insurance whereby the bank pays just under $54 thousand in annual premiums to fund permanent death benefits for his heirs. At the same time, Lewis is entitled to some of the ownership rights on the equity this policy builds up over time.

Secondly, Bank of America, which is to the author's knowledge the largest holder of cash value life insurance in the world, uses life insurance to fund Mr. Lewis' future pension—which is in the neighborhood of $3 million annually. Lastly, Bank of America owns life insurance on executives like Mr. Lewis to fund healthcare, disability, severance pay, and other welfare benefits costs.

Some of the household names outside of banking who are involved in corporate life insurance programs are General Electric; Walt Disney; Proctor & Gamble; Crown Holdings; AT&T; Amway; Nestle; Panera Bread; Prudential Insurance; MetLife; General Motors; Harley Davidson; H. J. Heinz; International Paper; Johnson & Johnson; Lockheed Martin; Lucent Technologies; McGraw-Hill; Norfolk Southern; Outback Steak House; Pfizer; Pacific Gas and Electric; Gannett Publishing; Dow Chemical; Lillian Vernon; Bed, Bath and Beyond; Cendant; CSX; Monsanto; BellSouth; Office Depot; Nike; Starbucks; United Healthcare; Ryder Systems; Anheuser-Busch; Newell Rubbermaid; KB Home; Avon; CVS; Comcast; United Technologies; Verizon; Wisconsin Energy; and many more.

At one point, even the *Boston Globe* and the *New York Times* had over two hundred employees covered with deferred compensation plans funded with life insurance. Although today, it appears that both plans have been terminated.

Not-for-Profits Use COLI Programs as Well

Not-for-profit institutions are also organizations that purchase a great deal of COLI. Hospitals, for instance, have been large purchasers of permanent life insurance programs. They have primarily used the product to fund selective executive retirement plans for key administrators, physicians, and so on. This is known as hospital-owned life insurance or HOLI.

Colleges and research facilities also purchase significant amounts of permanent life insurance as well. Many times, life insurance is used as a method of indemnifying a particular scientific institution for the economic loss it would suffer in the event of the premature death of a key employee. This author knows of one of the leading scientists in the United States who was insured for multiple millions for this reason.

COLI is also used as a form of compensation in not-for-profit institutions. In May of 2006, in a Boston University (BU) press release, it was reported that former university president *John Silber*, one of the highest paid academic professionals in America, received close to $6.2 million total compensation for the year ending 2005. This included $770,000 for sabbatical leave, $305,000 for imputed income for lifetime residence in a BU mansion, and $490,000 in imputed income for life insurance policies BU took out for him.[73]

Pushing the Tax Envelope

In the past, some corporations have gone too far in pushing the COLI envelope concerning the tax benefits that can be leveraged and received when using life insurance as a tax shelter. When *no economic substance* exists or when corporations push the tax code to the wall, it is unlikely someone will win—particularly when challenged by the IRS.

Steve Leimberg, a nationally known estate-planning attorney,[74] confirms that Wal-Mart named itself as a beneficiary for more than 335,000 life insurance policies and placed these policies in trust in Georgia in 1993. However, Wal-Mart was subsequently involved in various forms of adverse litigation in Texas and New Hampshire regarding the death benefits being paid to the corporation and not to the employee. Wal-Mart unwound the policies in 2000 after Congress eliminated the tax benefits for the policies.

---

[73] Marcella Bombardieri, "Rich Rewards Outlast Sibler's Reign-BU Has Paid Him $7M Since 2003," *Boston Globe,* May 10, 2006.
[74] Steve Leimberg, Esquire, www.leimbergservices.com or www.leimberg.com

In 1995, a Newsweek article[75] claimed that Winn-Dixie had over 33,000 employees covered with COLI policies; AT&T, 27,500; GTE, 22,000; Procter and Gamble, 14,000; Walt Disney and Eastman Kodak, 9,000 each; and Coca-Cola, 2,500. Four companies pushed the envelope by purchasing only the tax benefits of COLI. Since these purchases lacked economic substance other than tax benefits, it came back to haunt them.

Winn-Dixie, at one time, had taken out 36,000 policies in "janitors insurance." The Internal Revenue Service denied the company $4 million in tax deductions on its plan in 1999. The IRS requested that Winn-Dixie repay a $1.6 million deficiency it owed in taxes.

American Electric Power Company had a leveraged corporate-owned life insurance program covering 20,000 employees. The company was disallowed $66 million in interest deductions it claimed in 1996. Like Winn-Dixie, American Power was later assessed an additional $25 million in taxes by the IRS for the year in question.

Camelot Music, a company that purchased 1,500 policies with an annual premium of $14 million had its COLI program disallowed for excessive borrowing or leverage on the plan in 2000. However, if there ever was a landmark case in regards to COLI, it has to be the one associated with Dow Chemical.[76] In this case, the IRS maintained that Dow's corporate-owned life insurance program lacked economic substance. The IRS also claimed that no premiums were actually being paid due to netting transactions. The IRS claimed that Dow had no insurable interest and that its COLI program was an economic sham.

Dow Chemical actually had two COLI programs under its roof; the first covered about 4,000 management personnel, and the second covered 17,000 additional employees. In both COLI programs, Dow used complex premium payment-loan strategies to pay policy premiums. In the first three years, policy loans were used to pay premiums; in years four through seven, they used partial withdrawals to pay premiums; and in years eight and nine, Dow paid the premiums in full.

The IRS disallowed Dow's deduction for interest and expenses on its COLI program. However, Dow challenged the IRS in court and the court ordered the IRS to pay Dow $22.2 million and interest in its favor.

For the company, the victory against the IRS was short-lived. The IRS appealed the case and won. A primary reason was that Dow would have to inject significant amounts of capital into the life insurance program, and

---

[75] Allan Loan, "Deal of a Lifetime: How America's Biggest Corporations are Cashing In on Your Mortality," *Newsweek,* October 23, 1992.
[76] Steve Leimberg, "Dow-COLI Interest Deductions Denied by 6th Circuit," www.leimbergservices.com, January 24, 2006.

based upon prior history, it was unlikely Dow would do so. The court held that Dow's plan lacked a non-tax profit motive and economic substance.

New Requirements for Insurable Interest

Life insurance is here to stay as a long-term solution to fund the absorption of economic risk, long-term medical costs, executive benefits, and other corporate benefit programs. However, the so-called "janitor insurance" tax benefits and tax avoidance have likely come to an end. Tax legislation passed in 1986 limited deductibility of interest on policy loans up to the first $50,000 of indebtedness. Subsequently, in 1996, further legislation limited the deduction to only policies on five key people in a corporation or the lesser of either 5 percent of the total number of officers and employees of a business, or twenty individuals.

Pension legislation enacted in 2004 requires written consent by an employee to be covered under corporate-owned life insurance programs. On August 17, 2006, with the signing of the "Pension Protection Act of 2006," new rules further defined the corporate requirements regarding COLI under IRC 101(j).[77] Certain new steps must be taken to insure that the company owning the life insurance receives the income tax-free death benefit. Companies risk losing the valuable tax benefits, namely the income tax-free life insurance proceeds if they do not comply with the regulations. Among other things, the new law requires that:

1.   The employee must be notified in writing that their employer intends to insure the employee's life.
2.   The employee must provide the employer with written consent to be insured under the contract and that the insurance may continue after the employee terminates employment.
3.   The employee must be notified in writing that the employer will be the beneficiary of any death benefits. This notification and consent must take place before the policy is issued.
4.   In addition, employers who own such contracts will also have to file a return with the IRS each year for the contracts owned, which states, the number of employees within the company, the number insured under the COLI contracts, the total amount of insurance in force under these contracts, the employers name, address, tax identification number and a valid form of consent for each employee covered.

---

[77] Steve Leimberg, "New Code Section 101(j) Treatment of Death Benefits from Corporate-Owned Life Insurance," www.leimbergservices.com, August 9, 2006.

Enron Life Insurance

Enron purchased about $500 million in life insurance on its employees. According to the Senate Committee on Finance document prepared in February 2003 regarding the collapse of Enron, during the 1980s and 1990s, the company purchased approximately 1,000 life insurance contracts covering its employees. Documents obtained from Enron show that in 1994, Enron set up an irrevocable rabbi trust to purchase life insurance agreements from Cigna to cover about 100 employees for deferred compensation agreements. Subsequently, a new trust agreement was entered into with Wachovia Bank, N.A. as trustee dated January 1, 1999, to protect the life insurance assets and benefits if Enron came under new ownership. Policies were purchased from Cigna, Great West Life, Mass Mutual, Pacific Life, and Security Life of Denver. Right before the collapse, these policies were highly leveraged, with about $432 million in debt from policy loans having total death benefits of $512 million.

In addition to its own policies, Enron acquired Portland General Electric and its affiliates. Portland General had individual life policies covering 2,315 employees with aggregate cash surrender value of $139 million. Those policies were surrendered in 2003 for cash. Enron's were surrendered in 2002.

Enron also entered into executive split-dollar life insurance agreements with key employees, Kenneth Lay, Jeffrey Skilling, and Clifford Baxter. In the first split-dollar life insurance agreement, dated April 22, 1994, Kenneth Lay entered into a collateral assignment split-dollar arrangement whereby the Lay Family partnership owned $30 million of joint life insurance on Kenneth Lay and his wife, Linda. Enron agreed to pay nine $280 thousand plus annual premiums to Transamerica Occidental Life Insurance on behalf of the Lays. The Lay Family partnership assigned the life insurance to Enron as collateral. This gave Enron economic interest in the cash surrender value of the policies and the premiums.

In a second split-dollar arrangement dated December 13, 1996, Kenneth Lay entered into another arrangement whereby the family partnership was again listed as the owner with collateral assignments given to Enron. This policy had a face amount of $11.9 million and Enron paid five annual premiums for $250,000. Upon Lay's death, Enron could recapture the $1.25 million it paid in premiums.

Finally, a third split-dollar life insurance policy was arranged again for Kenneth Lay. The Enron compensation committee approved it May 3, 1999. The policy would insure Kenneth Lay for an additional $12.75 million. It was a way of compensating Lay for opting out of his Houston Natural Gas executive benefit agreement. Although Enron purchased the life insurance in 2000, no split-dollar agreement was ever entered into with Mr. Lay.

On May 23, 1997, Jeffrey Skilling entered into a split-dollar life insurance agreement with Enron and the Jeffrey Keith Skilling Trust, whereby Mark Skilling served as trustee. This policy was owned by the Skilling Family Trust and collaterally assigned back to Enron for cash value and premium payments. This policy, with a face amount of $8 million, was issued by Massachusetts Mutual Life Insurance Company. It had annual premiums of more than $115,000, which Enron paid for five years between 1997 and 2001.

Lastly, Clifford Baxter also agreed to a split-dollar life insurance arrangement with Margo Baxter as trustee. This also had collateral assignments with Enron paying in excess of $50,000 in annual premiums for a policy face amount of $5 million. The insurance had an effective date of January 26, 2000.

Enron went bankrupt under Chapter 11 on December 2, 2001. Mr. Baxter took his own life January 25, 2002, as he was the focus of much of Enron's fall. Kenneth Lay died in July of 2006. The life insurance, which he owned, including the split-dollar he had taken out in December of 1996, survived. Under Texas law, the ten million or so net death benefit will pass on unencumbered to his wife Linda as a protected asset.

Others with Corporate-Owned Life Insurance

Former Treasury Secretary Ken Snow, although it was never finalized before he took office, was in the process of acquiring $25 million in life insurance to fund deferred compensation with his previous employer, giant railroad conglomerate CSX Corporation.[78] The overwhelming majority of large publicly traded companies have special retirement plans for their key people. In reading, reviewing and studying dozens of proxy statements, the author concluded that these SERPs are, in part, and many times, fully, funded by life insurance and annuity contracts.

Retirement pay for key executives is laid out in a defined benefit pension format, using guaranteed income streams, single and joint life annuity factors, and so on. All pensions, whether they are qualified or non-qualified for executives, are based on life annuity calculations. It makes sense, based on overwhelming evidence, that life insurance and life annuities are the most logical and favored instruments to fund executive benefit programs.

Life insurance is definitely a cornerstone of overall compensation funding for executives in America. It should be. However, even with all the

---

[78] David Cay Johnston, "Loophole: Death Still Certain but not Taxes," *New York Times,* July 28, 2002.

so-called "transparency" in proxy statements filed with the SEC, executive compensation with public corporations can be obtuse, diversionary, and difficult to comprehend. For example, sometimes the only disclosure in proxy statement is the *value* of the life insurance and not the exact premiums paid on the executive's behalf.

Here is what some companies reported in regards to life insurance compensation in 2005 for their key people, whether it is the economic value of premiums paid, or the actual premiums themselves. Additional notes are included where applicable to verify life insurance and related compensation benefits which go with it.

Executive	Company/Position	Annual Premiums 2005
Michael S. Jeffries	Abercrombie & Fitch/CEO	$51,590
Robert S. Singer	Abercrombie & Fitch/former COO	$13,388
Kenneth I. Chenault	American Express/CEO	$ 2,271
A.F. Kelly, Jr.	American Express	$ 1,380
E. P. Gilligan	American Express	$ 1,313
G. L. Crittenden	American Express	$ 1,958
L.M. Parent	American Express	$ 2,491

(Note: Proxy Statement reports value of split-dollar life insurance.)

George J. Morrow	Amgen	$29,894

(Company has also agreed to assume or provide alternate to split-dollar life insurance arrangement with previous employer.)

Roger M. Perlmutter	Amgen	$10,450
Brian J. Harker	Alliance One International, Inc./CEO	$49,374
Steven B. Damels	Alliance One International, Inc./COO	$12,302
James A. Cooley	Alliance One International, Inc./CFO	$23,509
H. Peyton Green	Alliance One International, Inc./VP Sales	$26,051
Thomas C. Parrish	Alliance One International, Inc./VP Legal	$18,061
P.T. Stokes	Anheuser-Busch/President/CEO	$24,603
A.A. Busch III	Anheuser-Busch/Chairman of the Board	$41,802
A.A. Busch IV	Anheuser-Busch/VP/Group Executive	$ 6,314
W.R. Baker	Anheuser-Busch/VP/CFO	$16,691
D.J. Muhleman	Anheuser-Busch/VP Brewing & Operations	$ 9,956
Andrea Jung	Avon Products, Inc./CEO	$ 3,941
Susan J. Kropf	Avon Products, Inc./President/COO	$ 6,954
Elizabeth Smith	Avon Products, Inc./Executive VP	$ 5,114
Robert J. Corti	Avon Products, Inc./Executive VP	$ 8,103
Gilbert L. Klenman	Avon Products, Inc.	$ 7,617

(Note: Avon sponsors the Supplemental Executive and Life Plan of Avon Products, Inc. Avon "SERP" covers a select group of senior officers of the Company. Three of the named executives accrue retirement benefits under the SERP, namely Ms. Jung, Mrs. Kropf, and Mr. Corti. Mr. Corti retired from the Company effective February 28, 2006. He is entitled to receive benefits described under "Retirement Plans." In addition, under the terms of the SERP, Mr. Corti has elected his $1 million life policy under the Supplemental Life Insurance Program (SLIP) to himself, as the owner of the policy, on September 1, 2006. This policy will be transferred in the form of a paid-up whole life insurance policy with a cash surrender value of $254 thousand. (Under the terms of the SERP, Avon is required to gross up cash surrender value of the policy for income taxes in the amount of $197,957.)

| Kenneth D. Lewis | Bank of America/CEO | $53,093 |

(Note: Value of split-dollar life insurance only. Kenneth D. Lewis has one of the largest private pensions of any executive in America. Bank of America is one of the largest, if not the largest owner, of cash value life insurance in America.)

Ronald M. Dykes	BellSouth/CFO	$13,000
Mark L. Feidler	BellSouth	$ 4,900
Richard A. Anderson	BellSouth	$ 1,700
Francis A. Dramis	BellSouth	$23,000

(Note: Proxy statement reflects the value of life insurance for Bell South executives.)

Henry R. Silverman (2004)	Cendant Corporation/ Chairman/CEO	$3,959,334
Ronald L. Nelson (2004)	Cendant Corporation/President/CFO	$96,233
Kevin M. Sheehan (2004)	Cendant Corporation/Chairman/Vehicles	$119,473
Richard A. Smith (2004)	Cendant Corporation/Chairman/Real Estate	$96,582
Samuel L. Kate (2004)	Cendant Corporation/CEO/Travel	$73,734

| Brian L. Roberts | Comcast/Chairman/CEO | $190,917 |

(Note: According to the employment agreement which Mr. Brian Roberts has with Comcast, the Company has agreed to and supplied him with term, universal, and split-dollar life insurance, which is in the aggregate face amount of $223 million. According to notes in the proxy statement, the split-dollar life insurance is fully paid up. This agreement to provide Mr. Roberts this amount of insurance does not terminate with his termination of employment.)

170

| Ralph J. Roberts | Comcast/Chair of Executive/Finance | $3,319,936 |

(Note: Current life insurance benefit for Mr. Roberts is $39.3 million under a split-dollar arrangement. Although company is obligated to pay past and future premiums, Mr. Roberts has waived his right to a restricted share award.)

| Julian A. Brodsky | Comcast/Non executive VP | Unknown paid up Split dollar |

| Lawrence S. Smith | Comcast/Executive VP/Co-Chief CFO | $2,325/unknown Split dollar |

| John R. Alchin | Comcast/Executive VP/Co-Chief CFO | $2,136/unknown Split dollar |

John W. Conway	Crown Holdings/President/CEO	$15,311
Frank J. Mecura	Crown Holdings/President/Americas	$ 8,522
William H. Voss	Crown Holdings/President/Asia-Pacific	$20,248

Thomas M. Ryan	CVS Corp./Chairman	$18,200
David B. Rickard	CVS Corp/CFO	$ 8,889
Larry J. Merlo	CVS Corp/Executive VP	$ 2,200
Chris W. Bodine	CVS Corp/Executive VP	$ 2,200
Douglas J. Sgarro	CVS Corp/Executive VP/Legal	$ 1,745

(Note: Proxy statement says imputed income only.)

A.E. Liveris	Dow Chemical/President/CEO	$ 2,031
W.S. Stavropoulos	Dow Chemical/Chairman of the Board	$121,404
J.P. Reinhard	Dow Chemical/Executive VP	$270,779

(Note: Proxy statement says that amounts were approved for unanticipated tax liability from the Company's termination of the Executive Split-Dollar Life Insurance Program Pension Plans. The table on the following page illustrates the estimated benefits payable to executive officers receiving their entire service in U.S. plans, combining benefits from the DEPP(Dow Employees Pension Plan), ESRP (Executive Supplemental Retirement Plan) and KEIP (Key Employee Insurance Program.) KEIP is a life insurance program that secures benefits otherwise available under an ESRP that was offered to certain management employees as an alternative to the ESRP. The benefits shown in the table are single-life annuities for participants who retire at age 65. While a single-life annuity provides a higher retiree benefit, most participants elect pensions with survivorship provisions. Additional Benefits Following Retirement. A provision of the U.S. Internal Revenue Code may impact the death benefit and cash values to participants of the KEIP plan for two years following the retirement or the completion date of their KEIP program if a participant elects to take

171

possession of the life insurance policy. The company will make two annual payments to such participants to compensate for any shortfall. Mr. Reinhard is among the participants who may receive payments. The amount of payments to Mr. Reinhard cannot be determined until retirement. The company will continue to provide life insurance coverage until death in an amount equal to annual salary at the time of retirement to certain employees including each of the executives listed in the compensation tables.)

Franklin D. Raines   Fannie Mae/Chairman/CEO $2,444 & $15,003

(An amount allocated to the premiums paid by Fannie Mae for the term life portion of split-dollar life insurance. According to Form 8-K filed with the SEC on December 31, 2004, Franklin Raines and his spouse will receive $114,393 monthly pension for life as well as deferred compensation, medical and dental coverage for life with no cost to Mr. Raines. Premiums to fund $5 million in life insurance until age 60 and $2.5 million benefit thereafter, which is consistent with Fannie Mae's Executive Life Insurance Program.)

J. Timothy Howard   Fannie Mae/CFO $0.00

(No split-dollar premiums reported. According to Form 8-K in which Mr. Howard had an employment agreement until January 31, 2005. Mr. Howard will receive estimated monthly pension for life as well as his spouse for $36,000 plus medical and dental insurance at the same rate as other retirees and consistent with Fannie Mae Executive Life Insurance Program, and Fannie Mae will pay premiums for $2 million until January 2009 and a benefit of $1 million thereafter.)

Daniel H. Mudd	Fannie Mae/Vice Chairman/COO	$816
John Cochran	FirstMerit Corporation/Chairman/CEO	$31,542
Terrence E. Bichsel	FirstMerit Corporation/Executive VP	$15,361
Robert P. Brecht	FirstMerit Corporation/Sen. Exec.VP	$16,961
David G. Lucht	FirstMerit Corporation/Exec. VP	$ 9,165
George P. Paidas	FirstMerit Corporation/Sen. Exec.VP	$19,600
Douglas H. McCorkindale	Gannett Publishing/Chairman	$11,370

(Note: Premiums in 2004, $80,692 and 2003, $114,200)

Craig A. Dubow	Gannett Publishing/President/CEO	$27,056
Susan Clark Johnson	Gannett Publishing/Pres/Newspapers	$18,219
Craig A. Moon	Gannett Publishing/Pres/USA Today	$21,584
Gracia C. Martore	Gannett Publishing/VP/CFO	$20,544
Jeffrey R. Immelt	General Electric/Chairman/CEO	$57,070

172

Robert C. Wright	General Electric/Vice Chair/Executive Off.	$413,652
Dennis D. Dammerman	General Electric/Vice Chair/Executive Off.	$232,507
Benjamin W. Heinman, Jr.	General Electric/Senior VP/Law	$162,969

(Note: The above for General Electric is an executive bonus arrangement and is provided to 4,400 company executives. Also, as part of former CEO Jack Welch's retirement package, GE, in 2001 agreed to pay more than $1 million in annual life insurance premiums for Mr. Welch.)

James L. Ziemer	Harley Davidson/President/CEO	$ 2,717
James A. McCaslin	Harley Davidson/President/Motor Company	$ 622
Donna F. Zarcone	Harley Davidson/President/HDFS	$112,914
Gail A. Lione	Harley Davidson/VP/General Counsel	$ 639
Jeffrey L. Bluestein	Harley Davidson/Chairman/CEO, former	$ 3,238

| Richard Nardelli | Home Depot | Unknown |

(Nardelli received $ 55 million in life insurance in part of his $200 million exit package from Home Depot).

John V. Faraci	International Paper	$ 62,998
Robert M. Amen	International Paper	$ 42,212
Newland A. Lesko	International Paper	$ 27,939
Marianne M. Parrs	International Paper	$ 19,027
Maura A. Smith	International Paper	$ 21,416

(Note: The Company's ESIP provides certain employees, including named corporate officers, with an individually owned permanent life insurance policy. The amounts included in the column above for the annual executive officers include the entire cost of the premiums grossed up to cover income taxes due on the premiums. The pre-retirement death benefit is two times annual salary and post-retirement is one times final salary.)

William C. Weldon	Johnson & Johnson/Chairman/CEO	$ 5,495
Robert J. Darretta	Johnson & Johnson/Vice Chairman/CFO	$ 7,057
Christine A. Poon	Johnson & Johnson/VC/Worldwide	$ 9,099
Michael J. Dormer	Johnson & Johnson/Worldwide Chairman	$18,264
Per A. Peterson	Johnson & Johnson/Chairman/R&D	$22,872

Patricia F. Russo	Lucent Technologies/Chairman/CEO	$12,910
Frank A. D'Amelio	Lucent Technologies/Exec VP/CFO	$ 5,230
James K. Brewington	Lucent Technologies/President	$32,014
Cynthia K. Christy-Langenfeld	Lucent Technologies/President	$ 971

| Harold McGraw III | McGraw-Hill | $504,000 |

| Robert J. Bahash | McGraw-Hill | $357,000 |

(Note: Messrs. Harold McGraw III and Robert J. Bahash participate in the Senior Executive Supplemental Death, Disability and Retirement Benefit Plan or the "Supplemental Benefits Plan.")

David R. Goode	Norfolk Southern/Former Chairman/CEO	$61,251
Charles W. Moorman, IV	Norfolk Southern/Chairman/Pres/CEO	$11,403
L.I. Prillaman	Norfolk Southern/VP/CMO	$81,302
Stephen C. Tobias	Norfolk Southern/Vice Chairman/COO	$16,087
Henry C. Wolf	Norfolk Southern/Vice Chairman/CFO	$11,980
Dr. McKinnell	Pfizer	$159,429
Ms. Katen	Pfizer	$151,950
Mr. Shedlarz	Pfizer	$116,415
Mr. Kindler	Pfizer	$116,051
Dr. LaMattina	Pfizer	$ 31,202

(Note: The Other Benefits and Perquisites column represents the employer portion of active employee benefits including medical, dental, life insurance and disability coverage, which are available to all U.S. employees, as well as the value of perquisites and tax gross-ups.)

James E. Rohr	PNC Bank/Chairman/CEO	$189,484
Joseph C. Guyaux	PNC Bank/President	$ 12,007
William S. Demchak	PNC Bank/Vice Chairman	$ 40,534
Timothy G. Shack	PNC Bank/Exec. VP/CIO	$ 7,693
Thomas K. Whitford	PNC Bank/Exec. VP/Chief Risk Officer	$ 13,950
Thomas W. Dickson	Ruddick Corporation/President/CEO	$ 54,196
James B. Woodlief	Ruddick Corporation/VP/CFO	$ 86,557
Frederick J.Morganthall	Ruddick Corporation/Pres.Harris Teeter	$ 63,907
Fred A. Jackson	Ruddick Corporation/Pres. American Efird	$ 65,131
C.M. Connor	Sherwin-Williams Company/CEO	$ 10,311
S.P. Hennessy	Sherwin-Williams Company/VP/CFO	$ 3,025
J.G. Morikis	Sherwin-Williams Company/Pres.	$ 1,779
L.E. Stellato	Sherwin-Williams Company/VP Counsel	$ 5,851

(Note: Above are just split-dollar benefits for 2005.)

| Joseph W. Luter, III | Smithfield Foods/Chairman/CEO | $ 91,421 |

(Note: $91,421 only reflects the economic value of life insurance benefits received under a split-dollar agreement, which was terminated between Smithfield Foods and

certain irrevocable trusts with Mr. Luter. Prior premiums were $240,490 in 2004 and $314,765 in 2003. The split-dollar agreement was terminated and the cash surrender value of $14,158,837 reverted to the Company.)
.

James M. Wells III	Suntrust Banks/President/COO	$ 61,003
William J. Ryan	TD BankNorth/Chairman/President	$1,260,000

(Note: Lump sum premium to purchase and deliver $5 million of whole life insurance paid up per employment agreement with Mr. Ryan in December 2004.)

William D.McGuire, MD   United Healthcare/Chairman/CEO $ 79,557

(Note: Additional disability premiums for Dr. McGuire in 2005 were $100,883.)

Stephen J. Hemsley   United Healthcare/President/COO $ 43,673
(Note: Additional disability premiums for Mr. Hemsley in 2005, $17,741.)

Louis R. Chenevert	United Technologies/Chairman/CEO	$ 77,903
Ari Bousbib	United Technologies/Pres/Otis Elevator	$ 38,925
Gerard Darnis	United Technologies/Pres/Carrier Corp.	$ 40,782
William L. Bucknall, Jr.	United Technologies/VP/Human Resources	$ 29,750

Ivan G. Seidenberg	Verizon/Chairman/CEO	$221,507
Lawrence T. Babbio	Verizon/Vice Chairman & President	$201,667
Dennis F. Strigl	Verizon/President/Verizon Wireless	$201,420
William P. Barr	Verizon/VP/General Counsel	$124,272
Doreen A. Toben	Verizon/Executive VP/CFO	$118,350

G. Kennedy Thompson	Wachovia Corporation/CEO	$ 56,850
Robert P. Kelly	Wachovia Corporation/Senior VP	$ 99,348
Stephen E. Cummings	Wachovia Corporation/Senior VP	$ 36,587

(Note: In addition, under prior split-dollar arrangements with Wachovia, under the filed proxy statement, G. Kennedy Thompson, CEO, Benjamin Jenkins III, Vice Chairman, David Carroll, Senior Vice President, Robert Kelly, Stephen Cummings, and Wallace Malone Jr. received $22,674, $21,785, $12,679, $10,963, $8,197, and $168,757, the largest being for Wallace Malone under a prior arrangement with the merger with Sun Trust. The split-dollar agreement has been terminated, but the above is additional income for 2005.)

Notes from Various Proxy Statements Regarding COLI Programs

Anthem (WellPoint) Blue Cross/Blue Shield. *Footnote #2 Keith R. Faller, President and CEO Central Region, in addition to receiving above market interest on deferred compensation of $46,022 and above market interest paid on long-term incentive* *payments of $101,618, also includes a $249,851 in a tax gross-up payment relating to the rollout of a former split-dollar insurance program to a full whole life policy.*

KBHome. *In 2001, we implemented the DBO Plan. Currently fifty-six executives, including all of the named executive officers, participate in the DBO Plan. The beneficiary of a DBO Plan participant is entitled to DBO Plan Benefits if the participant either (1) dies while actively employed by us or an affiliate or (2) dies after completing ten years of service with us or an affiliate, including at least five consecutive years of service while a DBO Plan participant. Each participant is provided a net after-tax benefit from $500 thousand to $1 million. The death benefit of each of Messrs Karatz, Mezger, Freed, Moss, and Widner is $1 million. We have purchased life insurance policies on the lives of the participants in the DBO Plan.*

Lockheed Martin. *The Lockheed Martin Post-Retirement Death Benefit Plan for Elected Officers provides a death benefit for retired elected officers at a level of 1.5 times the officer's base salary at the time of retirement. During active employment, our elected officers are provided personal liability insurance coverage for $5 million and accidental death and dismemberment coverage for $1 million.*

Marshall & Ilsley Bank. *Because of changes in the federal income tax law governing the taxation of split-dollar life insurance benefits, in 2003, M&I entered into death benefit award agreements with Mr. Kuester and certain other senior executives under which a non-qualified death benefit plan was substituted for their previous life insurance arrangements. Originally, the life insurance arrangements were provided in lieu of certain benefits to which Mr. Kuester was entitled under the Deferred Compensation Plan. Pursuant to the death benefit agreements, the beneficiaries of Mr. Kuester are provided with a "death benefit" that is a formula based primarily on certain life insurance proceeds. On a present value basis, the new arrangements were structured to be economically neutral to M&I as compared to the life insurance arrangements.*

Newell Rubbermaid, Inc. *The SRP (Supplemental Retirement Plan), which is funded by cost recovery life insurance, covers executive officers and other key employees, including the Named Officers. The SRP benefit adds to retirement benefits under the Pension Plan so that at age sixty-five, a participant receives a maximum aggregate pension equal to 67 percent of his or her average compensation for five consecutive years in which it was the highest (multiplied by a fraction, the numerator of which is the participant's years of credited (not to exceed twenty-five)) and the denominator of which is twenty-five), reduced by primary Social Security, the benefit received under the Pension Plan and the SRP Cash Account described below.*

Outback Steak House. *The company entered into a Split-Dollar Agreement and Limited Collateral Assignment ('Split-Dollar Agreements") as of November 7, 1999, with each of the respective trusts established by Messrs. Sullivan, Basham and Avery (each, a "Policy Employee'), pursuant to which the Company was to pay the premium costs of the life insurance policies that pay a death benefit of not less than $5 million to one or more of the members of a Policy Employee's family upon death of that*

176

Policy Employee...In 2005, the Company and the Policy Employees entered into an Endorsement Split-Dollar Agreements pursuant to which the collateral assignments were released and the ownership of the policies was transferred to the Company.

Pacific Gas and Electric Company. *During 2002 and 2003, annuities were purchased to replace a significant portion of the unfunded retirement benefits for certain officers whose accrued benefit could not be provided under the Retirement Plan due to tax code limits. The annuities will not change the amount or timing of the after-tax benefits that would have been provided upon retirement under the Supplemental Executive Retirement Plan (SERP) or similar arrangements. In connection with the annuities, tax restoration payments were made such that the annuitization was tax-neutral to the officer.*

Polo Ralph Lauren Corporation. *Footnote#3. The amounts reported under "All Other Compensation" in fiscal 2003 include $501,154 premiums paid by the Company on split-dollar life insurance policies on the lives of Mr. Lauren and his spouse. We ceased paying such premiums during fiscal 2003. We will recover all premiums paid by us at the time the policies death benefits are paid, and may recover such amounts earlier under certain circumstances. (Note: In 2001, premiums paid for Ralph Lauren & his wife Ricki exceeded $3 million under split-dollar arrangements.)*

Starbucks. *The company also provides executive life insurance and annual physicals to all executive officers. The Company has terminated its obligations to pay premiums with respect to existing split-dollar life insurance arrangements with the chairman, as described on page 28 of this proxy statement, in exchange for an annual cash payment to be used by him to acquire a like benefit. There are no additional perquisites available to the executive officers...On February 11, 2005, the Company entered into a letter of agreement with Mr. Schultz and the trustee of the Shultz Irrevocable Trust and the Howard D. Shultz Irrevocable Trust to terminate split-dollar life insurance agreements with each of the trusts and the underlying policies. To replace the loss of the benefit to Mr. Shultz under the agreements, the Company agreed to compensate Mr. Shultz $236,250 annually as other compensation to be used by him to acquire a like benefit, for so long as he remains a full-time employee of the Company. This amount equals the Company's annual premium obligation as of the date of the agreement with an adjustment for related federal income tax consequences.*

Valero Energy Corporation. *Amounts for Mr. William E. Greehey also include executive insurance premiums with respect to cash value life insurance (not split-dollar life insurance) in the amount of $12,212 for 2003, 2004, and 2005. Amounts for Mr. Kleese also include executive insurance policy premiums with respect to cash value life insurance (not split-dollar life insurance) in the amount of $14,681 in 2003, $12,051 for 2004, and $17,523 for 2005. Upon his retirement, in addition to retiree medical and other benefits payable to retirees generally, the agreement provided for Mr. Greehey to receive credit for eight additional years of service for purposes of calculating his pension benefits, vesting of certain outstanding equity and equity-based awards and the right to exercise vested stock options for the remainder of their* *original term, office and secretarial services, tax planning services, and $300 thousand of permanent life insurance.*

Wisconsin Energy Death Benefit Only Plan. *The Company maintains a Death Benefit Only Plan ("DBO"). Pursuant to the terms of the DBO, upon an officer's death, a benefit is paid to his or her designated beneficiary in an amount equal to the after-tax value of three times the officer's base salary if the officer is employed by the Company at the time of death or the after-tax value of one times final base salary if death occurs post-retirement. All of the named executive officers participate in the DBO.*

LIFE INSURANCE IS SOMETHING GOOD FOR THE CONSUMER

"No great thing is ever created suddenly."
Epictetus

"There are three steps in the revelation of any truth: in the first it is ridiculed; in the second, resisted; in the third, it is considered self-evident."
Arthur Schopenhauer, German philosopher, 1788-1860

Permanent life insurance, particularly dividend-paying whole life, insurance is one of the rare financial products within America that has evolved and improved over the years. A testament to whole life is that it has endured for more that 150 years. It has survived multiple recessions and economic upheavals such as the Great Depression. The vast majority of financial products cannot make this claim. Most, eventually, break down and collapse under various economic strains.

A primary reason why dividend-paying whole life insurance has worked well throughout the years, is that it is not based upon stock market returns, the latest fad or consumer hype. The product has been designed with structural truths, rules, mathematical certainties, and conservative economic assumptions. It has also endured because the product is designed and engineered by life insurance actuaries who are the brains, architects, and rocket scientists of all life insurance products. Unlike a typical investment manager, who simply chases investment returns, the qualifications and standards to become an actuary are more comprehensive, rigorous, and selective.

Actuaries must pass numerous difficult exams in mathematical science. An actuary must also coordinate and integrate mathematical assumptions, mortality, morbidity, expenses, investment returns, economic factors, reserve ratios, and a multitude of regulations, which can vary from state to state. These individuals must also reduce speculation and risk to a science, while making permanent whole life insurance products profitable for the consumer who purchases them and for the life companies who manufacture them.

Actuaries can predict, with laser accuracy, how many people will die or live within a given sample of people over a period. The catch? Actuaries may be able to predict how many people will die within a given sample; they just cannot tell you who.

Actuaries and actuarial science are part of the economic and intellectual glues that hold any modern society together. Actuarial science is not only fundamental to the life insurance business, but the discipline is crucial to the development and pricing of all property and health insurance as well as being the mathematical methodology behind Social Security and all defined benefit pension programs.

Birth of Permanent Life Insurance

In the late nineteenth century, Henry B. Hyde, founder of the Equitable Life Assurance Society, developed the original model for cash value life insurance in this country. Hyde's work is the catalyst for all permanent life insurance products today. By adding a savings component to life insurance, Hyde successfully took away the apprehension that people had when considering the purchase of cash value life insurance. Most people thought they would never see any premiums for life insurance. Hyde developed the model whereby people would accumulate cash savings as well as life insurance benefits within one policy. These policies would mature into endowments of ten, fifteen, or twenty years.

This idea, marrying a savings component to a death benefit protection, made whole life insurance extremely popular in America and put Hyde's company on the map. From this success, the company would later extend its operations into England, Germany, and France.

Around 1900, approximately 50 percent of people's discretionary savings in America went into permanent life insurance and annuity products[79]. Thus, life insurance companies became some of the largest savings depositories. These products were not only attractive from an overall economic design, which a consumer could readily understand, but they also provided something else which the stock market and banks could not provide—safety and stability of principal.

Focus on Whole Life

This chapter primarily focuses on the benefits of dividend-paying whole life insurance, which is backed by the general account of a life company, and to a small extent, newer generation universal life insurance with secondary guarantees. Whole life *works*. As long as the consumer pays the premiums as scheduled, it will not break down and fall apart.

People often ask about variable life and variable universal life insurance. Variable life insurance is a relatively new financial product. In fact, the first variable life policy was sold in this country in 1976. There are numerous problems with variable life insurance and universal variable life insurance. With variable life, there are too many moving parts, expenses, and

---

[79] See "After the Ball, Gilded Age Secrets, Board Room Betrayals, and the Party that Ignited the Wall Street Scandal," by Patricia Beard, Harper Collins, New York, 2003.

unknowns. The ultimate success of the product is directly tied to stock market returns. Moreover, as we saw in the prior chapter on mutual funds, no one knows what the market will do. Long-term performance of variable life insurance is yet to be proven over a period of thirty or forty years.

Borrowing provisions and access to cash value can also be quite complicated with variable and variable universal life policies. Many times loan provisions of variable universal life are inferior to the loan provisions offered with traditional whole life. History gives us vital insight to all the things that can go wrong with life insurance policies that are tied to stock market returns. Take the case of John Maynard Keynes.

Keynes was one the twentieth century's leading economists. He also ran National Mutual Life Assurance Society, a leading British life insurance company. Keynes found himself in hot water by abandoning traditional bond portfolio management of life insurance and by embracing speculative returns of the stock market. Coincidentally, this is also how United Airlines wound up in trouble with its defined benefit pension; it abandoned traditional bond portfolio management of its pension. It abandoned traditional bond portfolio management, and like Keynes, chased the speculative return of the market.

Jesus Huerta de Soto, the international economist, writes about Keynes' problems in trying to manage life insurance reserves actively in a volatile stock market. In the book, *Money, Bank Credit and Economic Cycles,* he writes:

"During his chairmanship, he not only promoted an "active" investment policy strongly to variable-yield securities (abandoning the tradition of investing in bonds), but he also defended unorthodox criteria for the valuation of assets (at market value) and even the distribution of profits to policyholders through bonuses financed by unrealized stock market "earnings." All these typical Keynesian assaults on traditional insurance principles put his company in desperate straits when the stock market crashed in 1929 and the Great Depression hit. As a result, Keynes colleagues on the Board of Directors began to question his strategy and his decisions. Disagreements arose between them and led to Keynes's resignation in 1938, since, as he put it, he did not think, "it lies in my power to cure the faults of management and I am reluctant to continue to take responsibility for them."

If one of the past century's most renowned economists could not manage a variable life policy successfully, you have to wonder about the ability of the average consumer to manage one. Most consumers do not have the time, discipline, or expertise to monitor policy performance and maintain adequate buoyancy of these complex life insurance products.

This author has reviewed dozens of variable universal products. Far too many have been *underfunded*. Underfunded means these policies do not have sufficient cash equity or reserves to support the ongoing mortality and

181

expense charges in later policy years. The survival of these policies is based on unrealistic and over optimistic stock market returns. Many policies will never pay a claim, nor will they live up to their potential to be a vibrant living financial instrument.

With universal life and universal variable life, the consumer has the ability to *skip premiums*. This feature can be more of curse than a blessing. Historically, it has been demonstrated that the best life insurance policies from the best companies required *structured* deposits. However, because of this discipline, the policies also generate substantially more cash equity.

Variable life does have a place in financial planning, but it should be considered last. Variable life and a hybrid of variable life known as private placement life are popular with wealthy high net worth individuals and institutional purchasers. This product is essentially private money management with a death benefit wrapped around it.

The wealthy in this country are already convinced on the value of permanent life insurance. In an article written in 2002 in the *New York Times*, it was reported that certain individuals were depositing as much as $40 million into first-year life insurance premiums.[80] This author also knows of some extremely successful individuals who have purchased as much as $100 million face amounts of whole life, but for confidentiality reasons, cannot disclose their names.

The Pricing and Underwriting of Life Insurance

The pricing and ultimate cost of life insurance is based upon an applicant's age, gender, health status, job or hobbies, if it is exceptionally risky (e.g. hang gliding, rock climbing, parachuting, etc.). When one applies for life insurance, disability income, or long-term care insurance, this information is gathered and reviewed as part of the underwriting process.

The underwriting process allows insurers to group applicants with similar characteristics so they can calculate an appropriate premium to match the applicant's level of risk. Those applicants with similar risks pay the same premiums.

Life Insurance Is a Social Good

Life insurance companies provide an efficient, safe, and dependable means of pooling people's savings within a society. By efficiently amassing

---

[80] See "Loophole: Death Still Certain but not Taxes," by David Cay Johnston, *The New York Times*, July 28, 2002.

billions of dollars, life insurance companies become vital contributors to capital formation within society, and they do so with a high degree of integrity.

Life insurance companies are a social good because they provide highly skilled jobs right here in America and are able to maintain their infrastructure and back office operations within the United States.

Life insurance is a social good because ownership of life insurance makes policy owners and their beneficiaries less dependent upon the government for relief. Any time the government provides a service, it must confiscate the money from someone else in the form of taxes to pay for that service.

Life insurance companies are a social good as they have encouraged people to purchase war bonds in times of national need. They have also provided liquidity to the government when it has been short of cash. Life companies have also absorbed very high mortality costs when flu epidemics greatly increased death claims.

Life insurance companies had their reserves invested primarily in bonds after The Great Crash of 1929 and provided substantial liquidity for policyholders and the country as a whole. The stock market plunder only affected life insurance companies indirectly. When banks were literally going out of business on a daily basis, life insurance companies injected safe patient capital into the American economy. In addition, it was the life insurance companies that helped banks get back onto their feet financially, not the government.

Life insurance companies are a social good, as they have not strained the federal government for taxpayer subsidized deposit insurance or numerous bailouts. Many life insurance companies, who wrote group life insurance, but had not done business in the state of New York, were assessed and paid millions in life insurance claims for 9/11 victims as part of national reinsurance agreements.[81]

Life Insurance Is the Opposite of Gambling in the Casino Age

Amos Tversky, a Stanford University psychologist, has found that people would rather not make money than lose it. In a sea of speculation, life insurance is an oasis of safety and wisdom. Down through the ages, people have worried about risk. Nine out of ten times the greatest asset a family has is the ability of individuals within that family to make an income. Premature

---

[81] The author confirmed this payment by non-admitted life insurance companies who although they did not do business in the state of New York, still reimbursed millions of dollars for group life insurance claims as the result of the New York 9/11 tragedy.

death is one of the greatest gambles and risks any family or business faces. Ownership of life insurance transfers that economic risk to the life insurance company.

Life insurance proceeds cushion the family from uncertainty. As a savings program, life insurance gets better with age. Furthermore, contrary to conventional wisdom, permanent dividend-paying life insurance is one of the best inflation fighters there is, and banks' mammoth purchases of the product prove this.

Financial Strength

In 2004, Americans received over $335 billion dollars in benefits from life and health insurance companies. In 2005, the life and health insurance industry had over $4.3 trillion dollars invested in the United States economy. This included over $264 billion dollars in new investments. Insurance companies are the largest source of bond financing in this country, with $1.859 trillion dollars invested in corporate America. They also hold more than $911.9 billion in government bonds (including municipals) and over $700 billion in commercial and residential real estate.

The Great Depression was the most notable period of economic stress this country has ever witnessed. During that time, it can be rightfully said that policyholder deposits, from legal reserve life insurance companies were found to be more than 99.9 percent safe. No other financial intermediary within America can make this claim.

Give or take, there are around two thousand life insurance companies in the United States and life insurance companies employ about a half million people within the American economy. Life insurance companies are some of the largest providers of pension plans, 401(k) plans, and other retirement products for the American worker and a life insurance product of some type covers roughly 70 percent of the population. Although it is difficult to verify, it has been often said that these insurance companies control, manage or own more assets than all the banks or all the oil companies.

Life companies have consistently demonstrated superior financial strength over banks. Recent economic history verifies this. Based on figures obtained from the FDIC, starting around 1981-1982 banks were failing at a rate of about one hundred per year. The failure rate peaked at about five hundred per year in 1989, dropping down to about one hundred per year in 1991, and later petering out in 1996. All told, over twenty-nine hundred banks failed during this time.

184

Risk Management and Reinsurance

Life insurance companies manager their underwriting risks by using life reinsurance. Life reinsurance is insurance for the life insurance company. In other words, the life company transfers or cedes some of its risk to another company.

The company that receives the risk is called the reinsurer or assuming company. Reinsurance for life companies allows them to spread their risk, reduce their liabilities, and increase the asset base of the company. Without reinsurance, life companies could not issue the large face amounts or numerous types of life insurance policies offered today.

Inability to Inflate the Currency: An Additional Source of Strength

As previously documented, the Federal Reserve System, which is owned by the country's banks, creates money out of thin air when it sells treasury bills (IOU's) to our citizens and other investors. This power causes the worst tax of them all, known as *inflation.* It is inflation because the process dilutes the value of a country's currency and is similar to pouring water into a kettle of soup. You might still have soup, but you will need much more to get the same nourishment or purchasing power.

Banks further inflate the currency with *fractional reserve banking,* which means banks only have to retain a *"fraction"* of deposits on the money they lend out to the public. For every dollar of your funds the bank has on deposit, the bank can lend out *ten dollars to someone else.* This is the mystery of fractional reserve banking.

Although life companies lend out money as well, their loans are based upon 100 percent reserves. One hundred percent reserve ratio lending does not contribute to inflation, and this high reserve ratio reinforces the overall strength of the life company.

Professional Money Management

Life insurance companies, like other financial intermediaries, employ trained professionals to manage your money. With a life insurance company, the primary investment objectives are to pursue highest yield or rate of interest while maintaining preservation of capital. In 2000, gross investment income from life insurance companies was about 7.5 percent whereas it dropped to about 5.9 percent in 2004 largely because of falling interest rates. However, most life companies have at the same time drastically reduced expenses involved with investments and overall operation of their companies.

For life insurance companies to succeed, they need more than just competent money managers. They must also possess state-of-the art competence in economics, actuarial science, law, medicine, statistics, accounting, and finance. Life companies are not just looking ahead to the next quarter; they are looking out five, ten, or twenty years.

The General Account and Diversification

The general account of a life insurance company is the heart of a life insurance company. It is managed conservatively to get the highest rate of return with the maximum degree of safety. According to the National Association of Insurance Commissioners, the investments within a life and health insurance company (the general account average) in 2005 were comprised of 76.71 percent bonds, 3.38 percent stocks (common and preferred), 9.83 percent mortgage loans secured by real estate, 0.68 percent real estate, 2.21 percent cash and cash equivalents, 3.8 percent contract loans, 2.78 percent other invested assets, 0.11 percent receivables for securities and 0.45 percent aggregate write-ins for assets.

General accounts can also finance the construction of new buildings, office buildings, hotels, factories, shipbuilding, electronic transmission lines, affordable housing, historic redevelopment projects, and private placement loans to businesses. Funds can be invested in timberland, farms, and transportation systems. Notable projects, which were financed by the life insurance industry, were the Boulder Dam and the Sears Tower in Chicago.

Life insurance companies diversify investments to minimize risk. They diversify by industry, by maturity and by geography. Solomon S. Huebner, in his classic work, *The Economics of Life Insurance,* explained the way in which life companies diversify. Although Huebner wrote this fifty years ago, the same fundamentals hold true today for general account based participating whole life insurance.

Where a policyholder has $50,000 of cash accumulation under his policies and the contracts by as many as five companies, it is easily conceivable that his insurance estate may be spread out over some 200,000 different units of investment. In that case, it may be said that the policyholder has approximately 25 cents invested in each of some 200,000 different investments.

Even the wealthiest individual could not accomplish such a wide diversification. Yet the policyholder is given this splendid service, and at a very small cost. Strange as it may seem, most life underwriters seem to lose sight of this wonderful investment service connected with the investment side of the insurance account, and stress only the decreasing term protection element.

186

In addition, according to Conning Research and Consulting, the life insurance industry reported a statutory net operating gain of $32.8 billion in 2005, which was $1.7 billion above the record gain in 2004. Growth came from product innovation and increased fee-based revenue, even in the face of lower investment returns in its investment portfolios.

Guaranteed Interest and Mortality

All whole life policies contain contractual guaranteed rates of return. Most policies have guaranteed interest rates of about 4 percent. As low as this may seem, it was actually a competitive rate of return in 2003 when a ten-year U. S. Treasury bill dropped below 4 percent.

Mortality charges or the pure costs for death benefit, within a whole life policy are also guaranteed for the entire life of the policy. Initially one pays more for this permanent death benefit component. However, over time, particularly in later years, this guarantee becomes an extremely attractive economic benefit. It provides an unsurpassed compound after-tax rate of return to beneficiaries at the death of the insured.

This superior return of life insurance as an investment at death is the primary reason why banks, corporations, institutional investors, and even hedge funds have increasingly purchased older life insurance policies. However, for consumers, the guaranteed interest and mortality built into permanent whole life insurance is comforting, as other insurance coverage such as healthcare and auto continue to go up.

Sharing in Company Profits Through Dividends

Life insurance provides additional investment returns to the consumer with a dividend. Policies, which give the consumer a dividend in addition to the guaranteed interest rate, are classified as *participating policies*. Receipt of a dividend from a life insurance policy is a not taxable event, because under Internal Revenue Code, a dividend is classified as a *return of premium*. Dividends are generally paid to policyholders each year; however, they are not *guaranteed*.

A strength of a life insurance dividend is that it is guaranteed at *par value*. This is unlike dividends in other financial instruments such as common stocks. In that scenario, one could theoretically lose the entire value of the accumulated dividend if it was used to purchase additional stock of a company and if the price of the stock subsequently goes down.

187

Payment of the Dividend

Each year a life insurance company's board of directors determines what the dividend will be paid by a company to its policyholders, if any. There are three primary components to a life insurance dividend.

- The first component of the dividend—did the company make money, or is it doing better than average on its investments? If the company makes more money than it takes to run the life company, then generally a dividend will be paid.
- Secondly, claims can be a factor in a company declaring a dividend. If the life companies are underwriting their risks well, mortality costs improve and help maintain dividend levels.
- Lastly, administrative costs also are reflected in whether or not a company is going to pay a dividend. As life companies continually invest in new technology, administrative costs should go down. When administrative costs go down, they, too, help maintain the dividend.

Dividends are Less Volatile

An additional benefit of life insurance dividends, particularly from a mutual company where the policy owner is also a part owner of the company, is that they are based upon a blended aggregate yield on an entire portfolio. With this methodology, there are less *fluctuation* and *volatility* for the consumer. Dividend rates can vary from year-to-year but remain somewhat constant over a five- or six-year period.

Many life insurance companies adjusted their crediting policies in the distribution of dividends in the early 1980s when life companies faced excessive borrowing due to double-digit short-term interest rates. In order to curtail the outflow of dividends and cash values out of the life company by policyholder borrowing, many life companies developed what is called a *direct-recognition-method* of crediting dividends. This essentially credited the policyholder a slightly higher dividend rate if he or she does not borrow from the policy.

Some life companies today still credit the same dividend to a policyholder regardless of whether they borrow or not. This is called *non-direct-recognition* life insurance. Dividends vary from company to company, but generally are somewhere between two hundred and three hundred basis points (2 to 3 percent) better than a ten-year U. S. Treasury note. To give you an idea of how dividends have fared, here is a brief history of the note:

Year	10-Year Yield	Year	10-Year Yield
1986	7.71	1997	6.71
1987	8.61	1998	5.65
1988	9.09	1999	5.54
1989	8.86	2000	6.44
1990	8.76	2001	5.39
1991	8.07	2002	5.16
1992	7.39	2003	3.57
1993	6.04	2004	4.72
1994	7.18	2005	4.14
1995	6.63	2006	5.14
1996	6.74		

Accounting Treatment of Dividends

The life insurance contract has unique accounting in that dividends are treated in a FIFO (first in, first out) method of accounting.

No Lost Opportunity Costs with Whole Life Insurance

When we spend a dollar, there is a *lost opportunity cost* because we could have spent that dollar somewhere else with a more productive output. For instance, if we spend $10 thousand on an extravagant trip to Europe, there is a lost opportunity cost as we could have spent that $10 thousand somewhere else where the money could have been more productive, such as a new furnace, a deposit on a new car, or a new computer for a small business.

After a period, there is no lost opportunity cost within a permanent life insurance policy. Depending on the product chosen, which could be as soon as the third year, for every dollar one deposits into the life insurance program one realizes an additional dollar in savings as well as the enjoyment of tax deferral, death benefit protection, and so on.

Demutualization, Undivided Surplus and Closed Block Accounting

Although stock life companies can offer respectable whole life insurance products, the favorites of most experts and agents is a product from a mutual life insurance company because, technically, each policyholder is also an owner of the company. Profits from a mutual company go to policyholders versus stockholders.

However, in these times of industry consolidation, many large life insurance companies have migrated from the mutual form of ownership to a stock form of ownership whereby stockholders are owners of the company and not the policyholders. Large and familiar demutualizations include Metropolitan Life and Prudential. When a mutual life insurance company demutualizes, actuaries calculate how much money has to be set aside in reserves to pay, administer, and support all ongoing life, health, and annuity claims of the mutual insurance company. Existing mutual policyholders still enjoy payment of policy dividends just as if the company was still a mutual life insurance company under *closed block accounting* rules.

Once the company sets aside sufficient reserves to pay for claims, there are most often additional funds or profits left over. This is called *undivided surplus*. Upon demutualization of the life insurance company, this undivided surplus is set aside and distributed to policy owners on a pro rata basis. The more business the policyholder did with the company, the greater percentage of undivided surplus he or she will receive. This surplus amount can be quite an economic windfall. Each policyholder can generally receive their portion of undivided surplus in either cash, stock of the new company, or additional paid-up life insurance.

An example of the economic windfall is warranted. One Canadian life company who demutualized was extremely active in the bank-owned life insurance business. One major East Coast bank bought so much BOLI from the Canadian company that when the new life company demutualized and went into stock ownership, the bank became the largest stockholder.

State Reserve Pools as Deposit Protection

Although infrequent, several life insurance companies have gone into receivership. A few that the author is aware of are Mutual Benefit Life, Confederation Life, Executive Life, Fidelity Mutual, and Baldwin United. Although there have been failures, virtually no policyholders in the United States or Canada have lost any of their money in their life insurance contracts.

State reserve pools or guarantee associations have protected life insurance policyholders for over a hundred years. Reserve pools protect the policyholder just as much as the FDIC and have done so without taxpayer assistance.

Virtually all states participate in what is called a legal reserve pool. In a legal reserve pool system, member life insurance companies doing business in that state are assessed a portion of liability should they go defunct. For instance, if a life insurance company is doing 2 percent of business in a particular state, it incurs 2 percent of the liability of the failed company.

190

About forty-six states also have State Guarantee Funds, which guarantee up to $100 thousand of cash value in a policy and $300 thousand in aggregate life insurance benefits from a policy. The only states, which do not have guaranty funds backed up by assessments to life insurance companies, are Alaska, Colorado, the District of Columbia, New Jersey and Louisiana.[82]

State Regulation and the Armstrong Commission

The life insurance sector, like any industry, needs regulations to protect the consumer against things like misrepresentation, price gouging and so on. State regulators, who have a broad and deep authority over companies, oversee an insurance company's operations. Life companies must meet strict risk-based capital standards and abide by specific investment guidelines. Company financials are reviewed and analyzed with high accounting and actuarial standards.

A life company must first set up company and agent licensing requirements in the state in which it is domiciled and comply with solvency and product filing requirements. In order for a life company to do business in a multi-state arena, the company and its agents must apply for and receive licenses to do business in each state.

Major regulation today in the life insurance business has its roots stemming from the Armstrong Commission in the state of New York around 1905. A little history is in order.

At the turn of the century, the New York Life, the Equitable Life Assurance Society, and Mutual of New York were some of the largest custodians of capital in America. At the time, Americans put roughly 50 percent of their discretionary savings into life insurance and annuity products because of the safety and the stability the life insurance companies offered. The financiers at the turn of the century, bankers such as the Harrimans and J.P. Morgan, salivated over the amount of capital the life companies could raise and retain. This was also a time prior to the Federal Reserve, so money could not be created out of thin air. In any event, capital at times was scarce for financiers, and life insurance reserves were supposed to be put into safe and prudent bonds and not be fuel for the speculation of Wall Street.

As things would have it, Wall Street financiers managed to gain access to the life insurance funds and used this capital to finance railroad deals, bond deals and other speculative investments. Secret deals created behind closed doors between life insurance companies and Wall Street were exposed

---

[82] See "Getting Started in Annuities," by Gordon K. Williamson, John Wiley & Sons Inc., New York 1999.

through investigative journalism, and J. P. Morgan and George Perkins of the New York Life were right in the middle.

Massive resentment arose when average citizens discovered that financiers were using life insurance funds for their risky stock deals and takeovers. People worried that their funds were at risk. Investigations ensued and newspapers reported daily on the impropriety between Wall Street and the life insurance companies.

The major outcome of the investigations, through the Armstrong Commission, was that life insurance companies could no longer invest policy reserves in speculative financial deals like those that it had done with Morgan and New York Life. Since the Armstrong Commission, life companies, through various state rules and regulations, must prudently invest policyholder funds for life and annuity products in safe financial instruments. As a result, at least 90 percent or more of all life insurance funds are invested in investment grade bonds, mortgages, real estate, cash and a few percentage points in common stocks.

The track record of life insurance business has been ably managed and regulated at the state level for over a hundred years because of the Armstrong Commission. State regulators also impose restrictions on policy provisions, premiums, agent compensation, company investment strategies, and accounting.

Rating Services

There are rating companies, which monitor the financial stability of a life insurance company. The most widely known is A. M. Best Company out of New Jersey. It has rated the financial stability of life insurance companies since 1899. A. M. Best rates an entity based on its financial soundness and its ability to pay future life insurance and annuity claims.

The highest rating an insurance company can receive from A. M. Best is A+ + (superior), while A+ is excellent and A is very good. A. M. Best also gives lower ratings as well. In most instances purchasers of life insurance should stick with a life company with an A or better rating, although some carriers, which have a lower rating, may also be extremely sound.

Other rating services include Duff & Phelps, Moody's Investor Services, Standard & Poor's, and Weiss Research. There is also a Comdex rating, which is a composite numeric rating of all the rating services combined, with a score of one hundred being the perfect score of financial soundness.

You Are the Owner

From day one, you are the owner of a life insurance policy. As such, you have *immediate* contractual rights guaranteed by the policy. This differs from ownership rights within a retirement account like a 401(k) plan. Retirement accounts are subject to vesting schedules, entry dates, taxation, changes in tax code, and even employer integrity. In many ways, a retirement plan is not totally your own, particularly when you consider that the government, in one way or another is going to confiscate a large portion in the form of taxes.

Then there is the question of employer integrity. This author has witnessed several unscrupulous employers who used employee retirement funds as if they were their own piggy bank to start businesses and even to take their own families on skiing vacations out West. There was little government reaction to the employees' plight even when the problem was reported to the Department of Labor. In addition, to the best of the author's knowledge, no one was ever prosecuted for using employee retirement funds. It was just as tragic as the vaporization of the employee retirement plans at Enron, Global Crossing, and WorldCom.

The value of individual ownership within a society cannot be underestimated, as it is a *free contract among free people.* The contractual relationship between a well-capitalized highly regulated life insurance company and an individual can be much stronger than with an employer-employee relationship.

Utility of Your Money

Many financial products, perhaps the majority of those promoted in the media and by financial institutions today, put the utility of our money in a straight jacket for a very long period. Financial products which deny individuals access to their funds are products such as IRAs, Roth IRAs, 401(k)s, the Uniform Gift to Minors Account (UGMA), and 529 College savings plans.

By having total control of your money for a long period, financial institutions and other intermediaries are assured that they will make money. Quite often, the money within these accounts is only points on a scoreboard—you may not get to enjoy or use any of these funds.

If you are only thirty years of age and just starting an IRA or a 401(k), you are not going to have any enjoyment on this money for a very long time. In contrast, a major benefit of permanent cash value life insurance is that you have *access* or *utility* to your funds in case you need them. You may have access to the funds by borrowing against the policy, by surrendering dividends or even through total policy surrender.

Life Insurance is an Expression of Love, Caring and Wisdom

The vast majority of buildings never burn down, yet all people die—some of us later than others do—but we will all get one death eventually. Kwame Jackson, former star of the hit television show "The Apprentice," lost his mother when he was only fifteen years old. His stepfather and godparents raised him. Jackson said that the proceeds of his mother's life insurance initially funded his education at the University of North Carolina and a master's degree in business from Harvard University. This education helped Jackson secure a job working with high net worth individuals in financial planning at Goldman Sachs. Kwame Jackson has said openly, "Without life insurance, I'm not sure how things might have turned out."

Unexpected events happen all the time. Take for example, Olympic figure skating gold medalist Scott Hamilton. Hamilton lost his mother at age nineteen and knows well how a family's finances can be strained when there is no life insurance. Without his mother's income, he had to rely on an anonymous donor to help him compete. Today, Hamilton strongly believes in the value of life insurance. He has invested in the insurance since he was a young adult, and after a battle with testicular cancer, has become an even bigger believer.

Life insurance is the only financial product with feelings. That is right, feelings. It contains emotion and deep seated expressions of love. For the vast majority of us, nine times out of ten, the greatest economic asset is the potential earning capacity of the head or heads of a family. In this light, the family unit must be viewed as an economic enterprise. Purchasing life insurance on the breadwinners makes good economic sense. A life insurance purchase is a sign of wisdom, as only this financial product can perform many economic jobs *simultaneously.*

Moreover, as we have reviewed earlier, banks and corporations do not just buy high cash value life insurance just for the death benefits. They buy life insurance for a variety of economic reasons such as safety, liquidity, tax benefits and deductions, the ability to enhance the income statement, reserving for future benefits and cost recovery.

A Safe Harbor for Private Capital Formation

The modern-day American consumer desperately needs savings or private capital formation, which is safe, liquid, and not subject to the predatory nature of a deregulated, de-supervised, unstable fractional reserve banking system. Americans as a whole are swimming in debt and anywhere they can accumulate capital where it is not under the control of some bank will benefit them immensely.

Putting one's liquid savings in the stock market or real estate has serious drawbacks. The most obvious drawback with the stock market is the potential to lose some or even your entire principal in the market. The major drawback with real estate is the lack of liquidity. When you analyze it, there are only so many places you can legitimately store and warehouse liquid savings in America. Let's look at some of them:

1.   You could keep your cash under a mattress or in a cookie jar, but your money is vulnerable to theft and you will not be making any interest or earnings on that money.

2.   You could put your money in a bank or credit union. They will give you a miniscule amount of interest if the money is purely liquid. The government will *confiscate* a portion of your interest earnings at *top marginal tax rates*.

3.   You could put your money in the stock market and stock mutual funds. However, as we know, these are very volatile places for savings. There are no guarantees. Conflicts of interest are everywhere. Values can fluctuate wildly. You can lose some or even your entire principal. In addition, if you invest on margin, you can lose what you do not even have.

4.   You could put your money in a retirement account. However, if you are thirty years old, the money is in a lock box in someone else's vault for the next thirty years. Your money is only points on a scoreboard, and who knows what the market will do to your money, never mind inflation!

5.   Others still think it is safe to keep cash or equity tied up in a house or real estate by paying down or getting rid of the mortgage all together. There are problems with this thinking.

There is nothing more frozen than equity in raw land. Land and resale values can get devalued. Getting access to the cash or equity value in your home can take time, appraisal fees, new mortgages, higher interest rates and so on. A lender can also turn you down to the access on your equity if you lose your job or you have a drastic life change such as a new job or a divorce. Worse still, if you become disabled and can no longer work, lenders are not interested in you because your ability to repay the loan can be completely diminished.

We still hear the wisdom of having your home "paid off" as a great way to create a storehouse of wealth. What is perhaps more advantageous to the consumer is to be in a position to pay off the house but not necessarily paying it off.

First, by being in the position to pay off a house, you will still enjoy the home interest deduction, which is, for the majority of Americans, their

195

greatest tax deduction. When the home is paid off, there are no more deductions.

Secondly, if you have stored significant values in your life insurance policies using life insurance as a pool of capital instead of a home equity line as the owner you have more control. Life insurance values, particularly those within whole life remain at par value and are not subject to the contraction of real estate values.

Thirdly, you could suffer the consequences of a natural disaster. How do you get money out of your home if it burns down, is ripped apart in a tornado, or is totaled in a hurricane like Katrina? Good luck. As Robert Frost once said, "A banker will lend you an umbrella when the sun is out, but will take it away when it rains."

Don Blanton, President of Money Trax and one of the leading authorities on life insurance and financial planning in the United States, was at his residence in New Orleans during Hurricane Katrina, one of the greatest natural disasters this country has ever seen. Property damage as we know was of an incredible magnitude. Don gave permission to reprint part of his 2005 fall newsletter. It illuminates the benefits of having cash equity in your life insurance instead of a home.

"I could never have anticipated the impact of Hurricane Katrina. We have been in the paths of hurricanes many times but never dreamed a hurricane could change our lives forever. I have believed in the conviction that cash value is more valuable than home equity and have preached that message for over twelve years now. I have encouraged my clients over the year that having their home paid for is a desired position but doing so in a way that gives up liquidity, use, and control may not be the best way to reach that goal. My personal opinion is that when you have cash value equal to your mortgage balance your home is paid off. Having the money to write the check if you desire is most comforting. It is not necessary to have your home paid off. You need the money.

Hurricane Katrina has further solidified my personal convictions about where one's money should be located. I have clients on the Gulf Coast that lost everything in the storm. "Everything" is hard to imagine. You can't. If you could have heard the phone calls of some of my clients and their tears and cries, you would have a better idea. Those who had their homes paid for are in a rough time working with insurance companies and talking to attorneys trying to get back to square one. Property values most likely will not get back to pre-hurricane values even when the home has been replaced. In any case, it is going to take years. They had no mortgage, but now they have no money and many have no job. The entire equity is in the hands of the insurance adjusters. Many have been offered checks much less than what it will take to rebuild. Many have taken the money today in an effort to move on with their lives even at a loss.

Clients who had their equity in cash value had a much different reaction to their tragedy. Their mortgage company has frozen their payments due and even waived payments until the first of the year on homes in the area. Even on homes that were not even affected. Meanwhile, they have access to their cash value. They have secured loans on their contracts to put a down payment on a new home to live in until they receive their insurance settlements on their damaged home. This has provided a seamless opportunity to get their families and jobs back on track. They will one day sell the home they are in today, pay off the loan balance on the insurance policies and return to their original home. Those who did not have access to their money were not able to move fast enough to purchase the few homes on the market and available.

I have had clients who have used the money in their contracts to start side businesses related to the clean up and reconstruction while their current businesses are suffering. I have a physical therapist that has no clients to see so he started up a stump grinding business to make ends meet until his clients come back to town. I have a dentist who is driving a tractor-trailer to the dump to remove debris from all the trees have been blown down. He said he is starting his practice all over again with just a few people to see each week. People have moved to get their children in school and may not be back until Christmas, if at all.

I am more convinced now than the day I got in the insurance business. Insurance is the greatest product ever invented and cash value is much more valuable than home equity. If you do not believe it, come to New Orleans or the Gulf Coast of Mississippi and try to tell folks who have lost everything who thought having their home paid off is a safe position."

High cash value life insurance has many characteristics more common with banking than life insurance as we traditionally think of it. Maybe that is why the banks buy so much of it. However, when you analyze where your cash must reside, and your cash must reside somewhere, a life policy is in so many ways a superior warehouse, perhaps the best warehouse within our economic system. Again, you would be receiving these benefits simultaneously:

- The money is being professionally managed.
- There are guarantees on the money higher than a checking account.
- There is additional interest on the money in the form of dividends.
- The money growing within the policy is not being taxed like a bank.
- You have access to your money.
- There are death benefits in case someone dies and disability benefits to fund the program if someone becomes disabled.
- Depending on the state of residence, there are various protections on death benefits, disability benefits, and cash values in the case of lawsuits, bankruptcies, etc.
- Life insurance is an engineered system designed to accept additional deposits. It is the ultimate holding tank for money, yet you are not locked out of account because of government regulations.

197

Borrowing against Cash Value Life Insurance: A Guaranteed Line of Credit and a Way to Become Your Own Finance Company

"If you want to know the value of money, go out and try to borrow some."
Benjamin Franklin

"There is nothing sacred about the pay-as-you go idea so far as I am concerned, except that it represents the soundest principle of financing that I know."
Harry S. Truman.

Credit is the lifeblood of a family and a business. Once you understand the mechanics of permanent high cash value life insurance, you will understand that the product can become your own bank or the infrastructure of your very own finance company. Life insurance loans provide certainty in a very uncertain world.

Today the average American forks over about thirty-five cents of every dollar in interest costs paid to some bank or finance company. If we have a system to pay back that interest to ourselves versus a finance company, we will obviously become much wealthier.

When we have a large pool of accessible capital under our control, we become more confident and financially stronger because we are not dependent on a third party for approving our credit. When we are not dependent upon a bank, we can be better negotiators. When we have a pool of capital under our control, we *can act* on an opportunity versus *reacting to* an opportunity.

Loan Overview

Almost all whole life and universal life policies permit the policy owner to borrow a portion of the accumulated cash value with the insurance company charging interest on the loan. The interest rate charged to borrow the funds is often lower than market rates.

For instance, if one purchased a used car for $10,000 and financed most of it through a finance company, an interest rate could easily be 12 percent or more. However, if you borrowed $10,000 from a life insurance company secured by the collateral of your cash within the policy, your interest rate could be 6.5 percent, saving you 5.5 percent in interest charges. However, it gets even better; even though you have removed $10,000 from your life insurance policy, most companies still pay a dividend on those borrowed funds even though the money is not there. Most likely, the dividend would be 1 or 2 percent lower than the current interest rate of 6.5 or 5.5 percent. Therefore, if you are paying 6.5% gross interest to the life company on your loan, but the life company still pays you 4.5 or 5.5 percent on these borrowed

198

funds, your net loan rate is in effect, 1 or 2 percent, which is far superior to the 12 percent.

Deductibility of Interest

Personal interest, such as that paid on a credit card is not deductible. There are types of deductible interest, namely interest on loans to purchase *investment properties* (see IRC Sec. 1639(d) (4) (B) (iii)), interest incurred in the conduct of *your trade or business* (IRC. Sec 163) and *qualified residence interest.* A "qualified residence" is your principal residence and one other property such as a vacation home or a boat you live on which you use more than fourteen days during the year. (See IRC Sec. 163 (h) (5) (A).)

There are two types of deductible qualified residence interest. The first is *acquisition indebtedness,* which you incur when you purchase, build, or substantially improve a qualified residence. The limit on acquisition indebtedness is $1,000,000 and $500,000 for married persons filing separately.

There is also *home equity indebtedness* where one may take loans against the equity of the home, which can be over and above acquisition indebtedness. The maximum for home equity indebtedness is $100 thousand and $50 thousand for married persons separately.

You can also deduct interest on qualified education loans. The deduction is taken as an "above-the-line adjustment" which directly reduces adjusted gross income (AGI). The deduction is limited to $2,500 for years 2001 and after, and is phased out for married taxpayers filing with incomes of $135 thousand or more, and phased out for single taxpayers making $65 thousand or more.

Life Insurance Loans in Action

This author has seen life insurance loans finance a number of things when conventional financing was too expensive or non-existent. In his own childhood, he saw his parents use life insurance loans to make home improvements, purchase automobiles, and even help with college tuition bills.

The author has also seen some very creative uses of life insurance loans such as financing forklifts, computer networks, inventories, partner buy-outs, investment real estate, and airplanes. One time, this author even saw some very large life insurance loans finance the purchase of a new car dealership. The only real limit to the amount you can finance is determined by the amount of cash, which is deposited into the policies.

One of the most successful entrepreneurs this author ever knew used his life insurance loans to finance just about everything. He had a manufacturing facility with several locations and some very big life insurance policies. The entrepreneur used life insurance loans on his personal and corporate-owned life insurance to purchase machinery, automobiles, and real estate.

He paid the loans back just like he was paying back a bank as he knew the interest payments were going into his pocket instead of the bank. The pool of capital within those policies just kept getting bigger and bigger. He built up so much equity in these policies that during the 1980s, when prime rate to businesses was as high as 20 percent, he was purchasing equipment to expand his business with the equity he had in his life policies at five percent. While everyone else was scrambling for funds, this man was patiently moving forward and vastly expanding his business. In addition, in the middle of a major real estate contraction, he used the life insurance loans to purchase an oceanfront home in Maine and a retirement home in Florida.

When this man died, all the proceeds of his life insurance went directly to his widow who avoided a very complex probate process.

J. C. Penney and Walt Disney: A Testimony to the Power of Life Insurance Loans

Then there is the case of J.C. Penney, who built a billion dollar empire in retail. When Penney died in 1971, the *Grand Rapids Press* wrote, "In the Great Stock Market Crash of 1929 he was almost wiped out, but with the money he borrowed on his $3 million dollar life insurance policy, he was able to rebound."[83] Rebound is a bit of an understatement.

The best of us can be turned down for loans. Take the case of Walt Disney. Few people know of the trials and tribulations of Walt Disney. During his career, the best animators walked out on Disney. One of his most popular characters was stolen. His studios were often in debt and understaffed. He also went bankrupt a number of times, the first time when he was twenty-one years old. Walt Disney's life was a constant adventure against the odds.

However, Disney had a lifelong dream of building a family park unlike any other in America during the early 1950s. Typical amusement parks of the time were dilapidated places with rusty Ferris wheels, creaky merry-go-rounds, rancid food smells, drunks, and filthy restrooms.

Walt had a dream. He wanted to have a sparkling and immaculate theme park where families were treated fairly, where they would not be afraid to eat the food and where he could charge an admission to be compensated to

---

[83] See "Die Broke & Wealthy, The Insurance Bonanza that Beats the Tax Man While You Are Still Alive," by Gopala Alampur, Chestnut Publishing Group, Toronto, Canada, 2003.

make a profit. From coast to coast, people told Walt he was off his rocker. They said he would never be able to charge admission to an amusement park. No one did that.

His brother Roy, his financial manager and partner, said that a theme park like the one Walt was talking about could not be done. Roy maintained that Walt would have to serve liquor to make money. He told his brother it would cost too much to keep the place clean as Walt imagined. Roy, even though he was extremely close to his brother, refused to back Walt Disney's vision of a clean family theme park. He told his brother they were in the animation business, not the theme park business.

Walt was determined to move ahead with the project and financed the company on his own. Therefore, in 1952, Disney cleaned out his savings, sold a vacation home in Palm Springs, and recruited the help of a few employees. However, the most important asset to help propel his dream was his life insurance loan. Walt Disney used a $100,000 loan from his life insurance policies to start Walt Disney, Inc.[84]

Walt used the money from his life insurance loan to fund feasibility studies with Stanford Research Institute to pinpoint an ideal place for Disneyland. In the end, they decided that Anaheim, California, would be the best place to build a park due to location and climate.

Later Walt would raise additional millions through television. However, the life insurance loan started the initial dream known as Disneyland. The rest, as we say, is history.

Getting Started: Financing Automobiles

According to the Automobile Association of America, in 2004, the average car loan in this country was around sixty-three months compared to forty-eight months in 2001. J. D. Power & Associates reported that the amount of *upside down trades* (cars where the loan balances were greater than the value of the car) were 25 percent in 2001. By 2004, upside down trades had increased to 38 percent. In addition, there is no such thing as zero percent financing with interest or cash back. Most of these zero percent rates in actuality break down to 10-13 percent rates.

General Motors and Ford make more money on financing cars than they do building them. The most profitable segment of General Motors has been General Motors Acceptance Corporation (GMAC), which finances automobiles and home mortgages. General Motors also owns Ditech, the company who advertises non-stop for home refinancing.

---

[84] "The Man Behind the Magic, The Story of Walt Disney," by Catherine and Richard Greene, Viking Pengiun, New York, 1991.

Obviously, if we can find a way to finance the automobiles ourselves and pay the finance charges to ourselves instead of a bank or other finance company, the better off we will be. First, let us look at five ways in which we can finance the purchase of an automobile. (Credit must be given to R. Nelson Nash, best-selling author of the book, *Becoming Your Own Banker*). Here is just a summary of his work in regards to using life insurance as your own finance company.

The first way to purchase a car is via the lease method—in the long run, the most expensive way to purchase an automobile. If you go to a high-end luxury dealership, probably 75 percent or more of luxury cars are leased.

The second least expensive way to finance a car is via a bank or finance company. The third least expensive method is by paying cash, as you are eliminating finance charges altogether. The fourth least expensive way to purchase a car is by paying cash for the car and establishing a sinking fund for the next purchase after the existing car wears out. The final and most efficient method is to purchase your automobile for cash via a life insurance loan from a participating whole life policy and to pay back that loan at the rate of interest you would have normally paid a bank or other finance company.

For example, you may be paying 6.5 percent interest on a $25 thousand loan from a life insurance company. However, the company may be crediting you 5.5 percent on these borrowed funds, so in effect, you have a 1% loan. Not only are you getting a low loan rate, but also you are paying the vast majority of interest back to yourself instead of a greedy bank or finance company! By doing your financing this way, you are *recapturing* all the finance charges you would have normally paid to a bank or financial institution and putting them in your pocket instead.

Loans are made against the general account of a life insurance company. The cash values within your policies serve as collateral to secure the amount of the loan. The outstanding loan will reduce the total death benefit of the policy and surrender cash value. It is highly recommended you pay back the loan to restore your pool of capital.

The beauty of the life insurance loan is that it is flexible! You have more control. For instance, if circumstances change and you need breathing room, you can pay interest only and pay back the loan on a schedule that works for you. You can also pay back chunks of the loan without being penalized. The only limiting factor is that the financing available is limited to the money you have in your life insurance policy! Usually, that is not a true limitation.

Tax-Deferred Benefits

The savings element, interest and investment income in all permanent cash value life insurance grows tax-deferred just like savings in an IRA or a 401(k). If dividends are reinvested back into the policy, paid in cash, or used to reduce the annual premium due, there is no taxable event. However, when life insurance dividends are left within the policy to accumulate at interest, income taxes are due on the interest received on the accumulating dividends.

If a life insurance policy is never surrendered, there is no taxable gain. However, if a policy is surrendered and there is a gain within the policy, the policy gain is taxed at ordinary income tax rates within the year received.

Income Tax-Free Death Benefit

All life insurance benefits, regardless of policy type (term, group, whole life, variable, universal, modified endowment, etc.) are received income tax free by beneficiaries. The power of an income tax-free death benefit cannot be underestimated. This author, who has helped numerous clients settle an estate, has witnessed huge erosion in retirement plan balances due to income and estate taxes. With the proper advance planning, life insurance proceeds can generally be received free of estate taxes.

Tax-deductible Permanent Life Insurance

Permanent life insurance can be purchased with tax-deductible dollars under the Internal Revenue Code as a funding medium in a qualified retirement plan. The proceeds of life insurance in a qualified plan are also received income tax-free, but this follows the *net amount at risk rules*. The following is an example of how the rules work:

If the life policy within the retirement plan has cash surrender value of $10,000 but has a gross death benefit of $100,000, then the net amount at risk (death benefit minus cash value) would be $90,000. This amount would be income tax free to beneficiaries. The $10,000 would be fully taxable to the beneficiaries at normal income tax levels. Additional consideration will be given to life insurance in qualified retirement plans in a later chapter.

Unsurpassed Rate of Return in the Event of Premature Death

No one dies at the right time, and no one ever dies with too much cash. Although life insurance is not an investment per se, it is a superior economic workhorse that provides most beneficiaries with an exemplary return at death. The compound after-tax external rate of return on life insurance upon a premature death is phenomenal. This is why permanent life insurance policies and even term life insurance are now being actively purchased as investments by institutional investors and hedge funds, which we address in further detail shortly.

Since numbers often speak louder than words, the author is going to use an example of the actual rate of return upon death that one would have to get in an alternative investment to beat the power of life insurance. For this example, a mutual whole life policy from a respected Midwestern insurance company will be used. The policy is commonly known as Life Paid Up at 75 (Life@75). The insured is a non-smoking female in a preferred underwriting class at issue ages of thirty, forty, fifty, and sixty. A *money purchase* methodology will be utilized, which means premiums and deposits are identical at each age. The only variance is the total face amount of the policy. This example also has two riders attached to the policy. The first rider is a waiver of premium benefits provision on disability, which would pay the policy premiums of the insured in the event of a disability. The second rider is a long-term care rider, which would let the insured "pay down" up to $180,000 in long-term care expenses from the policy face amount. While these riders are valuable benefits to the insured, they place a drag on policy performance to the beneficiaries. Without these riders, the compound-after-tax rate of return to the beneficiary would be greater.

Compound After-Tax Rate of Return on Life Insurance Premiums to Beneficiaries
Life @ 75 Ordinary Whole Life, Participating
Money Purchase Methodology, Annual Premium/Deposit $6,895.00
Preferred Non-Smoking Female, 2001 Commissioner's Ordinary Standard Mortality
Riders: Waiver of Premium & Long-Term Care

Age Issue	30	40	50	60
Face Amount	$500,000	$345,562	$234,039	$153,699
Policy Year				
1.	7,191.00%	4,950.23%	3,327.59%	2,160.00%
2.	708.94%	565.92%	441.01%	332.12%
3.	282.35%	233.63%	188.34%	146.19%
4.	162.78%	136.28%	110.91%	86.60%
5.	110.35%	92.64%	75.42%	58.79%
10.	37.56%	92,64%	75.42%	58.79%
15.	21.17%	17.15%	13.29%	9.80%
20.	14.41%	11.52%	8.87%	6.45%

Settlements Confirm Superior Returns of Life Insurance

"Trading in life insurance policies held by wealthy seniors has quietly become a big business. Hedge funds, financial institutions like Credit Suisse and Deutsche Bank, and investors like Warren E. Buffett are spending billions to buy life insurance policies from the elderly. Other investors are paying seniors to apply for life insurance, lending them money to buy the policies, and then reselling them to speculators."
Charles Duhigg, Late in Life, Finding a Bonanza in Life Insurance
The New York Times, December 17, 2006

During the 1980s, when the AIDS virus broke out, investors started to buy life insurance policies from policyholders infected with AIDS. This was known as a *viatical settlement*. Individuals infected with AIDS received cash for their policies before death and investors who purchased these policies got a superior rate of return upon the death of the insured. With medical improvements, the life expectancy for people with AIDS has improved and, as such, the market for viatical settlements has dried up. However, an offshoot of the viatical settlement business later developed which is called the *life settlement business*.

The business of life settlements confirms the high rate of return that life insurance upon death provides. Life settlements are not limited to permanent life insurance policies. They can also apply to term life insurance.

Life settlements are generally for people who have a life expectancy of twelve years or less. An investor buys a life insurance policy at a discount. The investor takes over premium payments of the policy and collects the proceeds of the policy when the original owner dies.

Life settlements can work for senior citizens who need cash now. Life settlements can also rescue irrevocable life insurance trusts when product and interest assumptions change, particularly for older universal life policies. In addition, a life settlement may be a solution to an insurance trust when the funding requirements surpass the resources of the donor or exceed annual gift exclusions.

The purchase of older life insurance policies as investments is not a new business. Asian and European investors have been buying older life insurance policies for years. A working paper was published by the Wharton School of the University of Pennsylvania in October 2002 entitled "The Benefits of a Secondary Market for Life Insurance Policies," written by Neil A. Doherty and Hal J. Singer. The authors encouraged and praised the development of a secondary market for life insurance settlements, as it gives consumers new alternatives for those who have limited life expectancies.

Analysts Suneet Kamath and Timothy Sledge of Sanford C. Bernstein & Co. LLC published a call report in March 2005, entitled, "Life Insurance Long View—Life Settlements Need Not Be Unsettling." The analysts predicted a robust ten-fold increase in the market for life settlements over the next several years. In addition, Conning Research and Consulting estimates that in 2005, the total face amounts purchased in life settlements was about $5.5 billion, up from $2 billion in 2002.

Institutional investors in America are quickly getting into the life settlement business. Their involvement confirms that life insurance proceeds are a superior rate of return to beneficiaries. General Re Corporation (Gen Re), which is a subsidiary of Warren Buffett's Berkshire Hathaway, lent $400 million to Life Equity LLC, a life settlement provider based in Hudson, Ohio. Additional institutional interest and backing of the life settlement business is coming from Deutsche Bank (DB: NYSE), Merrill Lynch (MER: NYSE), the Advanced Settlements Division of National Financial Partners (NFP: NYSE) and American International Group (AIG: NYSE). Munich based HVB Group, Germany's second largest bank, is offering $1 billion to purchase Peachtree Life Settlements of Boca Raton, Florida—the largest institutional source of funding for life settlements.[85]

---

[85] See "Six Feet over/ Under," by Mathew Goldstein, TheStreet.com, posted online, www.thestreet.com, June 12, 2006.

Life Settlement Solutions, a major life settlement provider out of San Diego California, planned to purchase about $12 billion face amount of life insurance for about $4 billion in 2005. In a February 2006 issue of *US Banker,* Larry Simon, CEO of Life Settlement Solutions, said this about bankers' interest in the life settlement business.

"Banks in or considering the market include Citibank, Credit Suisse First Boston, UBS, Morgan Stanley, Deutsche Bank, Dresdner Bank, DZ Bank, Abbey, WestLB, KBC Bank and Fubon Bank. "All the major banks—I assure you, every one of the major banks, and I'm talking the investment banks and others—are in this asset or looking at the asset and following it very closely." Simon says. "They feel the yields will be higher than they got in most other places in the market. The non-correlated returns, which are of course everybody's concern today-[banks] don't want it tied to the stock market."

Due to a new accounting rule enacted in 2005 by the Connecticut-based Financial Accounting Standards Board (FASB), hedge funds are also investing in life settlements to boost the returns on their funds. New accounting rules let investors put life settlement policies on their books at purchase price. This eliminates the need for the first year initial write-down.

Some hedge funds that are purchasing life settlements include Dallas-based HBK, London's Pentagon Capital Management, London's Cheyne Capital, New York's Reservoir Capital, and New York-based DB Zwirn and Allsettled Group, Inc., a New York-based life settlement provider which is itself part of a hedge fund group, Oscar Capital Management, LLC. That fund has sold $500 million of life settlements to three hedge fund groups.[86]

Examples of Life Settlements

Life settlements can work with any type of life insurance. The 2005 fall issue of *Kiplinger's* magazine did an article about Richard Lowry[87], who once owned a computer chip company that went out of business. To protect his family and the company, Lowry had purchased two $1 million term life policies. He wanted to drop the policies, as he could no longer afford the thousands in annual premiums. However, Lowry also had had triple bypass surgery and a history of heart disease, so he was no longer insurable at reasonable pricing.

---

[86] "Hedge Funds Buy Life Insurance Policies to Ply New Profit Path," by Miles Weiss & Richard Teitlebaum, Bloomberg, December 1, 2005. www.qcapitalstrategies.com, July 26, 2006

[87] "New Life for Old Policy," by Mary Beth Franklin, *Kiplinger's Retirement Planning*, Fall 2005, p.92.

Lowry called his agent about canceling the policies; his agent had another idea. The agent found an investor and paid Lowry $280 thousand in cash for the policies in a life settlement. The article went on to explain how Lowry used the money he received from the life settlement to help pay for his children's education, replace lost income and fund a new venture writing a military book.

Another interesting life settlement came to light in *Business Wire* on June 29, 2005. A public company, X-Rite, Incorporated (NASDAQ:XRIT), out of Grandville, Michigan originally purchased $160 million of life insurance with fourteen policies to support and fund a shareholder redemption agreement with the original founders and their spouses. X-Rite spent $4.3 million annually on these policies.

In November 2004, the company terminated the shareholder agreement. As of April 1, 2005, the policies had a cash surrender value of $25.7 million. In June 2005, the company decided to sell off $30 million dollars in face amount of these policies to Coventry First, LLC and Maple Life Financial, Inc. X-Rite received $6.5 million net of closing costs and reported a $1.2 million gain in the second quarter but the gain would not be taxable due to prior company losses.

X-Rite's chief financial officer had felt that it was an excellent time to realize the value of some of the policies and acted upon it. Yet even after the $30 million in face amount was sold, $130 million remained, with $3.5 million in annual premiums. Obviously, this company understands the value of life insurance.

Life Insurance Accelerated Benefits

Many life companies are not very enthusiastic about life settlements, as they can have the potential to throw off lapse ratios and other actuarial assumptions, which can disrupt the profitability of a life insurance company. One alternative to life settlements that most life companies are now offering is *accelerated benefits*. Accelerated benefits are the acceleration of life insurance proceeds to an insured that is terminally ill before his or her death.

Under the Health Insurance Portability and Accountability Act of 1996, federal law (IRC Sec. 101(g)), an individual who is terminally ill is allowed to receive the death benefits from his or her life insurance as a living benefit prior to his or her death free of federal income tax. Taxes at the state level, however, still may apply.

Many life insurers have been offering accelerated benefits as a no-cost policy rider since about 1996 when the law was passed. Some companies let individuals spend down as little as 25 percent of life insurance proceeds, whereas others allow as much as 80 percent.

Minimal Administration Costs and Less Red Tape

Unlike retirement plans such as IRAs, 401(k)s, and simple and traditional defined benefit pensions, life insurance plans are relatively simple. Qualified retirement plans are extremely complex. Just when you seem to catch on to how they work, the government changes the rules.

The better retirement plans require filing for separate tax identification, preparation of trust documents, individual enrollment forms, discrimination tests, top-heavy test, actuarial certification, vendor selection, summary plan descriptions, spousal sign offs, 5500 filings, eleventh hour surprises, and miles of red tape.

Life insurance, in particular dividend paying whole life, is simple. You deposit your premiums and the life insurance company does everything else.

No Government Reporting

The purchase of life insurance for one's own use and privacy is not subject to invasive government reporting requirements.

No Discrimination; It Can Just Cover You

Another benefit of life insurance is that you can be *selective* as to whom is covered by it. Government-sanctioned retirement plans mandate that all employees must be covered. With life insurance, you do not have to cover everybody. You can be discriminatory.

Life insurance, particularly with the new improved designs, can be a cornerstone of a business owner's, or other key employee's, overall compensation and retirement package.

The Disability Problem

According to a study done by the Society of Actuaries in 1985, almost half (48 percent) of the homes in America are foreclosed on because of disability. The 1985 Commissioner's Individual Disability Table A, the probability of at least one long-term disability lasting at least ninety days prior to age sixty-five is as follows:

Age	30	40	50
	54%	45%	33%

When a disability occurs, this author has noticed the following troubling recurring patterns:

- Savings do not last too long, because Americans save so little.
- Banks will not lend to you, because they no longer believe you have the ability to repay.
- Social Security takes forever to qualify for. You have to go through a five-month waiting period; it must look like you cannot work for at least one year, and that your disability could result in death.
- Friends and relatives—well, this is charity and charity has its limits.
- Assets are sold and people settle for less.

Waiver of Premium Benefit: A Partial Solution to the Problem

For a modest price, a life insurance policy can have the waiver of premium benefit added as a rider. In essence, the waiver of premium benefit is a mini-disability policy. With the waiver of premium provision, when a long-term disability occurs, life insurance remains in force. The savings element continues within the policy. The asset protection and creditor protection remain with the policy. In addition, there is no indebtedness to the insured individual.

This author, who has designed, brokered, and installed well over a hundred individual and employer group disability plans is acutely aware of how easily people can become disabled. It happens all the time. Some of the most frequent disabilities that the author has seen are car accidents and other injuries, strokes and circulatory disorders, back injuries and degenerative musculoskeletal disorders, mental and nervous disorders, severe diabetes, cancer, and chronic fatigue syndrome. The benefit of waiver of premium rider is that when other savings programs and protection programs collapse, the life insurance continues.

An Example of Waiver of Premium in Action

An entrepreneur whose wife had some high cash value whole life insurance policies, which were being used to create stable college education funds, had consulted this author. The rationale behind the policies is that they would provide an efficient way to amass savings and that, in the event of the death of the wife, the funds would support the beneficiaries.

Unfortunately, the entrepreneur's wife, who had been actively working, had been disabled due to breast cancer for about three years. The entrepreneur

210

was still paying the premiums on the policies. The entrepreneur's agent had died so he asked this author for guidance and an explanation of his options concerning his wife's life insurance program.

The first thing we checked on was waiver of premium. The agent, who had originally sold the policy, got it right. The waiver of premium benefit was included. The entrepreneur subsequently filed a disability claim on his wife's life insurance. Since the entrepreneur was able to establish the existence of his wife's disability three years prior to the claim, the life insurance company, a large well-known national mutual company, refunded the entrepreneur's three years premium on his wife's policies. It was a large check.

In another instance, an agent friend from the Midwest said he had once had a doctor client, a high priced specialist who was making millions annually. This agent was successful in selling this doctor a very large life insurance policy with annual premiums of about $250,000. This doctor became disabled with a rare disease five or six years after he had bought the insurance. The policy had waiver of premium benefit and continues in force today. What better protection?

Long-Term Care Riders

Many life insurance companies today are offering the ability to add long-term care benefits to a life policy by rider. Long-term care benefits can be used to fund home healthcare, nursing home coverage, and so on. These riders are not meant to replace individual long-term care coverage, but to supplement long range planning efforts. Furthermore, with the "Pension Protection Act of 2006," legislation now allows and encourages the combination of permanent life insurance and annuities to be married to long-term care policies.

Long-term care riders on life insurance policies are generally an *indemnity benefit.* This is the best type of long-term care coverage as it contains the most liberal definitions of disability. With an indemnity benefit, one does not necessarily have to be confined to a nursing home to collect.

With a long-term care rider, your life insurance is doing another additional job, which most other financial products are incapable of. The use of the long-term care benefit reduces the face amount of a life insurance policy. For instance, one policy has a $5,000 a month long-term care benefit for a maximum of thirty-six months. On a $250,000 policy, the maximum payout in long-term care benefits would be $180,000. That would reduce the final death benefit to beneficiaries to $70,000.

Having a long-term care rider on a life insurance policy qualifies under IRC 7702B(c)(2) and IRC Sec.101(g).

211

Annuitization of Cash Values

All pensions are based upon life annuities and annuitization calculations. Annuitization is the spreading of payments of principal and interest over a set period, such as five or ten years—even a lifetime. The benefit of all pension benefits and individually owned annuities is that they can be designed into a guaranteed income stream that you or your spouse can never outlive.

An individual can take his or her accumulated cash values from the life insurance policies at retirement and convert them into a guaranteed income stream for life. Transfer of cash values from a life insurance policy into an annuity is allowed by Section 1035 of the Internal Revenue Code without incurring any income taxes. However, once done, you cannot take annuity money and make a 1035 tax-free exchange into a life insurance policy.

Annuities are Stable and Protected Income Streams in a Volatile World

A common complaint by some popular financial gurus is that annuities are bad places for savings and not competitive in market returns. Nothing could be farther from the truth. Actually, safe guaranteed rates with annuities backed by a general account of a life insurance company can, over the long haul, outperform a mutual fund on an actual net rate of return and not expose the consumer to any risk of the stock market. Let's look at the quiet consistency of a fixed annuity compared to a non-fixed variable rate of return of a mutual fund in a tax-deferred environment like a 401(k) plan.

Quiet Consistency Versus Sporadic Brilliance of the Stock Market
Variable Rate of Return (Account A) versus Fixed Rate of Return
(Account B)
$100,000 Invested

	Account A	Account B
Year 1.	+14.00%	6%
Year 2.	+16.00%	6%
Year 3.	+ 7.00%	6%
Year 4.	- 9.00%	6%
Year 5.	+ 5.00%	6%
Year 6.	- 12.00%	6%
Year 7.	+ 9.00%	6%
Year 8.	- 3.00%	6%
Year 9.	+13.00%	6%
Year 10.	+10.00%	6%
TOTAL	$156,361	$179,081

At some point in life, people like guarantees and not worries. Life insurance companies can offer the consumer a competitive income stream, which is guaranteed for life. Only a life insurance company can offer a fully-insured annuity product.

People like the idea of annuitization of life insurance values as well as other retirement plan assets. Some of the benefits of annuitization are no market risk, no interest rate risk, and no worries about who will get the balance of the funds or the income stream in the event of death. Better still, the annuity *bypasses probate*. With dependable guarantees of income streams that an annuity provides, tax planning and budgeting can be done with confidence.

In reviewing dozens of proxy statements with public corporations, the author was amazed at how many highly paid successful executives had annuity payments or annuity calculations as a major component in their final retirement package. Annuities to fund executive retirement packages make excellent business sense. For one, payment to the executive is guaranteed when the risk is shifted to an insurance company. Secondly, the payment is not dependent upon how well the company performs in the stock market years after the executive retires. Third, annuity payments are a *valuable asset protection strategy* for the retired executive in the event of bankruptcy, lawsuits, and so on.

In the proxy statement for Walt Disney, we learn about Michael Eisner, former CEO, and now a talk show commentator on *CNBC*. Eisner is compensated with an annuity payment:

Mr. Eisner retired on October 3, 2005. Effective as of November 1, 2005, Mr. Eisner began receiving a combined annual annuity of $297,779 for life from the Disney Salaried Retirement Plan and the Amended and Restated Key Plan. The annual payment was calculated based upon Mr. Eisner's final average annual compensation of $1,003,846 and 21 years of credited service. Mr. Eisner's single life annuity was actuarially reduced to take into account commencement of the annuity prior to Mr. Eisner's sixty-fifth birthday as well as the 100 percent joint and survivor form of payment which provides continuation of annuity payments to Mr. Eisner's spouse for her life should Mr. Eisner predecease her.

A portion of William B. Harrison's (JPMorganChase) retirement package was also annuity payment. The proxy statement reads:

On December 14, 2004, the Board approved a single life annuity benefit of $2 million for Mr. Harrison to commence at retirement

The public needs to be reawakened to the benefits and strengths of life insurance and annuities in light of all the volatility in the stock market. As we have just read, annuities were used for two very sophisticated people who had access to the best advisors money could buy. Hundreds of other highly paid executives are not putting all of their retirement income at risk in the stock market.

Roger Lowenstein is one of the country's leading financial writers. Author of numerous books on financial issues, he wrote an article about the collapse of the American pension system in the *New York Times* magazine. The article called, "We Regret to Inform You that You No Longer Have a Pension,"[88] said this about using annuities or annuitization principles as part of the solution to fix the country's retirement plan problems:

If defined benefits (pension plans) are on their last legs, then it would make sense to try to incorporate their best features into 401(k)s. The drawback to 401(k)s, remember, is that people are imperfect savers...
Here there is much the government could do. For instance, it could require that a portion of a 401(k) account be set aside in a life long annuity, with all the security of a pension...If you could make an annuity a prominent choice, more people will convert their accounts into annuities...Promoting an annuity culture is probably the best single way to make up for the demise of pensions. Yet most companies that provide 401(k)s don't even give the option of purchasing an annuity when people cash in their accounts. As Brown, the Illinois professor, notes, "There is no box to check that says 'annuities'". That is a minor scandal. "I wish someone in Washington

---

[88] "We Regret To Inform You, You No Longer Have a Pension," by Roger Lowenstein, *The New York Times Magazine*, October 30, 2005.

were thinking bigger thoughts about the optimal retirement package should look like," says Watson Wyatt's Coronado.

What are Secretary Chao's (Secretary of Labor, Elaine Chao) thoughts? She bounced the question to the Treasury Department. Mark Warshawsky, the Treasury's top economist, has written about the need for annuities, and in an interview he allowed that as the 401(k)'s become the primary, or the only, source of retirement income for more people, "I think it is a concern that annuities are not being offered in those plans." When I asked what Treasury was doing about encouraging annuities, Warshawsky merely said that it was under study. Anything that smacks of regulation (like rules to make sure employees get a particular menu of choices, whether for annuities or their portfolios) gives the administration shivers. This is what you would expect, given the administration's strong free market tendencies...

But in the defined contribution world—the world of 401(k)'s—there are no rules. Employers can contribute or not. Employees can diversify or blow it all on the company stock (even if it is Enron). If nothing else, the century-long experiment with pensions has proved that in the absence of the right rules, the money will not always be there.

Exclusion Ratio

If an individual decides to annuitize their cash values within a life insurance policy, non-qualified annuities, or any other large sum of money, the individual annuity holder is given an *exclusion ratio* that is determined by the life insurance company and tables established by the IRS. The exclusion ratio does not apply to distributions from retirement plans such as IRA balances, 401(k), 403(b), and so on.

The benefit of the exclusion ratio is that in receiving an income stream or annuity payment from a life insurance company, which you can never outlive, part of the payment is considered original principal and is, therefore, not taxable. The second part of the payment is considered interest income and, therefore, taxable for income tax purposes.

Common Methods of Annuitization

There are several common methods for annuitizing cash values from a life insurance policy, an annuity, or other large sum of money. They are:

*   *Life only.* Using this option, checks continue until the death of the annuitant and the amount received would be dependent when it was taken out. The older annuitant would normally expect a larger check as they would have a shorter life expectancy.

*   *Joint & Last Survivor.* This is an income stream that both husband and wife can never outlive.

215

  * ***Life Income with Period Certain.*** This is where an income stream is paid to the annuitant, but if the annuitant were to die early within a certain period, say in the sixth year of a certain ten-year period, then the beneficiary would receive the balance of annuity payments, which would be approximately four years.

  * ***Fixed Number of Years.*** An annuity payment can be stretched out over a number of years, so long as it is a minimum of three, which is an IRS requirement. Fixed number of years annuities are not only used to fund retirement plans; they are also used to fund divorce payments, lottery winnings, and other types of structured settlements.

  * ***Fixed Dollar Amount.*** This is where a person could purchase an annuity for a fixed dollar monthly payment. They would ask for a quote from an insurance company and determine how long that annuity payment would last based upon the deposit given.

Life Insurance and the Avoidance of Probate

  Probate is a messy, expensive, and lengthy legal process, which is used to settle an estate. Probate is the process whereby the terms of a decedent are carried out under court supervision and made a matter of public record. At best, probate is wrapped up in six months. Probate cases taking a year or more are, however, very common. Probate can be a bonanza for the legal business. The estate of Howard Hughes, for example, took over fifteen years to settle. Marilyn Monroe's took around ten. John Wayne's probate process was so lucrative that the law firm involved closed after it was all over.

  A major benefit and strength of life insurance is that it *bypasses* the probate process because life insurance is a *legal contract* and *a will unto itself*. Another major benefit of life insurance is that it will not be included in your gross estate when it is being probated unless the insured's estate is the named beneficiary of the life insurance or all other beneficiaries predecease the insured.

  Other assets such as retirement accounts, annuities, and assets held with joint tenancy with rights of survivorship also bypass the probate process. Additional methods to bypass the probate process are by using lifetime gifts or using a revocable living trust. Some states have also enacted Uniform Transfer on Death (TOD) security registration acts whereby permitted securities accounts that are registered can pass on to the beneficiaries at death.

  The optimum estate plan for an individual or a family is one that minimizes taxes, legal and administrative costs, and disburses assets quickly. In this regard, life insurance as legal property has no equal.

  Probate costs can add up. A state like California has particularly high probate fees, which start at around $6,300 for the first $100 thousand in estate assets. Probate costs escalate over $82 thousand when an estate approaches $3 million in value[89]. In addition, probate is based upon all the assets in your estate. It is not reduced by any outstanding mortgages or debts. Probate fees are something that generally cannot be negotiated, as they are set by a schedule.

Probate costs are additional to other expenses, which can include administrative expenses, attorney's fees, executor's fees, state, and federal income, and estate taxes.

States such as Connecticut and Georgia are Byzantine concerning probate with systems that have changed little in three hundred years. Yale professor, John H. Langevin, claimed the probate system in Connecticut a "national scandal."[90] Others have criticized the Connecticut probate system as a sacred cow, which is full of inefficiencies and patronage. Probate systems such as these are expensive to maintain.

Probate judges are elected to four-year terms. The only qualification is that judges live in the district in which they serve. Salaries for the judges follow an arcane formula. Some make a maximum of $94,000 per year while others make only $32,000 per year. Some judges keep the probate court open only six hours a week. About 25 percent of the probate judges in Connecticut do not even possess law degrees. Some probate judges have had careers in martial arts and waitressing. One judge is even an orthopedic surgeon. Adding to the cost of the system is that probate judges, some of whom do not work more than one or two days a week, also get full health insurance benefits. The benefits are also offered to their staff and retirees.[91]

A major benefit of life insurance is that not only does it provide a timely exemplary rate of return for beneficiaries at death; it also avoids arcane and costly probate process.

In researching this book and reviewing public records, the author identified some individuals who recognized that life insurance would avoid the probate process. They are:

---

[89] See "Getting Started in Annuities," by Gordon K. Williamson, John Wiley & Sons, Inc. New York, 1999.
[90] "Changes in Probate Courts, Panel Sees Variation in Service," by Kim Martineau, *Hartford Courant*, December 11, 2005.
[91] "Report Calls For Shakeup of Probate System," by Keith Phaneuf, *Journal Inquirer*, Manchester, CT, March 1, 2006.

Name	Occupation	Residence Date of Death	Life Insurance in Estate
Franklin Roosevelt	Governor of NY U.S. President	Hyde Park, NY 1945	$29,726 $562,142**
Malcolm Forbes	Publisher	New Jersey 2/24/1990	$46,000,000 [92]
Andy Warhol	Pop artist	New York, NY 2/22/1988	$4,541,016
G. Allan Hancock	Industrialist Philanthropist	Los Angeles 5/31/1965	$1,755,408
Yul Brynner	Actor	New York, NY 10/10/1985	$408,000
John Belushi	Comic Actor	New York, NY 3/5/1982	$1,153,293
Jessica Savitch	NBC Anchor	New York, NY 10/24/1983	$1,203,487
Chet Huntley	National Newscaster	Big Sky, MO unknown	$995,960

**Franklin D. Roosevelt left $29,726 in life insurance to his widow and daughter. The Georgia Warm Springs Foundation owned $562,142 on Roosevelt's life. Given the fact that Roosevelt's net estate passed on to his family was only $1,366,132, the life insurance was an immense gift. Adjusted for inflation, that $562,142 would easily be worth $15 million or more in 2005 dollars.

Life Insurance: a Will unto Itself

The beauty of life insurance is that it is a will unto itself. A policy owner can easily change beneficiaries with little effort. Moreover, one can divide policy proceeds without having to go to a lawyer.

---

[92] See "Hancock to Investigate Claim on Forbes Estate," by Jennifer Landes, *The National Underwriter*, May 21, 1990.

High Cash Value Life Insurance

With respect to all, life insurance of the higher premium kind offers to our population a well-thought-out lifetime program involving a long-range view of the future as distinguished from mere temporary consideration.

Solomon S. Huebner

One of the most underutilized features within life insurance is the ability for policy owners to make additional deposits into a life insurance policy, which will greatly enrich the cash value. R. Nelson Nash, best-selling author of *Becoming Your Own Banker,* has commented that the problem with Americans is that they are just not putting enough cash into a life insurance policy. Yet America's banks are putting the maximum allowed into life insurance policies, and in many cases, exceeding the maximum. If one consistently makes additional deposits into the policy, the policy will become a superior economic instrument and take on more of the characteristics of one's own private bank.

Comments by pundits in the media that all premiums go to agent commissions in the first year are simply not true. Life insurance policy designs are extremely advantageous to the consumer. Different life insurance policies are designed for different applications. Here is an example of a favorable design for a consumer.

$100,000 Life Insurance Death Benefit
Male Preferred Non-Smoker
Participating Dividend, High Cash Value Whole Life
2001 Commissioners Standard Ordinary Life Tables

Age	Premium	First Year Guaranteed Cash Value	Cash Value as a Percentage of Premium	First Year Dividend*	First Year Dividend as % of Premium	First Year Cash Value/ % Prem
25	2,209	868	39%	759	34%	1,627 74%
35	3,166	1,250	39%	1,094	35%	2,344 74%
45	4,552	1,805	40%	1,579	35%	3,384 74%
55	6,454	2,566	40%	2,245	35%	4,811 75%
65	9,032	3,597	40%	3,147	35%	6,744 75%

*Dividends are not guaranteed and maybe higher or lower than current projections. Actual results will vary. Product may not be available in all states. Check with a qualified agent.

Snuggle up to the Modified Endowment Line, but Do not Go Over It

When working with a life agent, make sure that the policy is not a modified endowment contract. A qualified agent will be able to assist you in designing a life policy that passes the "7-Pay" test rules. Ideally, you would like to maximize the amount of cash going into the policy while minimizing the amount of death benefit. Ironically, later in the policy's life, it will develop a very large death benefit for your heirs. The trick is to snuggle up to the modified endowment contract limits, but do not cross over them.

A modified endowment means the Internal Revenue Service no longer considers your plan a life insurance policy for tax purposes. Early withdrawals, including loans, will be taxed as current income until all policy earnings have been taxed. There is also an additional 10 percent penalty tax under age fifty-nine and one half, unless payments are due to disability or annuity type payments. In the event of death, however, the life insurance benefits of a modified endowment still pass on to one's heirs income tax-free. A well-designed premium payment schedule can avoid the modified endowment contract treatment and retain the benefits, which are unique to the life insurance contract.

There are some situations where a modified endowment does serve a legitimate purpose; for instance, banks, since they use BOLI to maintain Tier One capital reserves, use the modified endowment strategy. Modified endowments can also be used in other single-premium life strategies. However, for most applications, the author and other experts recommend that consumers do not go over the modified endowment line.

1035 Tax-Free Exchanges of Life Insurance

With an Internal Revenue Code 1035 Tax Free Exchange, an insured can exchange a new life policy for an older one without a taxable event. This also allows one to defer the gain on any old policies at the time they are exchanged for the new ones. With increased life expectancies, improved underwriting, and preferred discounts, newer policies may be a better buy than older smaller policies. However, one must proceed with extreme caution when using a 1035 exchange.

New life insurance underwriting is required. If an insured has had a change of health for the worse, careful analysis will likely reveal that this is not in the consumer's best interest to replace or exchange older policies. In addition, new incontestability period and suicide provisions will most likely be based upon the new policy date versus the dates of the older life policies.

Ground Rules for 1035 Exchanges

There are ground rules for 1035 exchanges. New life policies must be on the same life as the old policies. If the old permanent policy has an outstanding loan, the new policy will have a loan as well with the same indebtedness. There are several potential benefits for the consumer under an IRC 1035 exchange of life insurance. They are:

1.   A newer policy could have significantly lower mortality costs or include secondary guarantees on mortality. Older universal life policies are known for higher mortality costs, which can drastically increase in later years.

2.   With a variable life or universal variable life, consumers may no longer want to have their savings component at risk in the stock market. Fixed premium whole life or secondary guarantee universal life may be a better option.

3.   The client needs or goals may have changed. For instance, a consumer could now be more concerned with reducing out-of-pocket premium costs. By adding the transferred values from the older policy into the new policy, the additional reserves may help reduce or even eliminate ongoing premium commitments. A consumer may also be interested in adding riders on the new policy, which cover benefits such as long-term care.

There are valid reasons for a 1035 life insurance exchange. However, before proceeding, it is advised that you consult with a well-qualified agent. Do not surrender any existing life insurance until you have qualified favorably for the new life insurance. Also, be sure to check surrender charges on older life insurance policies as they can be "back-end loaded" and charges can be significant for premature surrender.

Creditor & Asset Protection

"Their assets and liabilities balance out. The estate is going to be worth nothing. And there will be—the—the Lay family will have a new start with the life insurance policy."

Kurt Eichenwald,
New York Times journalist and author, Conspiracy of Fools, about the collapse of Enron. Eichenwald was commenting on how life insurance was exempt from the

221

claims of creditors in Texas. The policy had a face amount around $10 million.
National Public Radio, July 8, 2006.

In a country of constant litigation, in a time of vastly increased personal bankruptcies, and where a government, its regulatory agencies and its court system consistently rules in favor of financial institution profits over the rights of individuals, creditor and asset protection is critical. The new bankruptcy bill passed in 2005, titled "The 2005 Bankruptcy Abuse and Consumer Protection Act" has made asset protection more important than ever for regular consumers.

After spending over $100 million and ten years in lobbying in portraying themselves to Congress as the victims of credit card fraud, banks, credit card companies and mongers of debt have gotten the government to legalize usury and etch it in stone. The new law gives the consumer little protection to discharge credit card debt and other forms of usury with the new bankruptcy bill. However, new bankruptcy legislation has left some state protection for life insurance death benefits and cash values within policies. Other protection is given to the homestead exemption as well as retirement plans such as 401(k)s and IRAs. You will have to check with each state as rules do vary. Some highlights are:

Homestead Exemption. States that give considerable homestead exemptions include Kansas, Florida, Iowa, Oklahoma, South Dakota, and Texas. However, under the new law, if you have been charged with a securities fraud, financial fraud, any criminal act, or a judgment arising out of a tort, which caused serious physical injury or death, the homestead exemption is limited to $125,000.

Retirement Plans. Under the new bankruptcy law, the first $1 million of assets in IRAs or Roth IRAs are considered exempt assets of the bankruptcy estate, and unlimited exemptions for qualified plan balances (e.g. pensions, profit sharing, and 401(k) including rollovers into IRAs). However, under prior laws, proceeds of qualified pension assets were fully exempt from the claims of creditors. An excellent example of this protection was the case of O.J. Simpson where creditors were unable to attach the value of any of his pension plans.

Life Insurance. Fortunately, the new act makes no changes to the sometimes favorable state laws regarding the exemptions for life insurance and annuities. For those of you who are in the armed services, all group life insurance proceeds are exempt assets from the claims of creditors. Be sure to check with appropriate legal and other advisors in your state of residence.

222

The Sammy Davis Case. Life insurance has a proven track record in asset protection, particularly for beneficiaries. For instance, when the famous comedian-actor Sammy Davis, Jr. died, he had accumulated by 1997 over $7.5 million in IRS debt including penalties and interest. The IRS also seized his Beverly Hills home and most of his memorabilia. Davis had made bequests in his will to celebrities he knew, including Clint Eastwood, but nobody saw anything. Only members of his family, who were beneficiaries of his life insurance policy, received any money.

The Kenneth Lay Case. Perhaps the greatest example of asset protection provided by life insurance and annuities is the example of fallen corporate CEO Kenneth Lay, who died at age 64 in July, 2006, in Aspen, Colorado. When Lay died, he had about $9.5 million in assets, but he also had about $9.5 million in liabilities. Once his estate was settled, the estate essentially had nothing. At the time of his death, Ken Lay had about $10 million in life insurance. His wife Linda was the primary beneficiary. This would most likely be the split-dollar life insurance policy Lay had purchased on December 13, 1996, with an initial face amount of $11.9 million. Enron or the bankruptcy estate of Enron, however, was entitled to recapture about $1.25 million in premiums it paid for the initial coverage under the original agreement. In addition, prior to Enron going bankrupt, the Lays also purchased variable annuities in 2000 for $4 million, which are scheduled to mature sometime in 2007. Life insurance and annuities are protected assets and exempt from the claims of creditors under Texas law.

REVERSE MORTGAGES

In an era of greatly reduced defined benefit pension plans, Americans are looking for additional income streams for retirement income. The potential to achieve an income out of one's home is an additional option worth looking into, as Americans must get their assets working harder. When one has permanent life insurance in force in their lives, the reverse mortgage option becomes more attractive.

For many years, we work hard to pay off our mortgages. When paid off, the home becomes one of life's greatest assets. However, older homes do not generate income. They evolve into cost centers, where maintenance is always required and taxes still must be paid.

The process behind a reverse mortgage is simple. Once the house is paid off, it can start generating income for you. Reverse mortgages can generate periodic monthly payments, a lump sum of money, a line of credit, or a combination of all of three. However, the reverse mortgage is what the name implies; you get a payment coming out of the home in the *reverse direction*. The benefit is that, because you are paying down an asset, the money is income tax-free.

Qualifications

To qualify for a reverse mortgage, a home must be owned free and clear, or loans must be paid off from the proceeds of the reverse mortgage. The amounts available on a reverse mortgage can vary widely from lender to lender. Most reverse mortgage lenders generally require an applicant to be sixty-two years of age, and the home must be owner-occupied. Not all properties qualify, but all programs accept single-family detached homes as well as condominiums and manufactured housing. Some programs allow owners of two- to four-unit owner-occupied homes to use reverse mortgages. Only first mortgages are permitted. Any other debts against the home must be paid off or paid using the proceeds from the reverse mortgage.

The benefit of a reverse mortgage is that no repayment is required, as long as the home is a primary residence (owners reside in the home six months or more per year). Repayment is due when the borrower sells the home, permanently moves away or dies. The loan is typically repaid by either selling or refinancing the home, yet the borrower can never owe more than the value of the home.

Background of Reverse Mortgages

Reverse mortgages have gained traction in the United States and abroad. In England, there are about 71,500 reverse mortgages or "lifetime mortgages" as they are called there, secured with aggregate property values of about $6.1 billion. Reverse mortgages are also gaining popularity in Canada, where there is a reverse mortgage product known as the Canadian Home Income Plan (CHIP).

In the United States, about 80 percent of American seniors own homes. About three-fourths are owned free and clear. Estimates are that approximately $2 trillion in equity is tied up in American homes. A benefit of a reverse mortgage is that when a consumer receives the proceeds, they will not affect Social Security or Medicare eligibility because those programs are not based on need.

Reverse mortgages entered the spotlight in the United States in 1989, when the United States Department of Housing and Urban Development (HUD) launched a pilot program to insure the proceeds of reverse mortgages for investors. With HUD's backing, Wall Street and Fannie Mae began to invest in reverse mortgages. Now, Fannie Mae actually purchases every reverse mortgage that HUD insures.

In 2000, President Bill Clinton signed the American Homeownership and Economic Opportunity Act of 2000. In that act, if someone purchases a Home Equity Conversion Mortgage (HECM), the 2 percent premium is waived if a portion of the proceeds is used to purchase long-term care insurance.

There are two major reverse mortgage programs available, as well as some private lender programs. First, there is the Federal Housing Administration (FHA), which is part of the Home Equity Conversion Mortgage (HECM) mentioned above. If the lender stops making payments as promised, the FHA steps in and takes over the lender's responsibility for the payments. The HECM has loan limits and it is primarily targeted to help moderate-income families.

Secondly, there is the Federal National Mortgage Association, otherwise known as Fannie Mae. It operates the Fannie Mae Home Keeper Plan (FMHP), which has many similar features and benefits of the FHA programs.

However, there is also a downside to reverse mortgages. When one uses a reverse mortgage, the cash flows to the borrower from the lender. Over time, the balance due increases and hence the net equity decreases. Then there is the psychological effect. Some individuals do not like the idea of any debt. There is also the problem of a legacy. Most homeowners want to pass the home equity onto either their beneficiaries or a charity.

225

Tax Paradise with Permanent Life Insurance

This is where the benefits of permanent life insurance come into play. Permanent life insurance can replace the lost equity spent down in the reverse mortgage process. In a way, this is *tax paradise*, as the owner gets tax deductions when paying for the home and receives tax-free income checks out of the home. At death, with the existence of permanent life insurance in place, the children or other beneficiaries get income tax-free proceeds to replace the equity spent down.

A common philosophy today is that homes will continue to appreciate. We really do not know. However, if they do, the children will most often be the beneficiaries of the appreciation. Regardless, having permanent life insurance in force makes the reverse mortgage an attractive alternative.

The beauty of permanent life insurance in place is that it lets you spend down your assets for income and creates a liquid divisible income tax-free asset for your heirs. Studies reaffirm that people would rather live in their homes than go into a nursing home. Who wouldn't? Who wants to be in a new neighborhood, away from family and friends, without the comforts of home, in a sterile nursing home or long-term care facility? By giving seniors the opportunity to stay in their own homes with reverse mortgages, we will reduce the need for institutional care.

Reverse mortgages should grow in this country. Moreover, when you add permanent life insurance as a financial asset to strengthen the reverse mortgage process, you get the best of both worlds. Mom and Dad get more income to enjoy life and maintain their independence. The cash values of the life insurance become an additional line of credit. Kids get wealth quickly, efficiently, free of income taxes, and unfettered by the probate process.

The reverse mortgage combined with permanent life insurance is a very powerful strategy for additional retirement income. Additional resources you may want to consult with on reverse mortgages are:

*   American Association for Retired Persons (AARP). They have information about reverse mortgages. www.aarp.org.

*   National Center for Home Equity Conversion (NCHEC). Consumer information regarding the equity conversion process. www.reverse.org.

*   U.S. Department of Housing and Urban Development (HUD). Information on reverse mortgages available. www.hud.gov.

Pension Maximization

If you are covered under a defined benefit pension plan, not only should you consider yourself lucky, but also you should understand that the value of a lifelong guaranteed pension could have a high economic value. A healthy employee retiring in 2007, who is in his or her late fifties or early sixties and has a healthy spouse, can quite conceivably live another thirty years based on the latest mortality.

In addition, pension benefits in the private sector have the additional protection of benefit payments with the government agency, the Pension Benefit Guarantee Corporation (PBGC). Each year, private employers pay an insurance premium to the PBGC, which is reserve for companies who may at some point run into trouble funding their pension obligations.

High Economic Value

A defined benefit pension has a high economic value when there is a *guaranteed income for life* for the retiree and his or her spouse. For instance, this author recently calculated the approximate value for a female retiree, age fifty-seven who was retiring from a state government position. Under her defined benefit pension plan, the retiree qualified for a life pension of $57,000. The pension had the annuity or lump sum economic value of about $806,207, which is a significant asset. At retirement, the retiree, who is married, had to choose from three options.

Option One. Take the maximum income for life. However, no benefits would be paid to the surviving spouse in the event she predeceased her husband.

Option Two. Take a life pension of slightly less. In the event of her predeceasing him, he would get a partial recovery of her contributions to the plan.

Option Three. She could take a substantially reduced pension for the lifetime. However, the pension would cover her and her husband and it would guarantee them a pension for life. Many retirees in this situation feel compelled to take the reduced lifetime income or option number three which is commonly known as a *joint and survivor pension*. However, once this option is selected, a majority of the time, it cannot be changed.

Important Considerations before Taking the Joint and Survivor Pension Option

There are several important considerations to consider and analyze before making the decision to take the reduced pension benefits.

* If the retiree lives only a short time, the surviving spouse faces a lifetime of reduced pensions.

* If they both live a full life and die within a year or so of each other (which is common, the author has come to find), little benefit, if any, is realized after twenty or more years of reduced pension income.

* In either case, the children of the retiree and spouse will never inherit any benefits. This author did have a situation whereby the husband and wife were both killed instantaneously in an automobile accident after being retired only a couple of months. As a result, the surviving children did not receive a dime.

Analyzing the Costs of Pension Options

Let's look at the potential costs associated with the retiree who was considering the $57,000 pension for life. Please keep in mind that this is only an example. Each situation is different and precise care must be exercised when individuals analyze their options in pension planning.

228

Option One:	
Maximum annual pension:	**$57,000**
(No survivor benefit)	
Option Two:	
Maximum annual pension with	
recapture of contributions only	**$56,430**
Option Three:	
Joint and Survivor Pension Retiree:	**$49,692**
Survivor Pension, two-thirds	**$33,095**
Joint Life Expectancy:	
IRS Annuity Table VI, Employee 57, Spouse 57 years	**32.5**
Annual Cost of Survivorship Option	**$7,308**
Total Potential Cost of Survivorship	
Option over Life Expectancy	
(32.5 x $7,308=$237,510)	**$237,510**

In conclusion, the pension survivorship option equates to very expensive term life insurance that may never pay off.

Pension Maximization: A Better Way

A strategy or alternative to the joint and survivor pension problem is called pension maximization. The solution to this problem is to purchase permanent life insurance prior to retirement *in* an amount that would provide the survivor or other heirs with a similar monthly benefit.

For example, a person could purchase a universal life policy for about $471,000, which would fund a survivor pension/annuity option if current interest rates remained level at 4.25 percent for the next thirty years. The annual premium or deposit into the life insurance would be $7,308 annually.

Conversely, a low premium whole life insurance policy, which would absolutely guarantee the death benefit and provide cash values as an additional economic asset, would be approximately $11 thousand per year.

The Best Way

The best time to formulate retirement planning or pension maximization strategy is when someone is healthy four or five years before retirement. For instance, low premium whole life, could be about $8,600 per year if purchased five years prior to a person retiring.

The pension maximization strategy with life insurance works and is used throughout corporate America (as evidenced in the chapter "Corporate-Owned Life Insurance"). In his own practice, the author has implemented a number of pension maximization cases to appreciate the true value of permanent life insurance and the success of the pension maximization strategy.

In one instance, a retiree's spouse predeceased the retiree. The retiree still has the maximum pension. The life insurance proceeds are now directed to the retiree's adult children. This would never have happened under a traditional joint and survivor pension arrangement.

In another situation, a retiree has accumulated so much cash in her life insurance that the retiree can now finance the purchase of her automobiles with her life insurance loans versus using a bank. The retiree loves having this additional option. This retiree is in excellent health, but now, unfortunately, her husband's health is failing. The pension maximization strategy we put in place years ago will work much better for her adult children who are heirs to her estate.

Like other options, pension maximization does not always work. A person who has had deterioration in health will not be a good candidate for permanent life insurance, which is the fundamental component and economic workhorse to a structurally strong pension maximization strategy.

Pension Maximization through Life Insurance: A Good Option for a Number of Reasons

To recap, pension maximization with permanent life insurance can be a superior way to enhance retirement income and provide additional benefits to heirs. Some important points to remember concerning pension maximization are as follows:

1.   Life insurance proceeds to the survivor are *income tax-free* whereas survivor pension benefits are *fully taxable* as ordinary income.

2.   If annuitized at an older age, the survivor will have a *larger* monthly income than under traditional joint and survivor options. If life

insurance proceeds are annuitized, a large part of that benefit will be income *tax-free* as a return of principal under the *exclusion ratio*.

3.   If a retiree and spouse die simultaneously (rare, but does happen) insurance benefits could pass to other heirs such as children.

4.   Life insurance can also provide additional benefits such as long-term care benefits and accelerated death benefits in the event of a terminal illness. If terminally ill and the retiree is in a cash crunch, the policy could also be sold at a discount to a life settlement provider.

5.   If the survivor recipient of the pension predeceases the retiree, the life insurance policy can be put into a reduced paid up mode whereby no further premiums are required at a reduced life insurance benefit. The retiree could also surrender the policy for its cash value if need be, or borrow against the policy even in a reduced paid up mode.

6.   If the retiree's spouse predeceases the retiree and the retiree remarries later, the new spouse can be named beneficiary of the life insurance policy, whereas no benefits would exist under a normal joint and survivor pension.

LIFE INSURANCE IN QUALIFIED RETIREMENT PLANS

Unfortunately, personal retirement plans such as IRAs, IRA rollovers, Roth IRAs, SEPs, and Simple IRA arrangements may not use life insurance as a funding medium. In addition, according to the latest rulings from the Treasury Department, any annuity contracts for 403(b) plans may no longer provide life insurance as an incidental death benefit to the plan. However, annuity plans issued prior to February 14, 2005, may use life insurance as a funding medium. With employer-qualified business retirement plans, life insurance has been used successfully as a funding medium for decades.

Employer Advantages

For the employer, there are a number of advantages to using life insurance for funding purposes. For one, life insurance premiums are deductible as a plan contribution. In addition, a defined benefit pension plan, which uses life insurance as a funding medium, will also allow an employer to make a larger contribution and help lessen the problem of corporate retained earnings. If participating whole life contracts are used, the dividends of the contract are used to reduce premiums and the cost of maintaining the defined benefit program can be reduced over time.

If an employer decides to use life insurance and annuities as the sole funding medium for a defined benefit plan under 412(i) of the Internal Revenue Code, then there are some additional advantages. Since the plan is secured by the *general account* of a life insurance company, no actuarial certification is required. Very large contributions can be made for older employees even though they may be close to retirement age.

Employee Advantages

There are a number of advantages for employees who have life insurance within their qualified retirement plan. First off, the net amount at risk or the true insurance portion of the death benefit is still received free of income taxes by their beneficiaries. Over time, net investment returns of the life policies can be competitive with other investments.

Uninsurable participants (those who have health insurance problems and who would not generally qualify favorably under normal life insurance underwriting) may acquire quality permanent life insurance benefits under *guarantee issue provisions,* which the life insurance company may offer. At retirement age, an employee could also have permanent life insurance as an additional retirement benefit.

Rules and Guidelines

With business retirement plans, there are two broad classifications—a *defined contribution model* and a *defined benefit model.* Life insurance can be purchased as a funding medium for both types of plans but the insurance must be made available or purchased on a *uniform non-discriminatory basis.*

First, let's look at the defined contribution model because this is the most common type of retirement plan today in America. Defined contribution plans are commonly known as a 401(k) plan, a profit sharing plan, or a money purchase pension plan.

The contribution formula for life insurance within a defined contribution plan is limited to certain formulas. If whole life is used as a funding medium, then up to 49 percent of the annual allocation can be used to fund life insurance within the plan. If term life, variable or universal life are used, then no more than 25 percent of the total contribution can be used to fund life insurance within the plan. There is no limit to the face amount of insurance within the plan.

Within profit sharing plans, there is a special provision known as the *aged money rule,* where in some cases, allocations more than two years old may be *totally* invested in life insurance (IRC. Rev. Ruls. 61-164 1961-2 CB99).

With defined benefit pensions, the face amount of insurance may not exceed one hundred times the anticipated monthly retirement benefit. For example, if a $5,000 per month pension benefit were anticipated, the maximum amount of insurance would be $500 thousand. If the anticipated monthly pension benefit were $10,000 per month, then $1 million would be the maximum face amount. This is what is known in defined benefit funding as the *basic rule.*

There is also an *alternative rule,* where total premiums for whole life must be less than 66 ⅔ percent (or 33 percent for term, variable, and universal life insurance) of the assumed aggregate contributions. See IRS Rev. Rul. 74-307.

In addition, there can also be a fully insured defined benefit plan, where the sole funding medium is exclusively in annuities or a combination of annuities and life insurance. Special rules apply. Please retain professional guidance in this area.

Single Employer Welfare Benefit Plans Funded with Permanent Life Insurance

As we saw in the chapter "Bank-Owned Life Insurance," the nation's banks purchase colossal amounts of permanent life insurance to fund not only executive retirement plans, but also to fund current and post-retirement life insurance, medical benefits, disability benefits, and severance pay. Plans are available to small- and medium-size employers under Section 419 of the Internal Revenue Code. They are commonly known as single employer health and welfare plans, and they are sanctioned in the black and white sections of the Internal Revenue Code Sections 419 and 419(a).

Single employer health and welfare plans funded with permanent life insurance contracts are nothing new. They were actually the predominant form of welfare plan prior to 1984 when that year's tax year DEFRA severely limited deductions for plan contributions.

Since the tax deductions can be substantial to a corporation, promoters developed multiple employer welfare plans, which came under scrutiny of the Treasury. These health and welfare plans were sometimes marketed as retirement plans. The Department of the Treasury issued final regulations on July 17, 2003 (IRS TD9079) to halt the abusive marketing of multiple employer health and welfare plans.

Single Employer Plans

A single employer plan is still a viable option for employers wishing for a proven methodology to fund disability benefits, medical expenses, severance pay and supplemental unemployment and life insurance plans up to $50 thousand. The funding for these benefits is clearly sanctioned by the Internal Revenue Code yet these plans must have economic substance. Pure tax avoidance will be questioned as in the Dow Chemical COLI case. The advantage to the employer is that contributions to the plan are deductible, and they provide employees and their dependents with additional retirement benefits. Using a health and welfare plan to reserve for these future costs is a pro-active solution to the nation's growing healthcare problems.

Health and welfare plans funded under sections 419 also provide *asset protection strategies* that are generally allowed under normal employer group insurance benefit programs.

Candidates for Single Employer Plans

Businesses with strong recurring revenues are ideal candidates for these plans, which are very popular with banks and large industrial conglomerates as well as successful small businesses such as medical and dental practices. A requirement of health and welfare plans is that they be *non-discriminatory* and cover all *eligible employees*, although there are special rules regarding the funding of supplemental benefits for key executives.

There is a *qualified cost* associated with providing these benefits. These costs are actuarially determined by using level contributions and reasonable assumptions. These assumptions must be funded over the working life of the employees in the plan. An additional requirement is that each year participants in the plan be notified of annual economic or associated cost of these benefits.

Normal Employee Retirement Income Security Act (ERISA) rules apply when setting up a health and welfare plan. Benefits will tend to favor older, higher paid employees. Contributions to key employee's post-retirement medical benefits count against limits in defined contribution pension plans but do not affect defined benefit plans.

As witnessed with the banks' immense purchases of bank-owned life insurance or BOLI, life insurance is an ideal funding mechanism to finance post-retirement medical costs, severance pay, and so on. Any life insurance product can be used (whole life, term, single life, and even survivorship life) to fund these benefits. An employer can also use a combination of products as a funding methodology. For instance, an employer could use *term life* to fund high-turnover positions and use *permanent life* to fund long-term employees, managers and other key people.

This is not a do-it-yourself type of plan. A candidate for a 419 health and welfare plan must definitely retain a qualified third-party administrator or plan sponsor who will provide documents, design consulting, and calculations for initial and ongoing contributions. This third-party administrator will also assist in determining employee eligibility and qualification, review anticipated liabilities, track disbursements to plan participants, and file appropriate requirements with the IRS to maintain plan integrity and compliance.

LIFE INSURANCE AS A FUNDING SOURCE OF ESTATE TAXES AND SETTLEMENT COSTS

Estate taxes or taxing people at death is nothing new in America. Governments who desperately need additional revenues to pay for war debts and other government deficit spending problems have most often precipitated estate taxes.

The first estate tax was introduced in 1797 to raise money for a potential naval war with France. It was called the Federal Stamps for Wills and Estates, but it was repealed in 1801. In 1862, the estate tax was introduced again to raise money for the Civil War but that tax was repealed in 1870. In 1898, the estate tax was reintroduced again to help pay for the Spanish-American war. The tax was repealed in 1902.

In 1916, the estate tax was introduced yet again. It has been with us in some form ever since. When it was revived in 1916, the estate tax was levied on estates of $10 million or more and was used to pay for war debts incurred after World War I.

After World War II, the estate tax skyrocketed to the 70 percent level because of the immense government debt incurred during that war. In 1981, the estate tax was reduced to the current 55 percent level, which is the baseline for today's federal estate tax.

Much of America's current economic problems originated with the massive debts incurred with the Vietnam War. It was that war, in combination with a major Middle East oil crisis, which drove the country off the gold standard. Because we could no longer redeem our international debts in gold (oil-producing countries drained our gold bullion), in August 1971, President Nixon took the dollar off the gold standard—opening Pandora's Box.

This abandonment of the gold standard unfortunately gave the Federal Reserve System the ability to create massive amounts of currency out of thin air, as the dollar was no longer tethered to gold or any other hard asset. The abandonment of the gold standard also gave Washington politicians the ability to spend our country into oblivion. The military is one of the largest beneficiaries of this spending.

Unfortunately, it sometimes takes decades for these problems to raise their ugly heads, but the problems are clearly felt with the government's excessive taxation of lower and middle classes to pay for these cataclysmic war budgets. Eventually, these costs will have to be covered, but the problem is that the politician who creates these costs will be out of office when the final tab comes due.

According to figures provided by the Center for Arms Control and Non-Proliferation (www.armscontrolcenter.org), in 2006, the Bush administration asked for a military spending budget of $439.3 billion. It ended up getting $436 billion. The Office of Management and Budget predict that at this pace, military spending will exceed $502 billion annually by 2011.

Military spending in America is of biblical proportions, and some experts are saying the actual costs incurred are closer to $600 billion annually. Maintaining a standing army in at least 120 outposts around the world drains a treasury. In comparison, Russia spends $65 billion annually, while China spends about $55 billion. What makes this military budget even more frightening is that we are borrowing, as a country, $1.5 to $3 billion a day in world markets to keep the empire afloat. A major portion of this deficit spending is funds to fund the military.

America's greatest threat may not be terrorism; it may be massive unmanageable deficit spending. Someday, all of these bills will have to be paid. We were once the world's greatest creditor, now we are the world's greatest debtor. Confidence in the dollar is slipping. The world is taking notice, and as a result, the Euro, the main currency that competes with the dollar is gaining traction.

The Bush administration has exerted considerable energy to try to eliminate the estate tax, a tax that only really affects about the top 2 percent of the population. However, this is where a great deal of this country's wealth is concentrated. Various estimates maintain that the top 1 percent of the population owns and controls as much as 40 percent of the wealth within this country.

Estate Settlement Costs

Estate settlement costs are significant. Settlement costs are compromised of federal and state income, estate taxes, appraisal fees, probate fees, legal fees, executors, and so on. Settlement costs can cause significant shrinkage of assets passed to heirs. Public records show how quickly the estate fades away.

Name	Gross Estate	Settlement Costs	Net Estate	Shrinkage
J. P. Morgan	$17,121,482	$11,893,691	$5,227,791	69%
Walt Disney	$23,004,851	$6,811,943	$16,192,908	30%
William Boeing	$22,386,158	$10,589,748	$11,796,410	47%
Elvis Presley	$10,165,434	$7,374,635	$2,790,799	73%
Marilyn Monroe	$819,176	$448,750	$370,426	55%

Current Estate and Transfer Taxes

State and federal estate taxes are excise taxes on the right to transfer properties at death. Gross estates, which consist of all the fair market value of all assets at death, are taxed at a 46 percent rate when gross estates exceed $2 million for a single person and $4 million for married couples in 2006. This also includes life insurance policies. In 2009, the top federal estate tax rate will be 45 percent, and the exemption amount for a single person will be $3.5 million and $7 million for a married couple.

In 2010, there will be no federal estate tax. In the year 2011, as currently scheduled, the exemption amount for federal estate taxes will revert to $1 million for a single person and $2 million per married couple. The top tax rate will revert to 55 percent.

Most experts agree that total estate tax repeal is a long shot, and Pollyannaish in light of massive debts, which this country is incurring (in light of history).

Additional Problem: State Death Taxes

Furthermore, there are complications such as the elimination of the state death tax credit that was phased out from 2002-2004 and eliminated in 2005. Prior to 2002, a decedent who lived in a state, which imposed a state inheritance/death tax, was allowed to use this amount to offset his or her federal estate tax liability. Therefore, while a couple could theoretically be exempt from federal estate taxes, they could be liable for state estate tax.

The states listed below have less than the $2 million federal exemption. This could be a problem in the state of New York, which could pass a levy with a top estate tax of 16 percent. Some states which have less than the federal exemption are:

State Exemption

$1,000,000	$675,000	Other
Kansas	Rhode Island	Ohio: $338,000
Maine	New Jersey	
Massachusetts	Wisconsin	
Maryland		
Minnesota		
Nebraska		
New York		
Oklahoma		
Oregon		

Problems with Estate Tax Reform

Each time the government gives something with one hand, they usually take something away with the other. If estate taxes were repealed, they would probably eliminate tax preference items such as *step-up in basis.*

What is step-up in basis? Currently at death, preference items such as real estate and securities are given a new "step-up" in basis.

For instance, say a decedent purchased real estate originally for $100,000. At death, the property may be worth $1 million, which is common with today's highly inflated real estate prices. With the current *step- up in basis*, this real estate would have a new basis for capital gains taxes of $1 million. Thus under the current system, an individual would be eliminating capital gains taxes of approximately $135,000.

Under proposed estate tax elimination reform, there would be a *limited step-up in basis*. Therefore, while elimination of the estate tax could be possible, the government could be recapturing a good portion of the tax revenue *back* with additional *capital gains* taxes.

What Can One Do to Reduce Estate Taxes Legitimately?

Over time, with proper long-range planning, total estate taxes and estate settlement costs can be greatly reduced. You cannot do much in one year if you have a very large estate. Sam Walton, the founder of Wal-Mart, was the best example of this great long-term estate planning over an extended period. The heirs to Sam Walton, in the aggregate, make the Walton family the wealthiest family in the United States. Through a strategy of *gifting discounted limited family partnership interests* over decades, Sam *minimized* taxes to his heirs while maintaining *control* over his assets.

All people can utilize a $12,000 *annual exclusion amount* that can be given to any number of donees per year, which is free of gift/estate taxes. People can also donate, free of gift tax consequences, unlimited amounts for school tuition or qualified medical expenses. However, gifts for tuition or medical expenses must be paid directly to the school or directly to the medical provider.

Furthermore, transfers among spouses generally qualify for the *unlimited marital deduction* and are free of current tax. The problem, obviously, is at the death of the surviving spouse.

What Can Life Insurance Do?

What happens about the future of estate taxes is anybody's guess. However, in light of history, the total repeal of estate taxes seems highly unlikely. Regardless of whether or not there is estate tax repeal, there will always be huge estate settlement costs. You will always have state and federal income taxes, probate fees, legal fees, appraisal fees, executor's fees, and the problems caused by the lack of marketability of various assets, such as real estate and closely held businesses. This author has seen estates, which were relatively modest with no estate taxes due, be eaten up in legal fees, maintenance fees, improvements to properties, income taxes, and so on.

Anyone who has been an executor knows estate settlement costs can be enormous. An estate can easily have 20 percent or more of its value eaten up in various costs, which have nothing to do with estate taxes. However, when an estate is large enough and estate taxes are due, the executor of the estate has several options to pay estate taxes. When the estate tax form, known as *Form 706*, is filed, any taxes due are generally *payable within nine months of death*.

The question remains, how will the executor pay for these taxes? One option is that the executor could borrow the money for estate taxes and other settlement costs. However, this only defers the problem since money borrowed

240

will have to be paid back with interest. Interest rates will most likely be higher in the future.

Secondly, estate taxes could be paid under the installment plan which is a loan from the government that includes payment of principal and interest under IRC Sections 6161 and 6166.

Thirdly, an executor could pay for estate settlement costs using cash. Rarely does an estate have excess cash.

Fourth, an executor could liquidate investments in the stock market. This could be a wise strategy if the market is up. However, it could be a disaster if some investments are just involved in a temporary setback.

Fifth, the executor could liquidate other assets. Yet there is always a *marketability* problem. Often there is not a ready market to turn investments immediately into cash. Many times assets have to be sold at fire sale prices to get immediate cash.

Lastly, the executor may have the benefit of having life insurance to pay for estate taxes and other settlement costs. There are numerous advantages of having life insurance to pay for these fees, namely:

- Heirs virtually always get more money out of the life insurance than was put into it
- The payment is prompt
- There is no *income tax* on life insurance proceeds. If structured properly, often there will not be any *estate taxes* either
- Life insurance proceeds are not subject to *probate court*
- Life insurance becomes an economic shock absorber for the inevitable and unpredictable costs that most estates incur.

As always, seek proper counsel to address these issues. However, when reviewing the options, life insurance is always extremely valuable in any estate.

INDEX

242

246

BIBLIOGRAPHY

"The 50 Smartest Things to Do With Your Money." *Money Magazine*, July 2005.

"The 400 Richest People In America." *Forbes*, October 9, 2006.

"The 401(k) Illusion." *Wall Street Journal*, April 15, 1999.

Adkisson, Jay and Chris Reisser. "Bankruptcy Act Impact on Life Insurance and Domestic Protection Trusts." (May 3, 2005). Leimberg Information Services. http://www.leimbergservices.com.

Alampur, Gopala. *Die Broke & Wealthy, The Insurance Bonanza that Beats The Taxman While You're Still Alive.* Toronto: Chestnut Publishing Group, 2003.

Associated Press. "Merrill Lynch Settles Stock Research Lawsuits." (February 17, 2006). MSNBC. http://www.msnbc.msn.com/id/11407434/from/RSS/.

Augar, Phillip. *The Greed Merchants: How Investment Banks Played The Free Market Game.* New York: Penguin Group, 2005.

Bach, David. *The Automatic Millionaire.* New York: Broadway Books/Random House, 2004.

Bailey, Steve. "Harvard Money Managers' Pay Draws IRE." *Boston Globe*, December 11, 2003.

Baldwin, Ben G. *The New Life Insurance Investment Advisor.* New York: McGraw-Hill, 2002.

"Banking Association Endorses Bank-Owned Life Program." *Insurance Advocate*, April 18, 2003.

Barrett, William P. "Sizzling Suze." *Forbes*, December 28, 1998.

Batra, Ravi. *Greenspan's Fraud: How Two Decades of His Policies Undermined the Global Economy.* New York: Palgrave MacMillan, 2005.

Beard, Patricia. *After The Ball, Gilded Age Secrets, Boardroom Betrayals, and the Party that Ignited the Great Wall Street Scandal.* New York: Harper Collins, 2003.

Berenson, Alex. "For Merck, Vioxx Paper Trail Won't Go Away." *New York Times*, August 21, 2005.

Bergman, Lowell, and Patrick McGeehan. "Expired: How a Credit King Was Cut Off." *New York Times*, March 7, 2004.

Biggs, Barton. *Hedge Hogging.* Hoboken, NJ: John Wiley & Sons, Inc., 2006.

Black, Kenneth, and Harold D. Skipper, Jr. *Life & Health Insurance.* New Jersey: Prentice Hall, 2000.

Black, William K. *The Best Way to Rob a Bank Is to Own One.* Austin: University of Texas Press, 2005.

Bogle, John C. "The Amazing Disappearance of The Individual Stockholder." *Wall Street Journal*, October 3, 2005.

———. *The Battle For The Soul Of Capitalism.* New Haven: Yale University Press, 2005.

————. "The Emperor's New Mutual Funds." *Wall Street Journal*, July 8, 2003.

————. "Fair Shake or Shakedown." *Wall Street Journal*, July 8, 2004.

————. "How Mutual Funds Lost Their Way." *Wall Street Journal*, June 20, 2000.

————. "Specialist Man." *Wall Street Journal*, September 19, 2003.

Bombardieri, Marcella. "Rich Rewards Outlast Sibler's Reign—BU Has Paid Him $7M Since 2003." *Boston Globe*, May 10, 2006.

Bonner, William and Addison Wiggin. *Empire of Debt.* Hoboken, NJ: John Wiley & Sons, Inc., 2006.

Borrus, Amy. "Credit Counseling: A Business Rife With Bad Guys." *Business Week*, July 11, 2005.

Bresiger, Gregory. "Unprotected Clients: The New Bankruptcy Law Changes the Rules of Asset Protection." *Financial Advisor*, December 2005.

Brown, Erika. "Going For Broke; Uncle Sam Is Helping People Make Money Off Those Who Are Bankrupt." *Forbes*, October 16, 2006.

Buford, Bill. "The Taming of a Chef." *New Yorker,* April 2, 2007.

Caffrey, Andrew. "Citizens Sets No-Gift Policy for Advisors: Firm Seeks to Avoid Conflicts of Interest."Boston Globe, August 20, 2005.

Chamberlain, John. "Family Counseling, Who's Better—Fidelity or Janus?" Forbes, September 18, 2006.

————. *The Outer Limits, Some of These Funds Go Way Beyond the Ordinary.* Forbes, September 18, 2006.

Chancellor, Edward. *Devil Take The Hindmost: A History of Financial Speculation.* New York: The Penguin Group, 1999.

Chatfield, William D. "Regulators Offer Roadmap to BOLI." *Community Banker*, April 2005.

Chen, David. "After Weighing Cost of Lives, 9/11 Fund Completes Its Task." *New York Times*, June 6, 2004.

Chernow, Ron. *The House of Morgan, An American Banking Dynasty and the Rise of Modern Finance.* New York: Simon & Schuster, 1990.

Cole, Mark Benjamin. *The Piped Pipers of Wall Street: How Analysts Sell You down the River.* Princeton, NJ: Bloomberg Press, 2001.

Der Hovanesian, Mara. "Amaranth's Loss, Wall Street's Gain." *Business Week*, October 9, 2006.

De Soto, Jesus Huerta. *Money, Bank Credit and Economic Cycles.* Translated by Melinda A. Stroup. Auburn, Alabama: Ludwig von Mises Institute, 2006.

Doherty, Neil A., and Hal J. Singer. "The Benefits of a Secondary Market for Life Insurance Policies." The Wharton Financial Institutions Center, University of Pennsylvania, October 14, 2002.

Dugus, Christine. "All Debt Counselors Are Not the Same." *USA Today*, May 28, 2002.

Duhigg, Charles. "Late in Life, Finding a Bonanza in Life Insurance." *New York Times*, December 17, 2006.

The Economist, Pocket World in Figures, 2007 Edition. London: Profile Books, 2006.

Edmiston, Kelly. *A New Perspective On Rising Non-Business Bankruptcy Filing Rates: Analyzing The Factors.* The Kansas City Federal Reserve Bank, www.kansascityfed.org, 2006.

Egan, Timothy. "Credit Card Offers Stacking Up At Homes of the Newly Bankrupt." *New York Times*, December 11, 2005.

"Executive Benefits—A Survey of Current Trends." Clark Consulting, Inc., posted online November 2005, www.clarkconsulting.com.

Fabrikant, Geraldine. "Cleaning Up Messes, Friend to Friend. Talking Money with Suze Orman." *New York Times*, March 5, 2006.

Feig, Nancy. "Bank-Owned Life Insurance." *Community Banker*, May 2005.

———. "Use of Bank-Owned Life Insurance Become More Popular Among Community Banks, Cash Values Rise." *Community Banker*, September 2004.

Feinberg, Kenneth R. "September 11th Victim Compensation Fund of 2001, Compensation for Deceased Victims." Posted online through 1/3/2004, www.usdoj.gov/victimcompensation/comp deceased html.

———. *What is Life Worth?* New York: Perseus Books, 2005.

"Financial Impact on Premature Death, The Value of Adequate Life Insurance Coverage when Tragedy Strikes." New York: Metropolitan Life Insurance Company, October 2003.

"Financial Institutions with $100M to $1 Billion, Using BOLI to Fund Retirement Plans." *Insurance Advocate,* December 8, 2003.

Fisher, Daniel. "A Dangerous Game: Hedge Funds Have Gotten Rich From Credit Derivatives. Will They Blow Up?" *Forbes*, October 16, 2006.

Francis, Theo. "COLI Revenue Declines Sharply at Large Insurers." *Wall Street Journal*, September 3, 2003.

Francis, Theo, and Ellen E. Shultz. "Big Banks Quietly Pile Up on Janitors Insurance." *Wall Street Journal*, May 2, 2002.

Franklin, Mary Beth. "New Life for An Old Policy." *Kiplinger's Retirement Planning*, Fall 2005.

Fraser, Steve. *Every Man a Speculator.* New York: Harper Collins, 2005.

Freeman, John P. "A Law Professor Comments on the Mutual Fund Fee Mess." U.S. Senate Governmental Affairs Subcommittee on Financial Management, the Budget, and International Security, January 27, 2004.

Freeman, John P., and Stewart Brown. "Mutual Fund Advisory Fees: The Cost of Conflicts of Interest." *Journal of Corporation Law*, 2001.

Fried, Carla. "The Rising Appeal and Falling Cost of Term Insurance." *New York Times*, August 29, 2004.

Galbraith, John Kenneth. *The Great Crash of 1929.* Boston: Houghton Mifflin Company, 1972.

Gasparino, Charles. *Blood on the Street: The Sensational Story of How Wall Street Analysts Duped a Generation of Investors.* New York: Free Press, 2005.

Gassman, Alan S., and Jonathan Alper. "New Bankruptcy Law-Who Pays It?" Steve Leimberg Asset Protection Planning Email Newsletter, www.leimbergservices.com , March 14, 2005.

Gitlin, Todd. *Media Unlimited.* New York: Henry Holt & Company, LLC, 2001.

Goldstein, Matthew. "Six-Feet Over/Under." The Street.com, www.thestreet.com, June 12, 2006.

Gordon, Marcy. "SEC Approves Market Shaping Merger of NYSE and Electronic Archipelago." Associated Press/Yahoo Finance, posted online February 2, 2006, www.yahoo.com.

Greene, Katherine and Richard. *The Man Behind The Magic, The Story of Walt Disney.* New York: Viking Penguin, 1991.

Greer, Carolyn T. "The Dollar Cost Fallacy." *Forbes,* April 10, 1995.

Gregg, Senator Judd. "It's Time to Stop Federal Overspending." *New Hampshire Business Review,* July 7. 2006.

Greider, William. "Secrets of the Temple, How the Federal Reserve Runs the Country." New York: Simon & Schuster, 1987.

Griffin, G. Edward. *The Creature From Jekyll Island, A Second Look At the Federal Reserve.* Westlake Village, CA: American Media, 1998.

Gross, Daniel. "How to Make the Deficit Look Smaller than It Is." *New York Times,* November 23, 2003.

———. "Like The Fund, Love The Company." *New York Times,* April 4, 2006.

Gross, Martin L. *The Tax Racket, Government Extortion from A to Z.* New York: Ballantine Books, 1995.

"Half of U.S. Households Own Equities, Study Finds." *Financial Advisor Magazine,* January 2006.

Halonen, Doug. "8 Big Companies Sued Over 401(k) Plan Fees." *Pensions and Investments,* October 2, 2006.

———. "Rule Hurts Advice Givers but Aids Fund Companies." *Pensions and Investments,* February 17, 2007.

Healy, Beth and Andrew Caffrey. "Fidelity Brokerage Arm Fined $2M." *Boston Globe,* August 4, 2004.

———. "Trustees on the Hot Seat, 8 Directors at Nations Funds (Bank of America) Urged To Quit.", *Boston Globe,* March 16, 2004.

Hertz, Noreena. *The Debt Threat: How Debt Is Destroying the Developing World.* New York: Harper Collins, 2004.

Himmelstein, David, Elizabeth Warren, Deborah Thorne, and Steffie Woolhandler. "Discounting the Debtors Will not Make Medical Bankruptcy Disappear." Health On-Line, www.healthaffairs.org, February 28, 2006.

———. "Illness and Injury as Contributors to Bankruptcy.", Health On-Line, www.healthaffairs.org, February 2, 2005.

257

Holden, Sarah and Jack Van Derhei. "401(k) Plan Asset Allocation, Account Balances, and Loan Activity in 2005." Investment Company Institute (ICI) and Employee Benefit Research Institute (EBRI), www.ic.org, August 2006.

Holderness, Hayes. "Bank-Owned Life Insurance Can Finance Executive Retirement, Enhance Shareholder Value." *American Banker*, August 1, 2003.

Holland, Gina. "Court Deals Blow to Investor Lawsuits." Nashua Telegraph/AP, March 23, 2006.

Holusha, John. "Huge Profit at Goldman Brings Big Bonuses." *New York Times*, December 12, 2006.

Huebner, Solomon S. *The Economics of Life Insurance.* Executive Asset Management. 3rd ed. 1996.

"Janus Chief Executive Resigns." *European Pensions & Investment News,* www.epn-magazine.com, April 26, 2004.

Johnston, David Cay. "Corporate Wealth Share Rises For Top-Income Americans." *New York Times*, January 26, 2006.

———. "In Loophole, Death Still Certain but not Taxes." *New York Times*, July 28, 2002.

———. "I.R.S. Says Americans' Income Shrank for 2 Consecutive Years."*New York Times*, July 29, 2004.

Johnston, David Cay and Christopher Drew. "Special Tax Breaks Enrich Savings of Many in the Ranks of Management." *New York Times*, October 13, 1996.

Jones, Lawrence. "Fund Times: Another Chapter in The Mutual Fund Scandals." *Morningstar*, www.morningstar.com , September 29, 2006.

Josephson, Matthew. *The Robber Barons .*New York: Harcourt Brace & Company, 1934, renewed 1964.

Kamath, Suneet and Timothy Sledge. *Life Insurance Long View—Life Settlements Need not Be Unsettling.* New York: Sanford C. Bernstein & Co. LLC, 2005.

Katz, Peter. "Life Settlements: Alternative for Troubled Irrevocable Life Insurance Trusts." *Life & Health Advisor*, September 2005.

Kesich, Gregory D. "Jury Awards $7.4 Million To Bank Client." *Portland Press Herald*, March 21, 2006.

Kelly, Tom. *The New Reverse Mortgage Formula, How to Convert Home Equity Into Tax-Free Income.* New York: John Wiley & Sons, 2005.

Kerber, Ross. *"Pay at State's Fund Firms Likely Up to 15%."* Boston Globe, November 24, 2006.

———. "Profit At Fidelity Rockets 20% in 2005, Revenue Also Up Amid So-So Year In Markets." *Boston Globe*, March 3, 2006.

Kindleberger, Charles P. *Manias, Panics and Crashes.* New York: John Wiley & Sons, 2000.

Kiviat, Barbara. "Going Under Folks Looking For A Financial Life Saver Are In For A Rougher Ride." *Time*, March 21, 2005.

Kolbert, Elizabeth. "The Calculator: How Kenneth Feinberg Determines The Value of Three Thousand Lives." *New Yorker*, November 25, 2002.

Kotlikoff, Laurence J., and Jagadeesh Gokhale. "The Adequacy of Life Insurance." Issue #72. TIAA-Cref Institute, www.tiaa-crefinstitute.org , July 2002.

Kratz, Ellen. "Profiting From the Bankruptcy Bill: New Law Provides Opportunity for Debt Collectors.", *Fortune*, May 2, 2005.

Labaton, Stephen. "10 Wall Street Firms Settle With The U.S. in Analyst Inquiry." *New York Times*, April 29, 2003.

Landes, Jennifer. "Hancock to Investigate Claim on Forbes Estate." *National Underwriter*, May 21, 1990.

Landon, Thomas, Jr. "The Man Behind Grasso's Payday." *New York Times*, March 14, 2004.

Leavenworth, Jesse, and David Owens. "Suit: Lawyer Bilked Widow: $2 Million Plus Taken." *Hartford Courant*, December 22, 2005.

Leimberg, Steve. "American Electric Power Company AEP-Taxpayer Loses COLI Case in Sixth Circuit." www.leimbergservices.com, April 29, 2003.

———. "DOW-COLI Interest Deductions Denied by 6th Circuit." Steve Leimberg's Estate Planning Newsletter, #920, www.leimbergservices.com, January 24, 2006.

———. "Important COLI Case Settled." www.leimbergservices.com, January 10, 2004.

———. "New Code Section 101(j)-Treatment of Death Benefits From Corporate Owned Life Insurance." www.leimbergservices.com, August 9, 2006.

Leimberg, Steve, and Robert J. Doyle, Jr. "Tools & Techniques of Life Insurance Planning." *The National Underwriter*, 2004.

"The Life Settlements Market: An Actuarial Perspective on Consumer Economic Value." Deloitte Consulting, LLP and The University of Connecticut. 2005.

Linn, Kurt. *The Trouble with Mutual Funds.* Seattle: Elton-Wolff Publishing, 2002.

Liptow, Jennifer. "Valuing Life in Dollars and Cents." *Financial Planning*, November 2004.

Loan, Allan. "Deal of a Lifetime: How America's Biggest Corporations Are Cashing in Your Mortality (Corporate-Owned Life Insurance)," *Newsweek*, October 23, 1995.

Lowenstein, Roger. *Origins of the Crash, the Great Bubble and Its Undoing.* New York: The Penguin Press, 2004.

——— "We Regret to Inform You that You no Longer Have a Pension." *New York Times Magazine*, October 30, 2005.

——— *When Genius Failed: The Rise and Fall of Long-Term Capital Management.* New York: Random House, 2000.

Lucchetti, Aaron. "Scrutiny Intensifies on Bond Fees: Wall Street Firm's Settlement Draws Spotlight on Murky World of Pricing Corporate Issues." *Wall Street Journal*, July 29, 2004.

Magi, Mina. "BOLI Is Still Great Tool for Financing Benefits (bank-owned life insurance)." *US Banker*, March 1, 2005.

Malkiel, Burton G. "Passive Investment Strategies and Efficient Markets." *European Financial Management*, Volume 9, November 1, 2003.

———. *A Random Walk Down Wall Street*. New York: W.W. Norton & Company, 2007.

Martineau, Kim. "Changes Urged in Probate Courts: Panel See Variations in Service." *Hartford Courant*, December 11, 2005.

Mayer, Caroline. "Bankruptcy Counseling Law Doesn't Deter Filings." *Washington Post*, January 17, 2006.

McDonald, Duff. Please, Sir, I Want Some More. How Goldman Sachs Is Carving up Its $11 Billion Money Pie." *New York Magazine*, November 28, 2005.

McLean, Bethany and Peter Elkind. *The Smartest Guys in the Room, The Amazing Rise and Scandalous Fall of Enron*. New York: Penguin Group, 2003.

Mekay, Emad. "Poorest Pay for the World Bank Corruption-US Senator." *Inter Press Service,* May 14, 2004. www.commondreams.org.

Morgenson, Gretchen. "At Putnam, The Buck Stays Put in the Pocket." *New York Times*, November 11, 2003.

———. "Dangers of a World without Rules." *New York Times*, September 24, 2006.

———. "Explaining Why the Boss Is Paid So Much." *New York Times*, January 25, 2004.

———. "Fidelity, Staunch Defender of the Status Quo." *New York Times*, October 10, 2006.

———. "Fund Managers May Have Some Pay Secrets, Too." *New York Times*, April 4, 2006.

———. "How to Find a Fund's True Colors." *New York Times*, September 10, 2006.

———. "In Wall Street Hierarchy, Short Shrift to the Little Guy." *New York Times*, April 29, 2003.

———. "The Fall of a Wall Street Ward Boss, Grasso Managed Through Fears and Favors." *New York Times*, October 19, 2003.

———. "When Winning Feels a Lot Like Losing." *New York Times*, December 10, 2006.

Morgenson, Gretchen, and Timothy L. O'Brien. "When Citigroup Met WorldCom—How A Money Superstore Courted A Prized Customer." *New York Times*, May 5, 2004.

"Most Americans Don't Know Investment Basics, Study Finds." *Financial Advisor Magazine*, January 2006.

Mrkvicka, Edward Jr. *Your Bank Is Ripping You Off*. New York: St. Martin's Press, December 1999.

Murray, Shailagh, and Jeanne Cummings. "Money Machine: Democrats Find a New Vein: Internet, Wall Street Tycoons; Sen. Corzine, as Fund-Raiser, Taps People Who're Rich, Youthful, Socially Liberal." *Wall Street Journal*, July 29, 2004.

"The Mutual Fund Scandals, Leaving the Little Guy in the Dark Made for Some Nice Payoffs, but the Comeuppance Stands to Be Even Heftier." *Business Week* Online, www.businessweek.com , January 12, 2004.

"Mutual Funds: Few Consistent Winners, S & P Finds Only a Small Number of Equity Funds Manage to Keep Top-Level Performance over Time." *Business Week* Online, www.businessweek.com , August 16, 2006.

Nash, R. Nelson. *Becoming Your Own Banker—The Infinite Banking Concept.* Birmingham, AL: Infinite Banking Concepts, 2000.

Nurenberg, Hugo. "Company-Owned Life Insurance in Business Continuations and Goodwill Testing." *CPA Journal of New York State*, March 2005.

O'Donnell, Jayne. "The Guy Who Blew The Whistle" *USA Today*, November 20, 2003.

Orman, Suze. *The Money Book for the Young, Fabulous & Broke.* New York: Riverhead Books, 2005.

———. *Nine Steps to Financial Freedom, Practical & Spiritual Steps So You Can Stop Worrying.* New York: Crown Publishers, 1997.

———. *The Road to Wealth, A Comprehensive Guide to Your Money.* New York: Riverhead Books, 2001.

Pacelle, Mitchell. "Growing Profit Source for Banks: Fees From Riskiest Card Holders." *Wall Street Journal*, July 6, 2004.

Palast, Greg. *The Best Democracy Money Can Buy, An Investigative Reporter Exposes the Truth about Globalization, Corporate Cons and High Finance Fraudsters.* Sterling, VA: Pluto Press, 2002.

Parker, David B. "The Rise and Fall of *The Wonderful Wizard of Oz* as a 'Parable on Populism.' " *Journal of the Georgia Association of Historians*, Vol. 15,1994.

Paul, Ron Rep. (R-Texas). "Paper Money and Tyranny." U. S. House of Representatives, September 5, 2003.

Perkins, John. *Confessions of an Economic Hit Man.* New York: Penguin Group, 2004.

"Personal Bankruptcy Hit Record High, Survey Finds That About One in Every 53 Households Filed for Bankruptcy in 2005." CNN, www.cnn.com, January 11, 2006.

Phaneuf, Keith M. "Auditors Fault Probate Court Administrators." *Journal Inquirer*, March 1, 2006.

———. "Report Calls for Shakeup of Probate Court System." *Journal Inquirer*, December 21, 2005.

Phillips, Kevin. *American Theocracy, the Peril and Politics of Radical Religion, Oil, and Borrowed Money in the 21st Century.* New York: Viking, 2006.

————. *Wealth and Democracy,* Broadway Books, New York 2002

Pound, Edward T. "Senator Bashes World Bank Corruption." *U. S. News & World Report,* March 26, 2006.

"Predatory Small Loans, The Problem, Legislative Strategies." National Consumer Law Center, www.consumerlaw.org, June 20, 2005.

Prince, Russ Alan. *Winning the War for the Wealthy.* Fairfield, CT: HNW Press, 1999.

"Quantitative Analysis of Investor Behavior 2003 Market Chasing Mutual Fund Investors Earn Less than Inflation." Dalbar, Inc., www.dalbarinc.com, July 14, 2003.

"Quick Tax Loans Skim Billions from Taxpayer Refunds." National Consumer Law Center, www.consumerlaw.org, February 2, 2006.

Quinn, Jane Bryant. "5 Ways to Fix the 401(k), Your Melting Money." *Newsweek,* August 19, 2002.

————. *Making The Most of Your Money.* New York: Simon & Schuster, 1997.

————. *Smart and Simple Financial Strategies for Busy People.* New York: Simon & Schuster, 2006.

————. "Talking Back to Life Insurance Agents: The Right Policy for You." *Good Housekeeping Magazine,* November 1, 1999.

Ramsey, Dave. *The Money Answer Book, Quick Answers To Your Everyday Financial Questions.* Nashville: Thomas Nelson Book Group, 2004.

————. "Why Is Term Insurance Better?" My Total Money Makeover, posted online, 5/19/2005, www.mytotalmoneymakeover.com.

Reilly, David, and Alessandra Galloni. "Big Banks Come Under Scrutiny for Role in Parmalat Scandal." *Wall Street Journal,* October 28, 2004.

Reingold, Dan. *Confessions of a Wall Street Analyst.* New York: Harper Collins, 2006.

Richardson, Karen. "'Viaticals' May Draw More Insurers." *Wall Street Journal,* May 18, 2005.

Richtel, Matt. "Wall Street Bets on Gambling on the Web: Investment Industry that is Illegal in the U.S." *New York Times,* December 25, 2005.

Risen, Clay. "The Campaign To Gut Sarbanes-Oxley." *New Republic On-Line,* www.tnr.com , October 17, 2006.

Rothacker, Rick. "Wachovia Looks to Life Insurance on Workers to Defray Costs." *Charlotte News Observer,* January 27, 2005.

Rothbard, Murray. *The Case Against The Fed.* Auburn, AL: Ludwig von Mises Institute, 1994.

————. *What Has The Government Done To Our Money.*Auburn, AL: Ludwig von Mises Institute, 1990.

Rozon, Tracie, and Joseph B. Treaster. "Insurance Plans for Top Executives Are Threatened." *New York Times,* August 29, 2002.

Salzman, Marian. "American Anxiety is High; Few Are Adequately Insured Against the Things They Fear Most." *Life & Health Advisor*, July 2005.

Sanders, Bob. "Ameriquest Deal Won't Make "Big Difference.*" New Hampshire Business Review*, March 3, 2006.

———.. "ING to Pay New Hampshire State Workers $2.75M." *New Hampshire Business Review*, October 27, 2006.

Sandler, Henry and Gregory Zuckerman. "Behind The Mutual Fund Probe: Three Informants Open Up." *Wall Street Journal*, December 9, 2003.

Sares, Ted. "CEO Severance Too Often Rewards Failure." *NH Business Review*, March 17, 2006.

Schmidt, Robert. "Treasury Secretary Paulson Aims to Protect Corporate Criminals." Bloomberg, www.peaceandjustice.org, October 10, 2006.

Schulte, Gary. *The Fall of First Executive, The House that Fred Carr Built.* New York: Harper Business, 1991.

Seward, Aaron. "Pimco Fund Chairman Found Guilty of Market Timing." Commerce Clearing House Online, www.cchwallstreet.com, July 13, 2006.

Shiller, Robert J. *The New Financial Order, Risk In the 21st Century.* Princeton, NJ: Princeton University Press, 2003.

Shoven, John B., and David A. Wise. Abstract, "The Taxation of Pensions: A Shelter Can Become a Trap." Stanford University, June 1997.

Siedle, Edward. "The Irrelevant SEC"—In Bed with the Industry It Is Supposed to Regulate, It Needs a Shake Up." *Forbes*, September 27, 2006.

Simon, Harry. "Making Law, Taking Action in Secrecy Are the Real Crimes." *Fort Worth Business Press*, June 14-20, 2002.

Simon, Larry. "Helping Your Clients Sell Unneeded Policies." *National Underwriter*, September 20, 2004.

———. "Wealth Management (Life Settlements), Banks Weigh in on Growing Baby Boomer Market." US Banker, February 2006.

Skidelsky, Robert. *John Maynard Keynes, Fighting for Freedom 1937-1946.* New York: The Penguin Group, 2000.

Slott, Ed. *The Retirement Savings Time Bomb...and How to Defuse It.* New York: Penguin Group, 2003.

Sorkin, Andrew Ross. "Goldman's Season to Reward and Shock." *New York Times*, December 17, 2006.

Stessman, Dennis. "Single Employers Can Benefit from 419(a) Welfare Benefit Plans." *Broker World*, April 2005.

Stiglitz, Joseph E. *Globalization and Its Discontents.* New York: W. W. Norton & Company, 2002.

———. *The Roaring Nineties: A New History of the World's Most Prosperous Decade.* New York: W.W. Norton & Company, 2003.

Stoffer, Harry. "Bankruptcy Bill Helps Industry." *Automotive News*, April 18, 2005.

Strauss, Gary, and Barbara Hansen. "CEO Pay Soars as a Select Group Breaks the $100 Million Mark." *USA Today*, posted 4/10/2006, www.usatoday.com.

Strauss, William. "2006 Annual Pension Plan Best and Worst Performance Report." FutureMetrics, www.futuremetrics.net, April 22, 2006.

Swensen, David F. *Unconventional Success: A Fundamental Approach to Personal Investment.* New York: Simon & Schuster, 2005.

"Today's Debate 30% Interest Rates: Sound Business or Loan Sharking. Our View: Effort to Punish Bad Borrowers Lets Reckless Lenders Escape." *USA Today*, March 11, 2005.

Traulsen, Christopher J. "Another Black Eye for the Mutual Fund Industry," *Morningstar*, www.morningstar.com , June 6, 2005.

United States Government. General Accounting Office (GAO). "Business-Owned Life Insurance, More Data Could Be Useful in Making Tax Policy Decisions," May 2004.

————. General Accounting Office (GAO). "Mutual Funds, Assessment of Regulatory Reforms to Improve the Management and Sale of Mutual Funds," March 10, 2004.

————. General Accounting Office (GAO). "Report to the Committee on the Judiciary, House of Representatives; Mutual Fund Trading Abuses & Lessons Can Be Learned From SEC Not Having Detected Violations At An Earlier Stage," April 2005.

————. Joint Committee on Taxation. "Report of Investigation of Enron Corporation and Related Entities Regarding Federal Tax and Compensation Issues, and Policy Recommendations." Senate Committee on Finance, February 2003.

Walbert, M.W. *The Coming Battle: A Complete History of the National Money Banking Power in the United States.* Merlin, OR: Walter Publishing & Research, 1997. First published Chicago: W.B. Conkey, 1899.

"Wall $treet Bonuses Balloon to New Record, New Record Set of $21.5 Billion, Beating Previous Record of $19.5 Billion Set in 2000." CNN, posted online January 11, 2006, www.cnn.com.

Walsh, Mary Williams. "How Wall Street Wrecked United's Pension, Money Managers Paid in Full, but (Oops!) Retirees Won't Be." *New York Times*, July 31, 2005.

————. "States and Cities Risk Bigger Losses to Fund Pensions." *New York Times*, October 12, 2003.

Wamberg, Tom. *Separate Account Bank Owned Life Insurance.* The American College Press, 2006.

Warren, Elizabeth, and Amelia Warren Tyagi. *All of Your Worth, The Ultimate Lifetime Money Plan.* New York: Free Press, Simon & Schuster, 2005.

Weber, Richard M. *Revealing Life Insurance Secrets, How the Pros Pick, Design, and Evaluate Their Own Policies.* Ellicott City, MD: Marketplace Books, 2005.

Wegner, Jonathan. "Selling a Policy for a Profit: Life Settlements Offer a Way to Get a Higher Return from No Longer Needed Policy." *Omaha World Herald*, August 5, 2005.

Weinberg, Neal. "Goldman Sachs Too Big? Too Powerful? Too Bad!" *Forbes*, January 29, 2007.

Weiss, Gary. *Wall Street Versus America, The Rampant Greed and Dishonesty that Imperils Your Investments.* New York: Penguin Group, 2006.

Weiss, Miles and Richard Teitelbaum "Hedge Funds Buy Life Insurance Policies to Ply New Profit Path." Bloomberg, 12/1/2005, posted on line, www.qcapitalstrategies.com, 7/26/2006.

Williamson, Christine. "All Talk, No Action So Far For Amaranth Clients." *Pensions & Investments*, October 2, 2006.

Williamson, Gordon K. *Getting Started In Annuities.* New York: John Wiley & Sons, Inc., 1999.

Winslow, Edward. *Blind Faith, Our Misplaced Trust in the Stock Market and Smarter, Safer Ways to Invest.* San Francisco: Berrett-Koehler, 2003.

Winter, Greg. "Richest Colleges Receiving Richest Share of U.S. Aid." *New York Times*, November 9, 2003.

Wolman, William, and Anne Colamosca. *The Great 401(k) Hoax.,* Cambridge, MA: Perseus Publishing, 2002.

Woodward, Dustin, "Bear Stearns Settlement on Fund Trading Scandal," About, Inc., a New York Times Company, www.about.com , October 16, 2006.

Young, Thomas W. *Life Insurance: Will It Pay When I Die?* Beaver, PA: Personality Press, 2005.

Your Estate Research Service. Chicago: Dearborn Financial Publishing, 1990.

Zaun, Todd. "Citigroup Tries to Repair Its Image in Japan." *New York Times*, October 26, 2004.

ADDITIONAL STATISTICS

Balance Sheet Comparison: Total Aggregate Hard Assets (Bank Premises, Fixed Assets & Other Real Estate) versus Bank Owned Life Insurance Sept. 30, 2007

Institution	Bank Premises Fixed Assets & Other RE Assets/$Billions Estimated Value	Bank Owned Life Insurance Assets/$Billions Cash Surrender Value
Bank of America	$8.051	$14.264
Wachovia	$4.293	$13.574
JPMorgan Chase	$7.371	$7.330
Washington Mutual	$3.759	$4.929
Wells Fargo, SD	$5.101	$4.448
Citibank	$6.142	$3.925
U.S. Bank NA	$1.913	$4.569
Keybank NA	$0.607	$2.660
Branch Banking & Trust	$1.571	$2.475
Bank of New York	$0.915	$1.771
Sovereign	$0.597	$1.766
PNC	$1.586	$1.953
National City	$1.575	$1.665
Regions	$2.537	$1.291
Harris National	$0.386	$1.236
The Huntington National	$0.608	$1.298
Manufacturers & Traders	$0.348	$1.106
Bank of the West	$0.580	$1.196
LaSalle-Chicago	$0.232	$1.019
LaSalle-Troy, MI	$0.335	$0.682
Fifth Third-Cincinnati	$0.806	$0.930
Fifth Third-Grand Rapids	$1.242	$1.066
TD BankNorth	$0.445	$0.845
Comerica	$0.650	$0.878
Mellon	$0.420	$0.801
Marshall & Ilsley	$0.437	$1.014
First Tennessee, NA	$0.505	$0.611
SunTrust	$1.887	$0.591
RBC Centura	$0.261	$0.565
New York Community	$0.161	$0.573
Compass	$0.668	$0.481
Colonial Bank	$0.468	$0.487
Capital One	$1.250	$0.476
Associated Bank-WI	$0.228	$0.428
Astoria-New York	$0.142	$0.393

266

ABOUT THE AUTHOR

BARRY JAMES DYKE, President & Founder of Castle Asset Management, LLC entered the financial services business in 1982 with Prudential after working with RCA Global Communications and high tech industries. At Prudential, he was one of the rookies of the year. Soon after he then became an independent agent with New England Life, founded a pension consulting business in 1986 called Chestnut Green Benefit that excelled in the design, installation and funding of both qualified and non-qualified retirement plans. He has also designed, communicated and administered numerous health and welfare plans, and in 1990 set up the first self-funded PPO plan for a Fortune 100 company for a major Boston HMO. Dyke also founded an administration firm in 1991, The Merrimac Benefit Group, Inc. which, specialized in flexible benefit and defined contribution health and welfare plans under Sections 125 and 105 of the Internal Revenue Code.

He has also written about financial planning and retirement plan issues in national publications such as *Pensions & Investment Age, Advisor Today, The National Underwriter* and *Broker World*, and in self-published newsletters.

As one of the leading agents in his field, he has worked with numerous closely held businesses, high net worth individuals, celebrities and major public corporations. In 2000, Dyke founded another corporation, Castle Asset Management, LLC that is a Registered Investment Advisor. Today, he spends the majority of his time in macroeconomic financial planning for his clients to help them maximize their opportunities, expose them to the severely damaging pitfalls of traditional "accumulation theory financial planning" most often promoted by major financial institutions, their agents and the media. He also assists clients in setting up their own finance companies. An ardent student in Austrian economics, Dyke defends the market economy, private property and sound money. He celebrates the freedom and productive power of capitalism, and views government intervention as socially and economically destructive.

Contact 555 Publishing

2 King's Highway
P.O.B. 95
Hampton, NH 03843-0095

Phone: 800-333-5013
Website: www.thepiratesofmanhattan.com
Email: info@thepiratesofmanhattan.com
Author's E-mail: barry@thepiratesofmanhattan.com
Shipping/Customer Service: mail@thepiratesofmanhattan.com

Look For Upcoming Titles From Barry J. Dyke

ORDER FORM

Send a Check and Order Form to:

555 Publishing or Order Online at www.thepiratesofmanhattan.com

Name _____

Address _____

City _____

State _____

Zip _____

E-Mail _____

Phone _____

Price $37.95 $ _____

Number of Copies   x _____

Sub Total $ _____

Shipping $ _____

Shipping + Handling Rates:

1. $8.90 2. $10.39 3. $11.12 4. $12.42 5. $14.16 6. $16.12 7. $18.16 8. $19.14 9. $22.22 10. $28.99

Total $ _____

Credit Card Type: Visa   MC   Discover   AMEX

Name_____

Number_____

Experation Date _____/_____

Security Code _____

Please Make Checks Payable to 555 Publishing

Please E-mail for Expedited or International Shipping: info@thepiratesofmanhattan.com

Volume Discount Phone: 800-335-5013